ANATHEISM

INSURRECTIONS: CRITICAL STUDIES IN RELIGION, POLITICS, AND CULTURE

Insurrections: Critical Studies in Religion, Politics, and Culture

Slavoj Žižek, Clayton Crockett, Creston Davis, Jeffrey W. Robbins, editors

The intersection of religion, politics, and culture is one of the most discussed areas in theory today. It also has the deepest and most wide-ranging impact on the world. Insurrections: Critical Studies in Religion, Politics, and Culture will bring the tools of philosophy and critical theory to the political implications of the religious turn. The series will address a range of religious traditions and political viewpoints in the United States, Europe, and other parts of the world. Without advocating any specific religious or theological stance, the series aims nonetheless to be faithful to the radical emancipatory potential of religion.

After the Death of God,
John D. Caputo and Gianni Vattimo, edited by Jeffrey W. Robbins

Nietzsche and Levinas: After the Death of a Certain God,
edited by Bettina Bergo and Jill Stauffer

The Politics of Postsecular Religion: Mourning Secular Futures,
Ananda Abeysekara

Wondrous Strange: The Closure of Metaphysics and the Opening of Awe,
Mary-Jane Rubenstein

*Religion and the Specter of the West: Sikhism, India, Postcoloniality,
and the Politics of Translation,*
Arvind Mandair

Plasticity at the Dusk of Writing: Dialectic, Destruction, Deconstruction,
Catherine Malabou

ANATHEISM

{ RETURNING TO GOD AFTER GOD }

RICHARD KEARNEY

COLUMBIA UNIVERSITY PRESS 〰 NEW YORK

Columbia University Press
Publishers Since 1893
New York Chichester, West Sussex
Copyright © 2010 Columbia University Press
All rights reserved

Library of Congress Cataloging-in-Publication Data

Kearney, Richard.
  Anatheism: returning to God after God / Richard Kearney.
    p. cm. —(Insurrections)
  Includes bibliographical references (p.   ) and index.
  ISBN 978-0-231-14788-0 (cloth: alk. paper) —ISBN 978-0-231-51986-1 (e-book)
1.   God. 2.   Death of God.   I. Title II. Series.

  BL473.K43 2010
  211—dc22

                                                           2009017886

For my sister, Sally,
who heals and cares

Sometimes the guest must leave the host
in order to remain a guest

—Fanny Howe, *The Lyrics*

He was my host—he was my guest,
I never to this day
If I invited him could tell,
Or he invited me.
So infinite our intercourse
So intimate, indeed,
Analysis as capsule seemed
To keeper of the seed.

—Emily Dickinson

CONTENTS

Preface xi
Acknowledgments xxi

ONE: PRELUDE

Introduction: God After God   3

1. In the Moment: The Uninvited Guest   17

2. In the Wager: The Fivefold Motion   40

3. In the Name: After Auschwitz Who Can Say God?   57

TWO: INTERLUDE

4. In the Flesh: Sacramental Imagination   85

5. In the Text: Joyce, Proust, Woolf   101

THREE: POSTLUDE

6. In the World: Between Secular and Sacred   133

7. In the Act: Between Word and Flesh   152

Conclusion: Welcoming Strange Gods   166

Epilogue   182

Notes   187
Index   235

PREFACE

> The space we stood around had been emptied
> Into us to keep, it penetrated
> Clearances that suddenly stood open.
> High cries were felled and pure change happened
>
> — Seamus Heaney, "Clearances"

When I arrived in Paris in 1977 to study with the philosopher, Paul Ricoeur, the first question he asked everyone is his seminar was: *d'où parlez-vous?* Where do you speak from? I would like to preface my thoughts on the "return to God after God" with some considerations of why this theme matters to me. Why anatheism and why now?

The God question is returning today with a new sense of urgency. One hears much talk about the "return of the religious" in contemporary world politics. Debates on the relation of the secular and the sacred are prevalent and arresting. Many speak of a "religious turn" in Continental philosophy or, contrariwise, of an "antireligious turn" in a new wave of critical secularism (Daniel Dennett, Richard Dawkins, Christopher Hitchens). Vital disputes about theism and atheism have not disappeared, as some expected, with the Enlightenment and subsequent declarations of the death of God by Nietzsche, Marx, and Freud. The God question keeps returning again and again, compelling us to ask what we mean when we speak of God. A deity of omnipotent causality or of self-emptying service? A mighty monarch or a solicitous stranger? A God without religion or a religion without God? A bringer of war or peace?

The question — where do you speak from? — may also be answered at a more personal level. So let me begin by trying to situate my own stance in this critical conversation. The God debate was especially important for me as a young philosopher living in Europe in the last decades of the twentieth century and moving to America shortly before the catastrophe of 9/11 and the renewed outbreak of war in the Middle East. The concern was as political as it was philosophical. And it carried an added charge for someone growing up in Ireland during a thirty-year period of violence with daily news reports of Catholics and Protestants maiming each other in the northern part of our island. The sectarian strife in Belgrade and Beirut mattered too, of course, but Belfast was just up the road. (I lived in Dublin for twenty years.) I couldn't ignore it even if I wanted to. But, in addition to witnessing sectarian violence, I also experienced the arrogance of certain Protestant and Catholic leaders speaking as if God was on their side. Home Rule is Rome Rule! What we have we hold! No Surrender! Not an Inch!

Such religious triumphalism did not, fortunately, prevent intrepid peace efforts and ecumenical dialogues occurring in my country, most notably in places like Glencree or Glenstal Abbey where I studied for five years. Indeed my education with the Benedictine monks of Glenstal played a formative role in my life. My mentors there took seriously the Rule of St. Benedict regarding uncompromising "hospitality to the stranger." Not only was this enlightened Abbey to serve as one of the focal points for ecumenical reconciliation between Catholics, Anglicans, Presbyterians, and Methodists in Ireland, it also opened doors to profound exchanges with the Oriental Orthodox Church and, further afield, with the non-Christian religions of the East. This Benedictine Abbey was a place where "strange gods" were welcomed and conversed with. And, when many years later I found myself tracing the footsteps of pioneering Benedictines like Henri le Saux and Bede Griffiths to the spiritual heartlands of India, I was reminded of the radical nature of interspiritual hospitality. These migrants entered into contact with foreign religions not to colonize or convert but to bear witness to their own God by learning from other Gods.

Happily, during my time in Glenstal, as later in Benedictine and Ignatian ashrams in India, the atheist too was a welcome stranger. How could one authentically choose theism if one was not familiar with the alternative of atheism? Or the agnostic space between? Indeed, in my first Christian doctrine classes at Glenstal I remember how liberated I felt when the monks had us read cogent arguments *against* the existence of God—by Feuerbach, Nietzsche, Sartre, and Russell—before any talk of why God *might* exist! Atheism was not only tolerated, it was considered indispensable to any wager of faith. And so I learned that, if it was indeed one of the most hostile religions in world history (the facts were legion), Christianity could also be one of the most hospitable.

This latter option was reinforced, I have to say, by the receipt of numerous Nobel peace prizes by spiritually inspired compatriots like Miread Corrigan, John Hume, and Sean McBride (a founder of Amnesty International). Such sustained witness to Christian peace in Ireland—echoing the international example of people like Martin Luther King, Gandhi, and Mandela—certainly influenced my belief that spiritual commitment had the means to provide one of the most effective antidotes to the perversion of religion. Thus while I certainly revolted at an early age against the ecclesiastical authorities of my land, and roundly rejected the God of Triumph, I never ceased to harbor a deep fascination for spiritual questions and an enduring admiration for religious peacemakers. So when I later found myself living in a radically secular society like France—where the principle of *laïcité* reigned supreme—I discovered myself coming back again to the God question. Was it possible, I asked after a meeting with Jean Vanier in Compiègne in 1978, to return to God after leaving God? And if so, what *kind* of God were we talking about?

This question continued to haunt me during my doctoral studies with Paul Ricoeur and Emmanuel Levinas in Paris. It informed my writings, from my first volumes in French—*Heidegger et la Question de Dieu* (1981) and *Poétique du Possible* (1984)—to more recent works like *The God Who May Be* (2001) and *Strangers Gods and Monsters* (2003). It was to remain an abiding concern in my numerous exchanges on "religion without religion" with my friends Jack Caputo and Jacques Derrida over the years. Indeed in 2005 the question of "which God are we talking about when we talk of God?" prompted me to undertake a journey to India and Nepal, resulting in conversations with swamis, yogis, and lamas recorded in *The Interreligious Imagination: A Hermeneutics of the Heart* (2008). This journey exposed me, firsthand, to the radical notion of "open-source Hinduism" as expressed in the spiritual and political legacy of Mahatma Gandhi and Swami Vivekananda.

In the present volume, I hope to weave some of these reflections into a renewed quest for a God after God. This is, I believe, an increasingly pressing inquiry for our "postmodern" age where the adversarial dogmas of secularism and absolutism threaten the option of considered dialogue. I like to think of this book as a small intellectual agora where theists and atheists might engage in reasonable if robust debate, acknowledging the possibility of what I call an anatheist space where the free decision to believe or not believe is not just tolerated but cherished. If anatheism signals the possibility of God after God, it is because it allows for the alternative option of its impossibility. So much depends, of course, on what we mean by God. If transcendence is indeed a *surplus* of meaning, it requires a process of endless interpretation. The more strange God is to our familiar ways, the more multiple our readings of this strangeness. If divinity is unknowable, humanity must imagine it in many ways. The absolute requires pluralism to avoid absolutism.

Looking back on my winding intellectual itinerary, I glimpse it as a set of widening circles. Brought up a Catholic in a devout but liberal Irish family, I experienced early on a deep sense of sacramental spirituality while also learning from the Protestant side of the family (my mother's father was of Scots Presbyterian stock) that religion should be a matter of individual choice and conscience as well as of consent and mystery. This sense of double belonging was confirmed by my exposure to the dual traditions of Irish literature—Shaw, Wilde, and Yeats hailing from the Protestant heritage; Joyce, Kavanagh, and Heaney from the Catholic. Indeed, as the peace movement gathered pace in Northern Ireland, seeking to resolve five hundred years of conflict, I was struck by how some of our finest poets, novelists, and playwrights began to reimagine the stories of the "other side." Catholics and Protestants got into each others' minds, swapped stories, and began to feel what the "enemy" felt. So that a sense of dual fidelity to the Catholic-Protestant heritage turned a curse into a blessing. Or, as Heaney put it, "Two buckets are easier carried than one—I grew up in between." I like to think that the eventual formulation of the Good Friday Peace Agreement in March 1998—permitting Irish citizens to be "British or Irish or both"— was greatly facilitated by the interconfessional and intercultural hospitality practiced by some of Ireland's finest artists. Personally, I admire this model of dual belonging and like to think of myself at times as intellectually Protestant and emotionally Catholic—seeking to combine what I learned "sacramentally" from the monks of Glenstal with the critical consciousness of Protestant mentors like Ricoeur and my dissenter ancestors.

The widening gyres of interreligious hospitality did not stop, however, at the Catholic-Protestant circle. In Paris my dialogues with Jewish thinkers like Emmanuel Levinas and Jacques Derrida were a crucial influence on my growing appreciation of emancipatory "messianic" horizons, and this was later extended to include a dialogue between the Judeo-Christian circle and the Islamic tradition (occasioned by my encounters with Sufi philosophers in Cairo and Kerala). Finally, this extension of my intellectual quest to embrace the three Abrahamic faiths was further amplified by meetings with Buddhist and Hindu thinkers like Choqui Nyma of Kathmandu and Swami Tyagananda of Bangalore. It is with this paradigm of extending and overlapping confessional circles in mind that I end my final chapter with some thoughts on Gandhi: a man who combined the Gods of East and West and was happy to call himself a "Hindu, Muslim, Christian, and Jew."

I rehearse this odyssey of widening circles merely to identify my own specific intervention in the God debate here and now. It is a matter of acknowledging the nature of my "hermeneutic situation" (from the Greek, *hermeneuein*, to interpret). And in seeking to answer the question *d'où parlez-vous?* I hope that readers of this book may be invited to situate their own perspectives and presuppositions. The most important thing I learned from hermeneutic philosophy is that interpretation goes all the way down. Nothing is exempt. If the Word was in the beginning, so was hermeneutics. There is no God's-eye view of things available to us. For we are not Gods, and history tells us that attempts to become so lead to intellectual and political catastrophe. Hermeneutics is a lesson in humility (we all speak from finite situations) as well as imagination (we fill the gaps between available and ulterior meanings). Hermeneutics reminds us that the holiest of books are works of interpretation—for authors no less than readers. Moses smashed the written tablets; Jesus never wrote a single word (only a scribble in the sand to prevent a woman being stoned); and Muhammad spoke, after much hesitation, but left writing to others. If Gods and prophets talk, the best we can do is listen—then speak and write in turn, always after the event, ana-logically and ana-gogically, returning to words already spoken and always needing to be spoken again. Hermeneutics was there from the beginning and will be there to the end.

Let me say, lastly, that my own hermeneutic stance in this work is philosophical rather than theological. I say this for two reasons. First, to identify the particular kind of philosophy I speak from: one nourished by the modern theories of phenomenology and existentialism, on the one hand, and by postmodern ideas of poststructuralism and deconstruction, on the other.

From the former I acquired, during my studies in Paris in the 1970s, an irrevocable respect for personal responsibility, choice, and agency; a belief in the possibility of thinking from concrete embodied experience; and a faith in the power of human imagination and action to transform our world. (The utopian energies of the sixties had not yet evaporated from the Parisian air.) From the latter, postmodern theories I learned that human selfhood and identity are always part of a larger linguistic-cultural process, a web of layered significations that constantly remind us of the unfathomable enigmas of alterity (Derrida, Levinas, Kristeva). Both of these stances—modern and postmodern—combined to inform my own narrative hermeneutic in dialogue with Ricoeur.

The second reason I stress the philosophical character of my reading is that I have no scholarly expertise in theology and little concern to legitimate my reflections with respect to one particular orthodoxy or another (with no disrespect to any). So when, for example, I endeavor to interpret the meaning of hospitality or sacramentality in various religions I am as likely to draw from the writings of agnostic thinkers and novelists as to invoke religious scholars and experts. Imagination and narrative play as important a role in my inquiry as do faith and reason. Hence my decision to introduce a "middle section" on the sacramental imaginary that explores, in some detail, the way in which three revolutionary authors (Joyce, Proust, and Woolf)—writing between two world wars when God seemed absent from this life—chart poetic journeys back to a new sense of the sacred at the heart of a "postreligious" universe. Logically and chronologically, this "literary interlude" might have been located before my chapter on the post-Holocaust writers. But my point is not to describe anatheism as some necessary historical dialectic—a pretentious temptation—but to indicate how certain bold minds of the twentieth century responded to spiritual questions of our age: namely, how might one speak of the sacred after the disappearance of God? Or how might one continue to have faith after the scientific enlightenment dispensed with superstition and submission and after two world wars exposed the fallacy of history as some Divine Plot?

After the terrors of Verdun, after the traumas of the Holocaust, Hiroshima, and the gulags, to speak of God is an insult unless we speak in a new way. (The fact that two of my uncles refused to mention religion after what they witnessed during World War II left a lasting impression on me.) That is what I mean by a return to God *after* God. God must die so that God might be reborn. Anatheistically. How this might happen is a matter of interpretation. A question of belief or disbelief—or some middle space between. I offer my own reading in the chapters of this book, according to my own particular wager. It is but one of many. And that is, I think, a grace of philosophy. It opens a space for the questioning of God where theists and atheists may converse. It invites us to revise old interpretations and reimagine new ones.

A brief word about method and structure.

As to method, this book takes the form of a hermeneutic narrative. While in previous works, *Poétique du Possible* and *The God Who May Be*, I sought to explore the ontological and eschatological dimensions of transcendence—addressing issues of metaphysical truth and being—in this work I am trying to tell a philosophical story of the God question, a story informed by my own journey through biblical theism, interreligious dialogue, modernist literature, the adventures of European thought and politics in the twentieth century, and the challenge of a return to the sacred at the birth of the third millennium. All of these way stations represent liminal spaces—what the French call *des zones frontalières*—where one tries to get one's bearings as one transits between two (or more) worlds. It is a question of orientation.

I would say that there are two main hermeneutic wagers at work in this book: 1. a philosophical wager regarding the interpretation of diverse voices, texts, and theories about the meaning of the sacred in our time; and 2. an existential wager that, I claim, is central to everyday movements of belief and disbelief, of uncertainty and wonder. These latter movements are often expressed as narratives when first translated into language: narratives that can take the form of cultural, religious, or artistic testimonies and, in Charles Taylor's words, offer a sense of "strong evaluation" about what matters most to us, what we consider most precious and "sacred" in our lives. (As in the common phrase *this is sacred to me*). Such narrative wagers—following Ricoeur and Taylor—differ from Pascalian wagers in that they are more about imagination and hospitality than calculation and blind leaps. They solicit fidelity not fideism.

In this sense, the present volume might be described as a narrative of narratives, that is, a philosophical story about the existential stories of our primal encounters with the Other, the Stranger, the Guest—encounters that in turn call for ever-recurring wagers and responses. This is the hermeneutic circle in which I find myself, and my particular choice of narratives in the chapters below is often, as this preface indicates, guided by personal and historical influences. My apprenticeship with Christian monks in Ireland and Continental philosophers in Paris, undoubtedly watermarks my selections. As does my exposure to non-Abrahamic wisdom traditions during my journeys to the Middle East, India, and Nepal. Moreover, when I choose Merleau-Ponty and Ricoeur as primary guides rather than Husserl and Heidegger, for instance, this has as much to do with my own pedagogical narrative as with any claim to epistemological or ontological priority. Likewise in my choice of Joyce, Proust, and Woolf: why not Mann, Munroe, or McCarthy? Or my choice of Vanier, Day, and Gandhi: why not Mandela, Bob Dylan, Capa, or Scorcese? Because in each case I write of those who marked me most (Joyce was my first real exposure to literature, Vanier the first guide on my return to faith). So much in a philosophical story has to do with history. And while history is often aleatory it is never arbitrary. We choose to remake our story according to the history that makes us. That is why we never exit from our hermeneutic circles—unless tempted by a God's-eye view not ours to possess. The acknowledgment of our finite hermeneutic situation saves us, I believe, from both relativism and absolutism.

As to structure, my narrative account is divided into three parts. The opening part, "Prelude," comprises exploratory accounts of the basic anatheist movement between theism and atheism, operating at a broadly macroscopic level. It culminates, in chapter 3, with an analysis of the drama between naive faith and the hermeneutics of suspicion (the "no" of atheism), a drama that opens up a space for a new encounter with the Other beyond possession and power.

The second part, "Interlude," takes a hermeneutic detour into more microscopic descriptions of the anatheist paradigm as it operates in a phenomenology of flesh (chapter 4) and a poetics of epiphany (chapter 5), both of which challenge the duality of the Sacred and the Profane. This section repeats the anatheist movement of first and second faith in terms of a natal pact where—through empathy and imagination—the human self and the stranger give birth to one another. The voices of protest and prophecy recorded in the "Prelude" are here supplemented by a more sacramental tone where everyday acts of sensation and epiphany allow for the mutual birth of oneself and a world that is other—human, natural, or divine.

In the third part, "Postlude," I return to the lived universe of political and ethical action. Here I seek to apply the anatheist paradigm to certain exemplary modern figures (Gandhi, Vanier, Day) who epitomize a commitment to sacramental praxis and, second, to current debates on secularity and sacredness.

All three parts hope to show how the anatheist response to the stranger may be witnessed in 1. primary lived experience, 2. poetic reexperience, and 3. a doubly renewed experience of ethical and spiritual praxis. Combined they seek to suggest how a faith beyond faith may serve new life.

ACKNOWLEDGMENTS

I would like to express my heartfelt gratitude to several colleagues and friends who greatly helped me by reading and commenting on various drafts of this book. Their generous scholarship and gracious solicitude were extraordinary at times and I am deeply in their debt. They include Joseph O'Leary, Mark Gedney, John Manoussakis, Jeffrey Bloechl, Eileen Rizo-Patron, Paul Freaney, Lovisa Bergdahl, William Desmond, Neal Deroo, Jens Zimmerman, Brian Gregor, and especially Kascha Semonovitch, Fanny Howe, and Christopher Yates, who guided me through the project from beginning to end.

I also owe a great debt to various mentors who have informed my thinking on the God question over the years. These include Mark Patrick Hederman and Andrew Nugent, two monks of Glenstal Abbey (Ireland) who introduced me as a teenager to the wonders of the sacred after the demise of oppressive Gods; Patrick Masterson, my first professor of philosophy at University College Dublin, whose teachings on Merleau-Ponty and whose book, *Atheism and Alienation*, left a lasting impression; Charles Taylor, whose supervision of my Master's thesis at McGill University helped me realize that creative imagination and spiritual belief are not mutually exclusive; and Fred Dallmayr whose *Dialogue Between Civilizations* guided my footsteps in the final chapters of this book. Finally, a word of deep gratitude to my Paris mentors, Paul Ricoeur and Emmanuel Levinas, who taught me that the most radical forms of phenomenology and hermeneutics have something timely to tell us about the disappearance and reappearance of the divine.

I wish to also thank my series editor at Columbia University Press, Creston Davis, for his commitment to this book and Wendy Lochner and Christine Mortlock for their editorial care, patience, and expertise. And as always my gratitude to my wife, Anne, and daughters, Simone and Sarah, for putting up with my ups and downs as I wrestled this anatheist manuscript to the ground.

{ ONE }

PRELUDE

INTRODUCTION

GOD AFTER GOD

Profundum, physical thunder, dimension in which
we believe, without belief, beyond belief.

—Wallace Stevens, "Flyers Fall"

What comes after God? What follows in the wake of our letting go of God? What emerges out of that night of not-knowing, that moment of abandoning and abandonment? Especially for those who—after ridding themselves of "God"—still seek God?

That is the question I wish to pursue in this volume. And, so doing, I propose the possibility of a third way beyond the extremes of dogmatic theism and militant atheism: those polar opposites of certainty that have maimed so many minds and souls in our history. This third option, this wager of faith beyond faith, I call anatheism. *Ana-theos*, God after God. Ana-theism: another word for another way of seeking and sounding the things we consider sacred but can never fully fathom or prove. Another idiom for receiving back what we've given up as if we were encountering it for the first time. Just as Abraham received back Isaac as gift, having given him up as patriarchal project. In short, another way of returning to a God beyond or beneath the God we thought we possessed.

The book is divided into seven chapters. The first, "In the Moment," asks what happens in the decisive instant when the sacred stranger appears: do we respond with hostility or hospitality? Fear or trust? Or both. The fact that inaugural moments of faith often begin with someone replying to an uninvited visitor—Abraham under the Mamre tree, Mary at the instant of annunciation, Muhammad in his cave—raises the question as to how religions respond to this advent of alterity in the midst of the human. By waging war or peace? By caring for the orphan, the widow and the stranger, or by hating and smiting one's enemies? To answer this question we must return, I suggest, to the anatheist wager between these two opposed responses to the Stranger. As signaled in the preface, I confine my current analysis of these responses mainly to the Abrahamic faiths—Judaism, Christianity, and Islam—which, in tandem with Greco-Roman culture, have determined the Western understanding of theism and atheism. This concentration is not intended in any exclusivist sense but simply reflects the particular hermeneutic parameters of my inquiry. On occasion, where appropriate, I will make passing reference to Buddhist and Hindu examples; for to do less would be to ignore the essentially "interreligious" nature of anatheism. To ignore strange Gods is, I will argue, to neglect the basic experience of God as Stranger.

My second chapter, "In the Wager," seeks to delineate five main movements in the anatheist wager: imagination, humor, commitment, discernment, and hospitality. On foot of this fivefold analysis, I proceed to extrapolate implications of anatheism for interreligious dialogue and for a new hermeneutics of the "powerless power" of God.

My third chapter, "In the Name," asks what we mean when we speak in the Name of God. Master or Servant? Sovereign or Stranger? Emperor or Guest? We explore the possibility here, with a number of postwar writers, of "faith without religion."

My fourth chapter, "In the Flesh," deals with a sacramental experience of the everyday as adumbrated by contemporary philosophers like Maurice Merleau-Ponty and Julia Kristeva. These thinkers operate from an agnostic space that revisits the sacramental structures of human sensation and embodiment so often occluded by the anticarnal dualisms of mainstream metaphysics and theology (soul versus body, spirit versus senses, mind versus matter). From such an agnostic space of inquiry—inspired by a phenomenological method of suspension and free variation—we may, I suggest, return anatheistically to a new appreciation of incarnate existence, as sacred word made flesh.

The fifth chapter, "In the Text," applies sacramental poetics to an anatheist reading of three novelists—Joyce, Proust, and Woolf—who retrieved sacred epiphanies at the heart of the ordinary universe.

The sixth chapter, "In the World," comprises a hermeneutics of political action covering recent controversies on the role of theism and atheism in matters of war and peace, democracy and violence, compassion and intolerance. Here we encounter the radical difference between a God who brings life and one who brings death, as played out in the history of the Abrahamic faiths.

In my final chapter, "In the Act," I extend this discussion to three exemplary modern figures who, in my view, refigure our understanding of faith by encountering the sacred at the heart of the secular world of action and suffering: Dorothy Day, Jean Vanier, and Mahatma Gandhi.

My wager throughout this volume is that it is only if one concedes that one knows virtually nothing about God that one can begin to recover the presence of holiness in the flesh of ordinary existence. Such holiness, I will suggest, was always already there—only we didn't see, touch, or hear it. This is what Jacob discovered after he wrestled with the stranger through the night, realizing at dawn that he had seen the face of God. It is what the disciples of Jesus discovered after they had walked with the stranger down the road to Emmaus before recognizing, retrospectively, after the breaking of bread, that this wanderer was their risen rabbounai (John 20:16). And it is a lesson recorded by many great mystics who traversed the dark "night of the soul" before discovering, like Teresa of Avila, that divinity dwells in the "pots and pans." *Ana-theos.* The return of God after the disappearance of God. A new and surprising divinity that comes all the way back, in an instant, to where we were without knowing it. Eternity in the epiphany of each moment. Repeating, recalling, returning, again and again.

Let me say at the outset that the moment of not-knowing that initiates the anatheist turn is not just epistemological. Nor is it a prerogative of elite intellectuals. The anatheist moment is one available to anyone who experiences instants of deep disorientation, doubt, or dread, when we are no longer sure exactly who we are or where we are going. Such moments may visit us in the middle of the night, in the void of boredom or melancholy, in the pain of loss or depression. Or simply in the "holy insecurity" of radical openness to the strange. Far from being the preserve of hypercognitive cogitos, the event of radical dispossession is felt by any human being who is deeply bewildered by what existence means. Anatheist moments are experienced in our bones—moods, affects, senses, emotions—before they are theoretically interrogated by our minds. And they are, I would insist, as familiar to believers as to nonbelievers. No human can be absolutely sure about absolutes.

Fortunately. Sages and saints repeatedly testify to encountering the divine in clouds of unknowing or caves of darkness. Believers typically pray to God "to help their disbelief" (Mark 9:24). And even Christ found himself questioning his Father on the cross—"Why have you forsaken me?"—before he could return to renewed belief in life: "Into thy hands I commend my spirit." No one is exempt from the moment of not-knowing. Anatheism presupposes this a-theistic moment as antidote to dogmatic theism. True faith, as Dostoyevsky put it, "bursts forth from the crucible of doubt."[1]

This inquiry, as noted, focuses primarily on the Abrahamic traditions as they respond to certain decisive events in Western history such as the encounter with Greek metaphysics, the modern Enlightenment and the Holocaust. This does not preclude, of course, the opening of a conversation with certain non-Western wisdom traditions, a conversation that, I hold, is imperative for anatheism. For how can one discover the God of hospitality in one's own tradition if one is not open to dialogue with others? The shortest route from self to self is through the other. And this is one reason why, in my final chapter, I look at how Western and Eastern spiritualities meet in the life and mind of Mahatma Ghandi. But this volume does not, I repeat, claim to cover non-Abrahamic religions in any significant or comprehensive fashion. That is work for two companion volumes, namely, *Interreligious Imagination* and *Caves: Filling the God Void*.[2]

But let me be clear. When I speak of anatheism I am not advocating some new religion. God forbid. Anatheism is not a hypothetical synthesis in a dialectic moving from theism through atheism to a final telos. Anatheism does not subscribe to a Master Narrative about the maturation of humanity from primitive religion through secular critique to a new spirituality for the third millennium (i.e., some postmodern faith composed of the "best" ingredients of all wisdom traditions). It is not predicated on a periodized progression from antique faith to rational postbelief. There is no Theology of Fulfillment here. Anatheism is not supersessionism. It has no patron saints and, if it did, Hegel or Fukayama would not be amongst them. Nor would the theosophists who endorsed a New Age spirituality analogous to the Esperanto project for a synthetic language. Anatheism eschews teleology as much as it does archeology. It resists perfect Origins and Ends.

So what *is* anatheism? As the prefix *ana* suggests, anatheism is about repetition and return. Not in the sense of a reversion to an anterior state of perfection—as in Plato's *anamnesis*, where we remember our preexistence with timeless forms. Nor, indeed, in the sense of a return to some prelapsarian state of pure belief before modernity dissolved eternal verities. There is nothing nostalgic at work here. We are, to borrow from Kierkegaard, not concerned with a "recollection" *backward* but with a "repetition" *forward*. The *ana* signals a movement of return to what I call a primordial wager, to an inaugural instant of reckoning at the root of belief. It marks a reopening of that space where we are free to choose between faith or nonfaith. As such, anatheism is about the *option* of retrieved belief. It operates *before* as well as *after* the division between theism and atheism, and it makes both possible. Anatheism, in short, is an invitation to revisit what might be termed a primary scene of religion: the encounter with a radical Stranger who we choose, or don't choose, to call God. What we discover in such encounters is, of course, a practice of infinite modulation. Moments of epiphany are always embedded in the conditions of culture and always require representation and reading. The event of the Stranger is not the only "scene" thus recorded to be sure; most accounts of Abrahamic religion, for example, have emphasized other defining moments of faith—Creation, Salvation, Miracle, Sovereignty, Judgment. But the scene of the Stranger is at the core of the anatheist wager that concerns us here, even if this epiphanic moment of awakening is often neglected in official theologies.

Anatheism, in other words, is nothing particularly new. It is simply a new name for something very old and, I hasten to add, constantly recurring in both the history of humanity and of each life. The anatheist wager has gone by different names throughout the course of human culture. We find it in various moments of creative "not knowing" that mark a break with ingrained habits of thought and open up novel possibilities of meaning. For without the suspension of received assumptions we cannot be open to the birth of the new. Without the abandonment of accredited certainties we remain inattentive to the advent of the strange; we ignore those moments of sacred enfleshment when the future erupts through the continuum of time.

This attitude of holy insecurity ranges, in Western history, from the Socratic practice of not-knowing—as precondition of the search for truth—through such decisive inaugurations of philosophical wonderment and questioning as Augustine's "Who do I seek?" Cusa's *docta ignorantia*, Kierkegaard's "objective uncertainty," and Husserl's *epoché* (which brackets the prejudices of the "natural attitude"). Such interrogative gestures—however distinct—testify to the indispensable significance of a moment of dispossessive bewilderment if one is to become attuned to the acoustics of the Other. Without non-knowing (*a-gnosis*) there would be no motivating urge to know more, to understand differently, to think otherwise, and therefore no possibility of seeking to re-cognize (*ana-gnorisis*) truth as it begins anew, again and again. Sometimes, such moments of not-knowing were seen as preludes to sacred insights beyond the scope of rational or metaphysical knowledge. As when Kant announced that he was "setting the limits to knowledge in order to make way for faith" or when Wittgenstein famously announced "whereof I cannot speak thereof I must be silent," so acknowledging the ineffable space of *das Mystische*. And Heidegger, no doubt, had something similar in mind when he spoke of deconstructing the abstract God of metaphysics—understood as *causa sui*—if we are to rediscover a God before whom we can dance and pray. But it is arguably Socrates who first indicated the philosophical doctrine of sacred not-knowing when he engaged in dialogue with the "Stranger" and suspended the mythical accounts of the Gods in order to commit himself to a second affirmation of divinity, a divine Good beyond accredited concepts and conventions. Philosophically speaking, therefore, the anatheist wager is marked by a moment of radicalized "innocence" (*in-nocens*) that opens the door to ulterior dimensions of truth. Without disorientation no reorientation.

What then of biblical Scripture, the other formative source of Western "wisdom" along with Greek philosophy? In my first chapter I will be concentrating on several key anatheist moments in the Abrahamic tradition—namely, Abraham's encounter with desert strangers, Mary's answer to the Annunciation, and Muhammad's response to a voice in a cave. These primal dramas of response serve as portals to faith, thresholds to new depths of divine recognition. All are instants of *anagnorisis*. And the subsequent history of biblical mysticism—Jewish, Christian, and Islamic—provides recurring testimonies to such liminal events. One thinks of the apophatic breakthroughs of theologians like Dionysius the Areopogite and Gregory of Nyssa or the various professions of mystical unknowing by the likes of John of the Cross, Julian of Norwich, Ruzihan Baqli, and Meister Eckhart (who went so far as to ask "God to rid him of God"). Almost all the great mystics and sages attested to a moment of agnostic abandonment as crucial transition to deeper faith. They called it by such names as *Abgeschiedenheit, Gelassenheit, nada*.

Such anatheist suspensions of theistic certainties allowed for a return (*ana*) to a second kind of faith, a faith beyond faith in a God beyond God. Michel de Certeau recognizes the importance of mystical experience in the West as a crossover point between the religious and irreligious, the secular and the sacred:

> Mysticism is less a heresy or a liberation from religion than an instrument for the work of unveiling, *within* religion itself, a truth that would first be formulated in the mode of a margin inexpressible in relation to orthodox texts and institutions, and which would then be able to be exhumed from beliefs. The study of mysticism thus makes a nonreligioius exegesis of religion possible. It also gives rise, in the historical relation of the West to itself, to a reintegration that eradicates the past without losing its meaning.[3]

The philosophical and biblical traditions that inform Western notions of the sacred stranger are not mutually exclusive. Athens and Jerusalem are both guests and hosts to one another. They question and amplify the respective notions of the sacred. Where Greek aesthetics emphasizes sacred immanence, biblical ethics cherishes holy transcendence. At times, of course, the relationship is adversarial. But it is not necessarily so. And in the measure that they extend hospitality to each other, welcoming the Stranger to their respective homes, they can intercranimate in inventive ways. The Greek house of philosophy, as Derrida notes, offers "hospitality to a thought that would remain foreign" in "welcoming alterity in general into the heart of the logos."[4] And the House of David has, throughout history, welcomed Greek logos into the heart of transcendence. The resulting crossovers have given birth to a double alliance that testifies to an "underlying rending of a world attached to both the philosophers and the prophets."[5] We might cite here the decisive work of translation from Hebrew into Greek—the Septuagint—as typical of such mutual hospitality. Likewise, the introduction of Greek notions of being into readings of Genesis 1 or Exodus 3:15 has allowed for amplifications and revisions of Platonic and Aristotelian categories of form and matter, potency and act. Greek and Jew put each other in question in a shock of strangeness that provokes endless new translations. One calls the other into anatheist openness. Or, as Joyce put, "Jewgreek is greekjew." The copula between these couples is the gap that separates and unites self and stranger. The *is* wrestles with the *is not* at its heart. And this is why anatheism may be said to operate according to what Paul Ricoeur calls a "tensional" model of *metaphor*: a fertile encounter between the familiar and the foreign.

But, in addition to philosophical and theological traditions, we can also speak of anatheist moments in Western art and literature. Here we might cite momentous literary breakthroughs from the invention of Greek drama to the revolution of romantic poetics (e.g., Keats and Hölderlin) and the radical experiments in modernist fiction by authors like Joyce, Proust, and Woolf (explored in chapter 5).

Greek tragedy reenvisions sacred stories of Gods and mortals with the benefit of poetic license. Tragedy—meaning "goat's song" in Greek—was a repetition of the powerful Dionysiac rites of fusion and sacrifice in the poetic guise of *mythos-mimesis*, that is, in narrative plots and imitations that reprised the old religious rituals while providing us with a formal agnostic distance. Suspending questions of belief and disbelief, we identify with heroic reenactments of the great religious myths *as if* they were true. But, because we are operating with poetic license, we—spectators (*thearoi*) of a staged theatrical event—enjoy a certain freedom from the events portrayed. The goat's head becomes a mask. No longer literally *believing* in the acts imitated on stage, we are able to balance our sympathetic identification with the actors with a critical awareness of the "secret cause" of their fate. Thus, while the music and imitation draw us into an act of "pity" (*eleos*), the chorus, script, and theatrical setting withdraw us into an attitude of "fear" (*phobos*).[6]

This counterbalancing of emotions allows for the famous "purgation by pity and fear" that Aristotle calls *katharsis*. Such purgation involves an experience of release that liberates the viewer into a space from which she or he may freely choose—after the poetic suspension of primary belief and after the magic has faded—to believe or not believe. The Gods invoked in religious myth are no longer seen as real "explanations" for our universe but as imagined beings who might or might not exist. They become gods who *may be* if we choose to believe. In short, it is only after we have put all religious "truth claims" in brackets, on entering the quasi-world of drama, that we have the option, *après coup*, of returning to those truth claims and assessing them anew. As we traverse the secular world of theater we find ourselves at liberty to decide for or against an assent to the sacred. Or, to be more accurate, we find ourselves free to interpret the ambivalent secular-sacred space, prized open by poetics, in favor of the secular or the sacred—or a mix of both. Drama may be described accordingly (and perhaps anachronistically) as an agnostic arena that may present us, after the event, with free options of theism or atheism. Emancipating the audience from the ideologies and mythologies of first belief, the aesthetic space liberates each spectator into possibilities of nonbelief or second belief. No longer a given, faith becomes a choice, a matter of interpretation. Poetics makes hermeneutics possible.

The history of Western art is replete with anatheist moments when the sacred and the secular meet to provide the recipient with a license to suspend the diktat of dogma in order to imagine different options of belief or disbelief (or both). John Keats articulates this poetic suspension in his famous formulation of "negative capability," namely, the ability to "find oneself in mystery, uncertainty and doubt without the irritable reaching after fact and reason." There is but a thin line, I suspect, separating Keats's formula of literary agnosticism from the analogous moves of apophatic mysticism in theology or the methodic suspension of accredited certainties in philosophy. And perhaps a certain poetics of negative capability is at the heart of all religious and philosophical exposures to "the strange"? For it is surely such exposure which prompts us to begin all over again, to surrender inherited sureties and turn towards the Other—in wonder and bewilderment, in fear and trembling, in fascination and awe.

Gerard Manley Hopkins calls this option of revisiting the sacred by various names—"aftering," "seconding," "over-and-overing," or simply "abiding again" by the "bidding" of the everyday. All these verbs are variations on the prefix *ana*, defined as "up, in place or time, back, again, anew" (OED). They designate a process of retrieving the divine in a world ostensibly estranged from God, recovering the sacred in a time of disenchantment (*Entzauberung*). Which is one reason Charles Taylor cites Hopkins in *A Secular Age* as exemplary of how the sacred can resurface in a secularized universe where God's existence is no longer taken for granted.[7] Hopkins felt this alienation from God in his very bones, of course. It was a personal, spiritual matter, not just philosophical or social. His dark nights of the soul—hauntingly recorded in sonnets like "I wake and feel the fell of dark" and "No Worse there is None"—were uncompromising testaments to the affliction of spiritual abandonment. But these nights were also interludes on a return journey to the ordinary universe as a place where one can give praise for "speckled, dappled things." They were occasions to reencounter

Christ not in some timeless heaven but "in ten thousand places, lovely in limbs and lovely in eyes not his, to the Father through the features of men's faces." And Mary is equally recovered by Hopkins in a second naïveté, after the forfeit of first naïveté. It is precisely as the mystical rose of the "five senses" that she is resacramentalized in quotidian encounters with others (*Rosa Mystica*). Poetic oscillations between loss and recovery, between turning away and returning typify Hopkins's oeuvre. And in his masterpiece, *The Wreck of the Deutschland*, we witness his most dramatic portrait of how a sense of abandonment can fold back into a passionate revisiting of the sacred. Here the nadir of descent (*katabasis*) becomes a moment of ascent (*anabasis*), a second "yes" to the "no" of dereliction:

> She was calling "O Christ, Christ, come quickly" . . .
> Is the shipwreck then a harvest, does tempest carry the grain for
> thee?
> For the lingerer with a love glides
> Lower than death and the dark;
> A vein for the visiting of the past-prayer, pent in prison,
> Our passion-plunged Giant risen . . . [8]

In Hopkins's poetic testimony to the dark night of the soul we witness a bold refiguring of first creation as second creation. The re-creation of the sacred in the carnal.[9] The retrieval of the divine in the very least of beings: every simple "Jack, poor potsherd, patch, matchwood . . . is immortal diamond."

Hölderlin's poetry of journeying also invokes a double movement of estrangement and epiphany. His poetry, as Heidegger notes, is the conscience (*Gewissen*) of the word of Being that upsets our natural consciousness and invites us to reexperience the strangeness of things. It brushes normal language against the grain, exposing us to the uncanny (*das Unheimliche*). By thus introjecting the strange into the homely (*das Heimliche*), Hölderlin calls us to new ways of speaking and being.

> The word strange we are using—the German "*fremd*"—really means forward to somewhere else, underway toward—onward to the encounter with what is kept in store for it. The stranger goes forth, ahead. But it does not roam aimlessly, without any kind of determi-

nation. The strange element goes in its search toward the site where it may stay in its wandering.

Heidegger elaborates on this poetics of the uncanny:

Almost unknown to itself, the "strange" is already following the call that calls it on the way into its own. The poet calls the soul "something strange on the earth." The earth is that very place which the soul's wandering could not reach so far. The soul only *seeks* the earth; it does not flee from it. This fulfils the soul's being: in her wandering to seek the earth so that she may poetically build and dwell upon it, and thus may be able to save the earth *as* earth.[10]

Poetics, in short, makes us strangers to the earth so that we may dwell more sacramentally upon it. For, as Hölderlin shows, unless we first experience an uncanny sense of homelessness (*Unheimlichkeit*), we cannot begin the journey of homecoming (*Heimkommen*); a journey that is never a return to a fixed origin (*Heimat*) but a turn toward a home always still to come (*Heimkunft* as *Ankunft*).[11] Without sundering, no arrival. Without dispossession no return. In this sense, the *ana* of anatheism may be read as a departure as much as a repetition, an odyssey that takes us away from home and back again. The shortest route from wonder to wonder is loss.

By way of a more liberal reference for anatheist poetics, we might also cite here Oscar Wilde's notion of a "religion of agnostics." Writing *de profundis*, having experienced deep humiliation and dejection, Wilde proposed the idea of a "confraternity of the faithless." He wrote: "Everything to be true must have a religion . . . but can there be a religion of agnostics?" Simon Critchley links this Wildean notion of aesthetic faith, in turn, with Wallace Stevens's claim that God is a "supreme fiction in which one believes." In an essay entitled "We Can't Believe/We Must Believe," Critchley compares the aesthetic imagination of Wilde and the ethical imagination of Christ. He writes:

The truth of art, according to Wilde's romantic aesthetics, is the incarnation of the inwardness of suffering in outward form, the expression of deep internality in externality. It is here that Wilde finds an intimate connection between the life of the artist and the life of

Christ. For Wilde, Christ is the supreme romantic artist, a poet who makes the inward outward through the power of the imagination. Wilde goes even further and says that Christ makes himself into a work of art through the transfiguration of his suffering in his life and passion. Christ creates himself as a work of art by rendering articulate a voiceless world of pain.[12]

Religion as art? Art as religion? Wilde does not answer this question, but he has this to say about the relationship between the artist and Christ: "To the artist, expression is the only mode under which he can conceive life at all. To him what is dumb is dead. But to Christ it was not so. With a width and wonder of imagination that fills one almost with awe, he took the entire world of the inarticulate, the voiceless world of pain, as his kingdom, and made of himself its external mouthpiece."[13] Otherwise put, in his limitless compassion for all alienated beings, Christ became the incarnation of love as an act of imagination. And this act of poetic imagination teaches us in turn how to open ourselves to an "experience of grace over which one has no power."[14] It is Christ the stranger, Wilde suggests, who is most susceptible to the estranged beings of our world and most ready to empathize with them, giving a voice to those without voice.

The moment of poetic faith does not necessarily entail a "second faith" in some divine Other (for Critchley it does not), though it may well serve, for those who choose, as prelude to such faith. While not requiring religious belief, such an aesthetic openness to the gracious and the strange does offer what Gide calls a "disposition to receive" (*une disposition à l'accueil*). And such an aesthetic *disponibilité* may also serve to remind us that any religious hermeneutics worth its salt needs art if it is to be true to faith. For art, however atheistic or agnostic, reveals that religions are anthropomorphic, composed of human images, names, stories, and symbols. In short, it reminds us that religions are imaginary works, even if what they witness to may be transcendent and true. Mindful of the inherent *art* of religion, we are more likely to resist the temptations of fetishism and idolatry—that is, avoid taking the divine *literally*, as something we could presume to contain or possess. The figural saves God from the literal. For faith is not just the art of the impossible but an art of endless hermeneutics. Spiritual art may thus teach us that the divine stranger can never be taken for granted, can never be reduced to a collective *acquis*, but needs to be interpreted again and again. Yet another modern poet, W. H. Auden, puts this well in respect to his own Christian anatheism: "Every Christian has to make the transition from the child's 'we believe still' to the adult's 'I believe *again*.' This cannot have been easy to make at any time and in our age it is rarely made, it would seem, without a hiatus of unbelief." Auden adds, tellingly, that while the liturgy says *We* in the confession of our shared responsibility for the sins of our neighbors, in the Creed it says *credo*, not *credimus*—for "nobody can put the responsibility of his faith upon others."[15] I shall return to the anatheist consideration of individual and social responsibility in my concluding chapters.

By including poetics, alongside philosophy and religion, as a special arena of anatheist experience, I do not mean to equate the anatheist wager with fiction. If poetics invites a "willing suspension" of first belief and disbelief, it neither includes nor excludes a leap of second faith. It may be said to clear a landing site for the divine stranger without either prohibiting or mandating a landing. The fictive *as if* is not the same as the anatheist *as* (where I see the stranger *as* divine); though the poetical may, as noted, serve as powerful prelude to the creedal for those who so choose. In fact, I would go further and say that without some poetic release into a free variation of possibles, the return to a God beyond God is virtually impossible.

But if faith is not reducible to fiction, it is integral to metaphor. Metaphor involves a transportation (*metaphora*) between self and other. And as such the metaphorical *as* contains within itself a mixed copula of *is/is not*.[16] The stranger before me both *is* God (as transcendent Guest) and *is not* God (as screen of my projections and presumptions). Out of this tension faith leaps. There can be no immediate appropriation of the divine Other as my "own," but only a relationship to someone other than myself who is, so to speak, *like me* while remaining irreducibly *unlike* me qua Other. It is precisely this metaphorical *as*, central to the grammar of faith, which in turn makes the relationship between the Self and Stranger a wager of transit between like and unlike, between a host and guest languages. I am suggesting, in short, that hospitality toward the Stranger as Guest always involves both the necessity and the limits of translation. For just as there is much gained in translation between self and stranger, there is always something "lost in translation." Only thus can the stranger be respected as stranger rather than simply reappropriated as another "myself" (i.e., as alter reduced to alter ego).[17]

Finally, let me add that if we venture into other sacred cultures, we find suggestive analogies to anatheist openness in what Buddhism calls emptiness (*sunyata*) in the famous Heart Sutra or in what the Upanishads refer to as the empty space (*akasa*) in the cave of the heart (*guha*). In these non-Western traditions, as in others, there is deep appreciation of the importance of withdrawing from creedal attachments — at least provisionally — in order to liberate oneself into an awareness of the holy beyond habitual constructions. But such comparisons and contrasts are, alas, beyond the limits of this inquiry.

So how, in sum, does anatheism differ from atheism? This is a key question for the deliberations that follow. But let me offer this preliminary conjecture: anatheism differs from dogmatic atheism in that it resists absolutist positions *against* the divine, just as it differs from the absolutist positions of dogmatic theism *for* the divine. It is a movement — not a state — that refuses all absolute talk about the absolute, negative or positive; for it acknowledges that the absolute can never be understood *absolutely* by any single person or religion. Anatheism acknowledges the emancipatory force of critical atheism as an integral part of theism, understood as a second faith beyond faith. And it also respects agnostic atheism that remains just that — *agnosis*, not-knowing — choosing not to make the second move of faith. What anatheism opposes is militant antitheism, which — as in the Reign of Terror or Stalinist persecutions — is just as pernicious as triumphal theism.

Anatheism is a freedom of belief that precedes the choice between theism and atheism as much as it follows in its wake. The choice of faith is never taken once and for all. It needs to be repeated again and again — every time we speak in the name of God or ask God why he has abandoned us. Anatheism performs a drama of decision whenever humans encounter the stranger who, like Rilke's statue, whispers, "Change your life!" And every moment is a portal through which this stranger may enter.

IN THE MOMENT

THE UNINVITED GUEST

Thus says the Lord: you shall not molest or oppress an alien, for you were once aliens yourselves.

—Exodus 22:20

She walks with him as a stranger, and at first she puts him to the test; fear and dread she brings upon him and tries him with her discipline . . . then she comes back to bring him happiness and reveal her secrets to him.

—"On Wisdom," *Sirach* 4.

Abrahamic religions testify to inaugural encounters with a divine stranger. In such primary scenes two responses are registered: hostility or hospitality. You decline the other or receive the other into your home. Let me give some examples drawn from the three Religions of the Book—Judaism, Christianity, and Islam.

THE JUDAIC WAGER

I begin with the story of Abraham. It is a dry hot day in the desert of Mamre. An old man is sitting at the door of his tent, pitched under the shade of an oak tree. His wife, Sarah, is inside the tent, sheltering from the midday sun. She is not happy; she is over a hundred years and she is barren. Her servant woman, Hagar, is younger, more attractive than she and more fertile: a rival. Abraham is brooding, about his unhappy wife, about the future of Israel. Suddenly a shadow flits across the sunlit ground in front of him. He looks

Figure 1.1. *Abraham and the Three Angels,* by Marc Chagall, 1954–1967

up to see strange men standing before him. He is filled with fear. Why have they come? he wonders. To kill him? There are three of them, and he has two women to protect, his wife and his servant girl. But instead of reaching for a weapon or retreating to his tent, Abraham finds himself running toward the strangers. He greets them, bows to the ground, and invites them to a meal. He asks Sarah to knead three measures of her best flour to make loaves while he fetches a calf and prepares it with curds and milk. Then Abraham stands under the oak tree and watches the strangers eat. When they have finished they announce that they will return in a year and when they do Sarah will be with child. Sarah, standing inside the entrance of the tent, laughs when she hears this; it is quite impossible that she be with child! But the Lord Stranger repeats the promise: "Nothing is impossible to Yahweh. I shall come back to you at the same time next year and Sarah will have a son" (Gen. 18:14).

The New Jerusalem Bible offers an interesting translation of this scene. As the narrative progresses, the "three men" who first appear out of the desert mutate into a single "guest" once invited to the table before finally appearing as "Yahweh" himself in the final scene of annunciation. In other words, the divine Other first reveals itself in the guise of three unknown strangers before Abraham's act of hospitality permits the further revelation of their promise to bring life not death. Potential hostility becomes actual hospitality. Abraham chooses a God of love over a God of fear. And this choice is, arguably, echoed in Sarah's laughter. For is not humor the acceptance of contradiction, of the impossible become possible, of the foreign finding a home within the familiar, of the Other entering the self and being reborn? Isaac, the son who results from this encounter with the Stranger, in Hebrew means "the one who laughs."

Abraham is the wanderer par excellence; he is the nomadic tent dweller celebrated in Psalm 119, "I am a stranger on this earth." Hegel famously describes him as "a stranger on earth to soil and men alike."[1] But, if Abraham is the first prophet of strangeness, he is also the first to experience the temptation of closure: namely, the urge to confound the sacred with the tribe. The temptation, in short, to fold his tent and build a fortress. To reduce divinity to territory and thereby exclude the stranger. Put in another way, Abraham is capable of both great and terrible things. While he welcomes the three strange men (*anashim*) who announce the birth of his son, Isaac, he does not hesitate, not long afterward, to cruelly expel his foreign slave girl, Hagar, into the wilderness with their son, Ishmael.

Later in the Genesis story, Abraham is compelled to make yet another dramatic choice. This time, on Mount Moriah, he has to decide between two commanding angels: one who tells him to kill his son Isaac, the other who bids him abandon the tribal ways of blood sacrifice and receive his son back as a gift. He chooses life over death, but only after much "fear and trembling." And one realizes on reading on—through Exodus and Kings and Deuteronomy and the Prophets and, further still, through Christian and Islamic Scriptures—that the decision for hospitality over hostility is never made once and for all; it is a wager that needs to be renewed again and again, anatheistically.

In sum, the great founder of biblical religion is capable of both hostility and hospitality. And Abraham's descendents have followed suit throughout history. Reject the stranger or embrace the stranger. In fact, the annual Jewish festival of Sukkot serves to remind the followers of Abraham that they are forever tent dwellers, strangers on the earth committed to the hosting of strangers. This is a reminder that needs to be made, again and again, year after year. Why? Because biblical religion, like most other religions, is capable of the best and of the worst. It all comes down, in the first and last instance, to a wager of faith—a hermeneutic reading of the word of God. I repeat: Abraham's heartless banishment of Hagar and Ishmael is totally at odds with his hospitable reaction to the arrival of the aliens from nowhere. Capable of the most cruel acts, Abraham is also capable of receiving potentially threatening nomads into his home with open arms. As a result of his radical turning around, he opens himself and his wife Sarah to new life.

The entire Bible, it could be said, is a story of struggles between different ways of responding to the alien. Saul goes out to bring destruction on the Ameliketes but, in the battle against the foreigners, decides to abandon bloodlust in favor of mercy. Jacob wrestles with an anonymous "someone" (*eesh*) through the night; he fights with what he perceives to be a threatening adversary, until he finally opens himself to the Other (Gen. 32:25). Receiving a divine mark upon his hipbone and the new name of Israel, Jacob opts for peace, ultimately acknowledging "the face of God" in the visage of his mortal enemy. Indeed it is significant that, the day after he wrestled with the angel, he is able to finally embrace God in the guise of his estranged rival brother, Esau. The message is this: the divine, as exile, is in each human other who asks to be received into our midst. The face that serves as trace of transcendent divinity is also a portal to humanity in its flesh and blood immanence. Or, as Emmanuel Levinas puts it, "The epiphany of the face qua face opens humanity. The face in its nakedness as a face presents to me the destitution of the poor one and the stranger."[2] My hospitable relationship with the stranger, in sum, gives meaning to my relations with all strangers, proximate or distant, human or divine. In this sense it is an option for justice over murder.

One of the most famous prayers of Passover says: "You shall not oppress a stranger, for you know the heart of the stranger, having yourselves been strangers in the land of Egypt" (Exodus 22). And another Passover text, *Sefer Ha-Hinukh* 431, explains this Exodus passage as a reminder that "we have experienced the great suffering that one in a foreign land feels. By remembering the pain that we ourselves have undergone, from which God, in God"s mercy, delivered us, our compassion will be stirred up toward every person in this plight." In support of this reading, we might recall how three of the earliest books of the Bible are about strangers—Job, Ruth, and the Song of Songs. Job challenges Yahweh before finally accepting his strange ways. Ruth is a Moabite alien accepted by Boas into his community, thereby initiating a long line of hybrid descendants including David and Jesus. While the last of these books, the Song of Songs, may be cited as paradigmatic of the coming together of Israel and its Egyptian adversary: King Solomon courts the foreign "Shulammite" woman, defying tradition to embrace this "black and beautiful" stranger as his bride. Indeed it is telling that the Song itself celebrates a Jewish love story about human-divine love in the borrowed form of a Babylonian-Egyptian marriage poem or epithalamium. Loving your Other is more divine than loving your own. Which is arguably why the Hebrew Bible has thirty-six commands to "love the stranger" (Deut. 27:19, 10:18, 24:17, 16:11, etc.) and only two to "love your neighbor."[3]

Deuteronomy is one of the richest books in references to the stranger. Let me cite a few examples: "He shows his love for the stranger by giving him food and clothing" (Deut. 10:18; the term *ger* here is rendered as *xenos* in Greek and *peregrinus* in Latin); "Cursed is he who distorts the justice due a stranger, orphan and widow"(Deut. 27:19; here *ger* is rendered as *advena* in Latin and variously as "alien" in English); "You shall not pervert the justice due a stranger or an orphan, nor take a widow's garment in pledge" (Deut. 24:17). Or again: "You shall rejoice to the Lord your God . . . and the stranger and the orphan and the widow who are in your midst, in the place where the Lord your God chooses to establish His name" (Deut. 16.11).

There are several telling things about these references. First, the stranger is associated with the name of God. Second, the stranger is invariably linked with allusions to orphans and widows—vulnerable and defenseless ones without family or guarantor. Third, the advent of the stranger calls for a "justice" that seems to go beyond normal conventions of homeland security, which tend to exclude strangers, orphans, and widows. The very fact that the Lord must repeatedly enjoin justice to prevent hatred of the foreign is itself an acknowledgment that initial responses to aliens are more likely to be fear than love. So that, if Deuteronomy recalls that "our father was a wandering Aramean" (Deut. 26:5), the same text is also guilty of the most egregious expressions of exclusion toward wanderers beyond the tribe (viz. the numerous exhortations to smite the enemy in the *milchemeth mitzvah*). Finally, the Latin translations of the Hebrew *ger* as *advena* and *peregrinus* are particularly suggestive in that they connote 1. one who comes from outside, from afar, from the future (*advena*) and 2. one who migrates across borders of nation, tribe, or home (*peregrinus* as in the English peregrination). The stranger, in short, is the uninvited one with nowhere to lay its head unless we act as "hosts" and provide a dwelling. There is a sense of

surprising irruption about the coming of this estranged and estranging outsider—a sense of unknowability calling for risk and adventure on our part.
Hospitality to the irreducibly Other does not come naturally. It requires
imagination and trust. So, while the Torah acknowledges the predictable
impulse to persecute intruders, it exhorts us to overcome our murderous impulses and accept the advening one. As one commentator remarks, "What
is hateful to you do not do to another. This is the whole Torah; all the rest
is commentary."[4]

It is noteworthy, I think, that the stranger is often treated as the *human*
persona of the divine. Indeed what appears as an all-too-human other,
emerging out of the night to wrestle with us, is only *subsequently* recognized
as divine. The Latin translation of the Hebrew *eesh/iysh* as *vir* in Latin and
anthropos in Greek carries this sense across multiple tongues. Though some
English versions speak here of "angels," most remain faithful to the original
biblical sense of the divine revealing itself in and through the human, e.g.,
"Jacob was left alone, and a *man* wrestled with him until daybreak" (Gen.
32:24). And, we recall again, it is only *after* the struggle with the alien in
the dark that Jacob realizes that he has been blessed by the "Face of God"
(*Peniel*). God is revealed *après coup*, in the wake of the encounter, in the
trace of his passing. And this episode demonstrates that if divinity moves toward us kataphatically in the face of the foreigner, it also absolves itself apo-
phatically from the immediate grasp of cognition. When God is revealed
as having been present all the time, God is already gone. That is why God
remains a stranger even in the most intimate embrace: "for my thoughts are
not your thoughts and my ways are not your ways" (Isa. 55:8). The Other
remains foreign in its most familiar guise. The divine and the human are
neither separable nor the same, neither divorceable nor identical.

The great stories of Israel are, I am suggesting, testaments to the paradoxical origins of religion in both violent conflict and peaceful embrace.
This, in effect, makes every dramatic encounter between the human and
the divine into a radical hermeneutic wager: compassion or murder. You
either welcome or refuse the stranger. Monotheism is the history of this
wager. The fact that the Abrahamic legacy has witnessed both traditions of
interpretation speaks for itself. On the one hand, we have ample evidence
for those critics who see monotheism as an irremediable source of intolerance and war (from Enlightenment atheists to the likes of Dawkins, Harris,
and Hitchens). On the other hand, the Abrahamic legacy provides powerful
resources for those—like this author—who wish to postcritically retrieve a

liberating message in the Bible, one that fosters radical attentiveness to the stranger as portal to the sacred.

THE CHRISTIAN WAGER

The double legacy of Abrahamic religion perdures in Christianity. Here too we witness an ambiguous history of love and hate toward the alien. For every Francis of Assisi there is an Inquisitor, for every Saint James a Jim Jones. And here again the drama of the Stranger—*peregrinus, hostis, advena*—is powerfully enacted in a "primary scene," in this instance, the Annunciation.

Recall: A young Nazarene woman meets an intruder. She is alone in her shuttered room. She is reading. The day is cool. In the air a fragrance of lilies. She is perhaps half thinking of her betrothed, Joseph, as she reads the Songs of Songs or the story of Rachel meeting Jacob at the well or the story of Sarah being with child. (We do not know; we only have paintings.) She hears a flutter of wings, puts down her book, half closes her eyes, listens.

Figure 1.2. *The Annunciation*, by Sandro Botticelli, 1489–1490

Suddenly, out of nowhere, someone appears. He is terrifying, and Mary is full of fear. She withdraws, steps back, pauses. Then, bowing her head and attending carefully to a voice that whispers "Do Not Be Afraid," Mary opens herself to the stranger and conceives a child. In short, Mary chooses grace over fear. She responds to the call, trusts in the promise. She dares imagine the impossible as possible. She says yes. Amen. A Nazarene echo of Sarah's laughter.

Denise Levertov captures this moment in her poem, "Annunciation," when she writes of Mary's audacious choice:

> We know the scene: the room, variously furnished,
> almost always a lectern, a book; always the tall lily.
> Arrived on solemn grandeur of great wings,
> the angelic ambassador, standing or hovering,
> whom she acknowledges, a guest.
>
> But we are told of meek obedience. No one mentions courage.
> The engendering Spirit
> did not enter her without consent.
> God waited.
> She was free
> to accept or to refuse, choice
> integral to humanness.

Mary is faced with a hermeneutic wager. She looks up from her lectern and reads the face of the stranger. She chooses to say yes, carnally, courageously. And word is made flesh.

Another poet, Andrew Hudgins, glossing Botticelli's Cestello painting of the Annunciation, adds a further variation on this scene:

> . . . angel to virgin,
> Both her hands held up, both elegant, one raised
> As if to say stop, while the other hand, the right one,
> Reaches toward his; and, as it does, it parts her blue robe
> and reveals the concealed red of her inner garment
> to the red tiles of the floor and the red folds

of the angel's robe. But her whole body pulls away.
Only her head, already haloed, bows,
Acquiescing. And though she will, she's not yet said,
Behold, I am the handmaiden of the Lord,
As Botticelli, in his great pity,
Lets her refuse, accept, refuse, and think again.

Ana, again, is the key. Mary's thinking again, believing again, trusting
again, is the first act of Christian anatheism. Repetition of Jewish anatheism, anticipation of Islamic anatheism. The term *thinking* is important. In
Luke 1:29 we read that Mary "was troubled and pondered" (*dietarachtek kai
dielogizete*) when she encountered the angel. The Greek term for "ponder"
is *dialogizomai*, meaning to think through, to be in dia-logue with oneself
and others. In most of the Renaissance paintings, it is significant that Mary
is usually portrayed reading a book as the angel appears. She is not violated.
She volunteers. She is not alone. She is conversing with holy ones and her
own heart. It is also significant, in this regard, that the same description
of being troubled and frightened when the angel appears, occurs in previous annunciations—for example, the annunciation of the birth of Samson
to Manoah's wife (Judges 13:2–25) and of the birth of John the Baptist to
Zechariah (Luke 1:15).[5] In short, Mary's response of fear and consent is
preceded by responses that she may well be recalling as she "ponders"—in
her body and soul—between "yes" and "no."

The fact that the birth of the Nazarene child is marked by the advent of
Three Foreigners from the East—the Magi—confirms the sentiment that
epiphanies of divine eros and natality involve an incursion of the foreign
into the frame of the familiar. And it is fitting that the trinity of strangers—
exemplified by the three visitors, first to Abraham, then to Mary—was chosen by the great painter of Russian Orthodoxy, Andrei Rublev, as the perfect
icon for the three divine persons of the Christian deity. In Rublev's *Icon of
the Trinity* (painted in AD 1411 and housed in the monastery of Zagorsk)
the three angels are seated in a circle around an empty chalice—symbol of
the gap in our horizons of time and space where the radically Other may
arrive, unexpected and unknown. And this empty receptacle at the core
of the circle is, arguably, none other than the womb-heart of Mary herself
(*khora*). As the Greek inscription of the *Mother and Child Mosaic* of the

Figure 1.3. *The Holy Trinity*, by Andrei Rublev, circ. 1410

Monastery of the Khora in Istanbul reads: *Khora akhoraton*—"Container of the Uncontainable." Mary is the *khora* opening the heart of divinity. The aperture, without which, as in all human openings to the stranger, the sacred could not be embodied.

The story of sacred strangers does not, of course, stop there. After the Incarnation comes the life of Jesus himself. Jesus was repeatedly experienced by his disciples as a terrifyingly alien apparition. On Mount Tabor when he was transfigured. On Lake Galilee when he appeared over the stormy waves or on the shores of the same lake when he appeared to his apostles after his death. In each of these episodes, Jesus's most intimate followers responded to him as if he were a foreigner; and he responds, repeatedly, with the words, "Do not be afraid." Each time Christ turns their terror into communion — preparing fish for them on the lakeshore, breaking bread for them at the inn of Emmaus.

The famous Emmaus scene of epiphanic love flaring up in the darkness of suspicion is graphically evoked in Rembrandt's series of portraits, most poignantly the Emmaus painting of 1628 where Jesus's black silhouette is offset against the light of epiphany, a light that counters the fear of the disciples recoiling from the irruption of divinity (as Jesus breaks bread). This irruption is, of course, a return of Jesus through the incognito of the departed one, the posthumous Christ. He has to leave in order to come back. He has to die as estranged outcast, as a broken reed, a nobody and nothing, before he can live again. Unless the seed dies it cannot grow. *Ana-theos.* The return of God after the death of God.

Christ, as Michel de Certeau puts it, is that "Other," present but also absent, whose "Follow me," in the penumbra of the empty tomb "comes from a voice forever irrecoverable." But, because of this irrecoverabilty (in any final sense), Christ functions as an endless invitation to translate, remember, and believe anew.[6] This crucial insight into the radical estrangement of Jesus's death is movingly captured in the Office of the Greek Orthodox Matins of Good Friday, which tells of Joseph of Arimathea seeking the body of Jesus from Pilate:

> Joseph came before Pilate, beseeching him, saying:
> "Give me this stranger (*dos moi touton ton xenon*),
> who from infancy guested (*xenisthenta*) in the world as a stranger,
> he cried,
> Give me this stranger,
> whom his own people have hated and slain as a stranger,
> Give me this stranger,
> at the sight of whose strange death I am estranged (*xenothenta*).
> Give me this stranger,
> who gave hospitality (*xenizein*) to the poor and the stranger."

Here we encounter the great paradox of the divine stranger as host *and* guest. Jesus is both the one who gives hospitality to the thirsting stranger and the one who calls to us to host him in turn as our guest (as Joseph does by receiving and caring for his scarred body). It is a paradox illustrated in this text by the linguistic play between the terms for "guested" (*xenisthenta*) and "estranged" (*xenothenta*), "stranger" (*xenos*) and "hospitality" (*xeneia*). Tellingly, for our purposes, the Greek *xenizo* means to offer hospitality by taking someone as guest, while the same verb in the passive voice, *xenizo-mai*, means to be struck by something strange, to be defamiliarized by the Other.[7] This double direction of hospitality—at once active and passive—is reiterated in the celebrated Maundy Thursday hymn, *Adore Te Devote*, that concludes with this double image of Christ as the one who *both* offers the eucharistic bread *and* is received by us as we consume the bread:

Blest are you, my friends, invited to my wedding feast . . .
Lord, make known to us your presence at this table blest.
Stay with us forever, God our host and guest.

But the stranger is not always recognized as either host or guest. In the case of Jesus, most of his contemporaries—friends and enemies alike—did not see him as divine. Even his close relatives, we are told in Mark 3:21, "set out to seize him, for they said, "He is out of his mind!" And if Jesus's immediate acquaintances had such difficulty acknowledging the presence of the divine, is it any wonder that so many of his followers down through the ages misinterpreted his message, that is, mistook his call to hospitality and service as an invitation to triumphal dominion? The radical hermeneutic liberty of the Christ event makes each Christian believer a pilgrim who must become, as Kierkegaard put it, *contemporaneous* with Christ himself to be a true recipient of his "scandalous strangeness." And perhaps it was out of fidelity to this role of radical Other that Jesus refused to be captured in written words. He never wrote anything down except some illegible words in the sand that prevented a woman from being stoned to death. He left the rest to imagination (as the diverse evangelists show).

Likewise, Jesus pointedly refused the temptations in the desert to become an emperor imposing a triumphant message on a credulous populace (a drama brilliantly portrayed by Dostoyevsky in the "Grand Inquisitor" chapter of the *Brothers Karamazov*). Surely Jesus was announcing his role as unfamiliar guest when he described himself not as illustrious Monarch but as the uninvited alien knocking at the door, or as the "least of these" (*elachistos*) wandering the streets, asking to be fed or housed. "If you give to the least of these you give to me" (cf. Matt. 25:41). The rest of the passage reads: "For I was hungry and you gave me food, I was thirsty and you gave me to drink, a *stranger* (*hospes*) and you welcomed me"—to which the righteous answer and say, "Lord when did we see you a stranger and welcome you?" (Matt. 25:35–44). For they had not recognized the divine embodied in the alien before them. They were looking up not down, obsessed by some fantasy in the skies rather than heeding a flesh and blood presence here on earth.

This is no casual comment by Jesus. The invocation of the surprising divinity of the *hospes* is actually repeated four times in the same passage as key for entry to the kingdom. Eschatology is realized in the presence of the alien in our midst. Love of the guest becomes love of God.[8] The cut comes, once more, in this crucial and ultimate choice: to welcome or repudiate the *hospes*. So it is not surprising that when Jesus, in another episode, is asked by the lawyer, "who is my neighbor?" he replies with the story of the Good Samaritan—the alien outsider who brings healing to the wounded and the dying (Luke 10:25–36). Theophany as the guest become host. And it is another "stranger," again a Samaritan, who is the only leper to acknowledge his healer: "Has none but this foreigner (*allogenes*) returned to give thanks to God," asks Jesus (Luke 17:18).

To "love those who love you" is normal, as Jesus says in Matthew 5:43–48. "To greet your brothers and sisters only" is expected. But to love the alien, even when it takes the form of the adversary, that is the most difficult—and most divine—thing of all. So, when Jesus says he is the Way, he insists it is the Way of the Stranger, not the Sovereign—with all that this implies in terms of radical hospitality and healing. This commitment to radical hospitality was central to the Christian mission of service throughout the centuries (down to the theology of liberation and the worker priest movements) as well as proving a core principle of St. Benedict's Rule in the sixth century, the founding guide of Western monasticism. The following passage of the rule is characteristic and pioneering: "Let all guests who arrive be received like Christ, for He is going to say: 'I came as a guest, and you received Me.' And to all let due honor be shown, especially to the domestics of the faith and to pilgrims. . . . In the salutation of all guests, whether arriving or departing, let all humility be shown. Let the head be bowed or the whole body prostrated on the ground in adoration of Christ, who indeed is received in their persons." The passage concludes with an invocation to the last becoming first: "Let both the Abbot and community wash the feet of all guests. After the washing of the feet let them say this verse: "We have received Your mercy, O God, in the midst of Your temple" (*Rule of St. Benedict*, chapter 53).

But, if the Benedictine legacy informed one Christian attitude to the stranger, the Crusades and Inquisitions informed another. The choice for Christians is as contemporary as it is historical.

THE ISLAMIC WAGER

Recall the primary scene of Islam: A respected businessman called Muhammad Ibn Abdullah retires to a cave on the summit of Mount Hira. It is the month of Ramadan, 610 CE. Here, as was his annual wont, Muhammad sets to praying, fasting, and providing alms to the poor and outcast members of Meccan society who visited him. This time, however, on the night of 17 Ramadan something extraordinary happens. Muhammad is woken from his sleep by a strange presence in the cave. Something grips him until he can hardly breathe. All his certainties desert him, dissolving into the walls of the cave. His entire body is convulsed; he sweats profusely in the cool of midnight. He struggles, fearing his life may be in peril. Then, suddenly, he stops and listens. Muhammad decides to trust the incoming presence. And no sooner has he overcome terror and surrendered (*islam*) to the stranger before him than he hears a voice speak through him. The voice of the angel Gabriel. His lips open and the first words of a new Arab Scripture issue from his mouth. The Prophet of Islam is born, discovering himself a foreigner within his mother tongue. "When I heard the Qur'an," he announced after, "my heart was softened and I wept, and Islam entered me."[9] The words that he heard he did not speak or write. Only much later did he cautiously recite them to various groups of followers who in turn recorded them in the sacred texts known as the Qur'an and Hadith.

The deep ambiguity of Abrahamic religion recurs in Islam, the third confessional response to biblical revelation. We need no reminder of the manifold expressions of Islamic faith down through the centuries. In the wake of 9/11 the bloodier, if unrepresentative, chapters of this history have been rehearsed ad infinitum. And of course certain fundamentalist interpretations of the Qur'an, from the early civil wars of the sixth century to the rise of Wahhabism in our modern era, have given sorry credence to this negative legacy. But it is only one legacy. Many forget that the words of the Prophet may be read in very different ways. Each episode of his Book, as of previous biblical testaments, is susceptible to different hermeneutic

Figure 1.4. *Muhammed Receiving a Vision Near Mecca,*
by anonymous Turkish artist, circa. sixteenth century

readings—namely, 1. those in the name of hospitality to aliens and 2. those
in the name of war against the enemies of faith. Muhammad himself, it
must be remembered, like Jesus and Abraham before him, never wrote anything down. His words were recorded and inscribed by witnesses, after the
revelation at Mecca. And he was, in fact, so overwhelmed by the voice of
the strange angel that for the first two years he spoke to no one about it
but his wife Khadija and her cousin Waraqa Ibn Nawfal. Only in 612 did
Muhammad feel ready to speak out more openly to a small group of family
friends and young merchants, thereby ensuring that his vision of a society

where the "weak and vulnerable were treated with respect" could extend to wider circles.[10] If the Divine Stranger was first experienced in fear and trembling by Abraham and by Mary of Nazareth, so too by Muhammad. The encounter, as noted, was painful and bewildering. "Never once did I receive a revelation," confessed Muhammad, "without thinking that my soul had been torn away from me."[11]

Through the centers over seventy branches of Islam have emerged from the primary scene of Muhammad in the cave. And common to all, it seems, is this holy teaching of the Prophet: "Islam began as a stranger, and it will become a stranger. So blessed are those who are strangers." The Arabic term used in this celebrated Hadith is *gharib*, in the sense of an "outsider," beyond tribal ties and determinations. It was used in multiple ways in later traditions, especially esoteric and mystical ones where it was considered a term of the highest praise. But it is not an isolated exception. Throughout the Islamic texts we find similar precepts of hospitality being cited again and again: "Not one of you truly believes unless you wish for others what you wish for yourself" ("The Golden Rule"). Or again: "We have made you into nations and tribes, so that you can get to know and befriend each other, not to be boastful of your heritage" (Qur'an 49:13). Hardly recipes for war or conquest! Moreover, the Prophet's teaching that no one knows the true interpretations of the Qur'an except God indicates that divine truth cannot be exhausted in any single human form; it "demands a variety of interpretations, especially by the spiritually adept, on themes concerning the nature of God and the nature of humanity."[12]

The liberating legacy of Islam is one that—as in Judaism and Christianity—has to be reclaimed rather than assumed. It is, once again, a matter of bold hermeneutic retrieval. And, in this instance, a retrieval oft contested in Muslim culture, arguably because Islam, unlike Judaism and Christianity, escaped the disenchanting rigors of a secular Enlightenment. A number of contemporary Islamic scholars have, nonetheless, engaged in this task of pioneering critical reappropriation, among them Maqbood Siraj, Abdolkarim Soroush, and other commentators discussed in chapter 6. In contradistinction to the bellicose readings of Islam in the sixth-century khalifat or later Wahhabi movements (from which Al Qaeda sprang), these thinkers offer alternative accounts of Islamic intellectual history.[13]

Such counternarratives—counter, that is, to fundamentalist assumptions—are more in keeping with the original intellectual legacy of Andalusian philosophers like Al'Farabi and Averroes (Ibn Rushd). Siraj, for example, explores the legacy of Islam on the Indian subcontinent as one of creative synthesis and imaginative accommodation. Particularly pertinent is his description of the interfaith vision of enlightened Mughal leaders like Babur and Akbar, or visionaries like Dara Shikoh, committed to a vast enterprise of "translation" between Islamic and Hindu texts (including renditions of the Ramayana, Mahabharata, and Upanishads in Persian). Akbar was even credited with the promotion of a new interspiritual philosophy known as *Din e Ilahi*, drawing from the wisest insights of the different faiths practiced in his jurisdiction. He engaged in frequent discussions with delegates of various religions in his court—from Purkottham Brahman and Sheikh Tajudden to Portuguese Christian missionaries and Zoroastrian representatives from Navsari in Gujarat.[14] These exchanges led Akbar to believe in the commonality of all religions or what he called a "general consensus" (*sulhe kul*) among different faiths regarding certain human values. Indeed it is humbling for Westerners to recall, especially in our time of anti-Islamic suspicion, that in the sixteenth and seventeenth centuries when Christian inquisitors were persecuting witches, Jews, Muslims, and heretics (Giordano Bruno was burnt alive in the Campo dei Fiori for his interreligious imagination in 1600), Akbar was convening multifaith symposia in his Indian palace! One sometimes forgets that there have always been multiple schools of Islam, not one monolithic authority. Indeed religious minorities and diversities were often better treated under the Mughal Empire than under most Western empires of the time.

One might also recall other Muslim leaders' willingness to engage in creative dialogue with their Christian and Jewish counterparts at crucial junctures in Western history. We could cite, for example, the fertile exchanges between Muslim and non-Muslim thinkers in Andalusian Spain in the twelfth century; the famous interreligious Council of Florence, convened by Nicholas of Cusa in the middle of the fifteenth century and attended by leading Islamic scholars of Constantinople and beyond; the welcome given to the Patrarch of Constantinople, Batholowmew, by the Grand Mufti of Sarajevo during the height of the Bosnian war; or, more recently, the intervention by 138 leading Islamic scholars in October 2007 in the debate following Pope Benedict's lecture at Regensburg, issuing in the path-breaking manifesto of interconfessional hospitality entitled "A Common Word."[15]

Arguably the most historically influential figure of a tolerant Islamic hermeneutics was the Great Averroes of Cordoba. Averroes, also known as Ibn Rushd, was one of the key figures of the famous Andalusian conversation between Muslims, Christians, Jews, and "pagans." Boldly opposing the fundamentalist clerics in his influential text, *Fasl al-maqal*, Averroes argued for a harmonious debate between Islamic religion and secular (at that time mainly Greek) philosophy. Faith, he insisted, needed to be kept in critical dialogue with reason (however "pagan" it might seem to certain clerics) if the rich plurality of meanings, human and divine, were to be properly respected. Indeed Fred Dallmayr has suggested that the most apt translation of Averroes's formative work is *The Book of Differences.* Referring to the pagan Greeks (the intellectual "others" of his own Islamic culture), Averroes argued that "those who do not share our religion" were as likely to reach truth through the ways of reason as those who follow Islam. For Averroes the ideal philosopher was one who could combine "religious integrity" with "natural reason" (available to all humans). And, as a consequence of this intellectual latitude, he was an audacious proponent of nonliteral and metaphorical readings of the Qur'an. Where conflicts of interpretation occurred, as was inevitable, the matter should be consigned, he argued, to philosophers; for not only were they most attuned to the rational clarification of complex, multiple meanings—i.e., "depth interpretation"—but they were also directed toward the same horizon of "truth" as that disclosed in revealed scripture.[16] In this sense, one might say that Averroes recognized the importance of the "anatheist" wager within the ambit of Islamic faith. He knew that without the critical distance of philosophical inquiry revelation risked lapsing into authoritarianism.

With this commitment to intellectual freedom, Averroes and other critical scholars advanced a thoughtfully tolerant brand of Islamic hermeneutics against those literalists who, in his acerbic words, "threw people into hatred, mutual detestation and wars."[17] Open philosophical inquiry was hailed as the "friend and milk-sister of religion," not its sworn enemy as the literalists held. Islam needed to learn from critical outsiders—in particular the earlier Greek philosophers—if it was to be true to its mission of respecting the alien and the stranger. The *Fasl* concludes, significantly, with a moving paean to "a loving relationship that respects difference without fusion or mutual separation."[18] I shall return to the contemporary relevance of such Islamic hermeneutics in our discussion of the relation between the sacred and the secular in chapter 6.

But Averroes is not the only thinker to advance a critical hermeneutics of Islam. Much contemporary scholarship by figures like Henri Corbin, James Morris, and Hannah Merriman has reemphasized the interfaith resources of progressive Islam conceived as a multisided pyramid whose apex is reachable by different paths. Commenting on the extraordinary insights of Islamic sages like Ghazali, Biruni, and Ibn 'Arabi, Morris shows how they ingeniously reconciled the historical multiplicity of religions with the unity of the One *Din*. Ibn 'Arabi, in particular, treasured the process of "creative imagination" and promoted the reciprocal translation between languages and religions as a means of articulating the invisible human-divine reality the Qur'an called the "Heart" (*al-qalb*).[19]

The Islamic tendency toward intellectual pluralism and "cultural blending" also found cogent expression in the poetic-spiritual works of Sufi mystics like Rumi, Hallaj, Hafiz, and Kabir Das. Here the motif of hospitality to the stranger is pivotal and recurring. Indeed throughout their poems and ghazals we find God being referred to as an "uninvited Guest." Let me briefly mention two of these figures.

Hafiz of Shiraz was a fourteenth-century poet who wrote in Persian. His name is short for "one who knows the Qur'an by heart," and his famous ghazals explored the central Islamic notion of the heart (*qalb*) as locus of encounter with the Beloved Guest. Hafiz expresses his readers thus: "If God invited you to a party, and said, 'Everyone in the ballroom tonight will be my special Guest,' How would you treat them when you arrived?"[20] In other words, if we are all God's guests on this earth how should we behave toward each other and how do we know who is our host? God, suggests Hafiz, is the beloved host of hosts who teaches us hospitality by coming to us in the guise of the "guest," inviting us to host him in turn as we would a Lover. Terror before the stranger is thus translated into fascination for a new beloved whom we meet at a nocturnal feast full of musk, music, wine, and dance. By visiting the house of the Other, taking on the role of guest, we learn the art of hospitable refinement and attentiveness toward others. "What happens to the guest who visits the house of a great musician," asks Hafiz. "Of course, his tastes become refined."[21] Refinement, in this context, means becoming apprenticed to the art of welcome, daring to embrace aliens and newcomers whose identity is unfamiliar and surprising. That is why Hafiz exhorts us, on meeting with a stranger, not to ask his or her history or allegiance. On the contrary, he says, make a wager of trust. "O my dear, Do not ask how we are, be a stranger and ask of no comrade's story."[22]

In Hafiz's universe God plays variously the role of guest and host and invites us to do likewise. And if God has invited many different people to celebrate in his house, "we must respect them no matter how strange their games."[23] We may not even know from time to time who is the divine lover and who the human. Who the friend and who the trickster. There is always a risk in the game of love; and the divine lover needs us, it seems, as much as we need him. Hafiz's God is a "voyaging friend" who comes and goes, calling and courting his creatures: "God has made love with you and the whole universe is germinating inside your belly."[24] God consummates his desire in the love between humans as they mutually and endlessly exchange the roles of guest and stranger, giver and receiver, lover and beloved. In Hafiz's world of mystical poetics the sacred and profane go hand in glove. He has taken the Qur'an so much to heart that his own heart has become one of its privileged voices, translating each time into more novel and startling symbols. This is Islamic hermeneutics at its most transgressive, daring, and imaginative.[25]

Our second poet, Kabir Das, was a fifteenth-century visionary raised in Islam in northern India. His life and work brought together what he considered to be the most promising aspects of both Muslim and Hindu faiths in the spirit of bhakti and Sufi practices. A prophet of "dual religious belonging," Kabir composed poems renowned throughout all his native India in his time. He wrote in a hybrid language that broke down barriers to experiencing the divine. This is important: for unlike some of the more expert scholars and philosophers, Sufi poets like Hafiz, Rumi, and Kabir were known to millions of Muslims throughout the world, learned by heart, recited at weddings, funerals, and feastdays. Their songs of the Qur'an were part of a lived religious imaginary, operating beneath and beyond official ideology (literalist or fundamentalist). Some of them, exposed to clerical courts, were executed for their imaginings. But they have lived on in popular Islmamic cultures to this day.

Kabir, and his friend and mystic poet Mirabai, denounced the bigotry of narrow religious sects and invited people to seek God within themselves in simplicity, integrity, and love. Indeed Kabir described himself as a hybrid "child of Allah-Rama," considering these two deities as different names for the same unnameable God. Interestingly, Kabir refers frequently to God as a stranger at the door, an unexpected visitor from afar, a migrant lover with nowhere to lay his head. The traversal of otherness is, he believes, one of the surest signs of spiritual courage. "There is one thing in the world that satisfies," writes Kabir, "and that is meeting with the Guest." The welcoming of the divine Guest in our everyday midst is a constant theme for Kabir, leading him to transcend doctrinal constraints and tribal restrictions:

> I do not ring the temple bell:
> I do not set the idol on its throne . . .
> When you leave off your clothes and
> Kill your senses, you do not please the Lord.
> The man who is kind and practises righteousness
> Who considers all creatures on earth as his own self,
> He attains the Immortal Being,
> The true God is ever with him.[26]

Nurtured in the culture of Sufi Islam, Kabir pushed the doors wide open to interreligious belonging:

> If God be in the mosque, then to whom does this world belong?
> If Ram be within the image which you find upon your pilgrimage,
> Then who is there to know what happens without?
> Hari is in the East: Allah is in the West.
> Look within your heart,
> For there you will find both Karim and Ram;
> All the men and women of the world
> Are His living forms.
> Kabir is the child of Allah and of Ram.

Legend tells how on his death, when Hindu and Muslim sects rushed to appropriate his body for rival funeral rites, they found no one lying beneath the shroud—only a bed of jasmine.[27]

We have seen how the three Abrahamic religions testify to a basic ambivalence in human responses to the divine stranger. You can kill the alien as a threatening enemy or overcome the initial fear and respond with a gesture of welcome. Western religion is the history of this either/or, and most of its

chapters offer evidence of both. That is why it remains to this day a battle-
ground of interpretations. In the beginning was the Word; which means
in the beginning was hermeneutics. Emile Benveniste acknowledges the
drama of this inaugural ambivalence toward the stranger in his analysis of
the common root of our terms, hostility and hospitality. In Latin "guest" is
called both *hostis* and *hospes*. The first, *hostis*, can mean variously enemy or
host, adversary or guest. As Benveniste explains, referring to the Indo-European genealogy of the term: "The primitive notion conveyed by *hostis* is one
who repays my gift with a counter-gift. Thus, like its Gothic counterpart,
gasts, Latin *Hostis* at one period denoted the guest. The classical meaning "enemy" must have been developed when reciprocal relations between
clans were succeeded by the exclusive relations of *civitas* to *civitas* (cf. Gr.
Xenos "guest" — "stranger")."[28] In this manner, according to Benveniste, the
"word *hostis* assumed a hostile flavour."[29] The related Latin term, *hospes*,
as noted, also carries the ambivalence of both host and guest: that is, the
host who receives, or refuses to receive, the stranger as guest. This second
term consists of the compound elements *hosti-pet-s*, from both "guest" and
"master," so that *hospes* literally means "Guest-Master." The root *pet* or *pot*
in turn carries the meaning of power and mastery (*potestas*) or capacity
and potential (*potest*). So *hospes* can mean one who is master of the house
(*demipot*) or of his own identity (*pats*). But it also means one who "can," one
who is "capable" of difference, otherness, of receiving the stranger into the
home. And the "one who receives," as Benveniste observes, "is not the one
who is master of his house."[30] On the basis of these rich ambivalences in the
root terms, *hostis* and *hospes*, Benveniste can conclude that the connection
between "guest" and "enemy" supposes that both derive their meaning from
"stranger," a sense that is still attested in Latin. The notion of "favourable
stranger" developed to "guest"; that of "hostile stranger" to "enemy."[31]

   "Every angel is terrible" Rilke says in the *Duino Elegies*, and it is our
decision as to how we respond. In many religions, we are told, the holy is experienced as a terrifying yet compelling event: *"fascinans et tremendum"* —
both inviting and fearsome.[32] From its inception then, religion tells a double story of violence or compassion, of genocide or justice, of *thanatos* or
eros. And often both at once.

   The challenge, I am suggesting, is to struggle with angels of death and
life, turning the pressures of night into the promise of natality. But to return
after nocturnal not-knowing, after the abandonment of old Master Gods,
to a second light, to a second faith, we must first traverse the dark. And to

do this in our time we must engage, I submit, with critical and iconoclastic atheism. For if one does not fully acknowledge the murderous potential of religion, exposed by robust atheistic critiques, how can one hope to embrace the stranger who comes from the desert rather than condemning him or her to exclusion or oblivion? That is why I understand open atheism as a-theism, namely, a salutary moment of estrangement, a departure from God (*a-dieu*) that struggles with God (*contre-dieu*). It may thus allow the possibility of a return to a God beyond God (*hors-dieu*), a God who may come back to us from the future.[33] Without such a-theism we would not have the *option* of ana-theism. The former is a condition of possibility (if by no means necessity) for the latter.

2

IN THE WAGER

THE FIVEFOLD MOTION

When a great moment knocks on the door of your life it is often no louder
than the beating of your heart and it is very easy to miss it.

—Pasternak, *Letter to Olga*

FIVE MOMENTS

The anatheist wager I am trying to describe has five main components:
imagination, humor, committment, discernment, and *hospitality.* I will say a
word about each in turn, though strictly speaking they do not constitute five
sequential moments, chronologically separate in time, but rather equiprimordial aspects of a single hermeneutic arc. Wagers occur in an instant, all
at once. But they are complex, shrouded in a halo of multilayered motions.
And there is much, we shall see, that precedes and follows them.

Imagination

One cannot wager unless one has freedom to choose. Such choice presupposes our ability to imagine different possibilities in the same person,
to see the Other before us *as* a stranger to be welcomed or rejected. This
sense of primordial openness to the Stranger means that our perception
is *already* a hermeneutic "seeing as." From the start, it is a primary interpretation inscribed in our bodily response, emotion and affect, before any
theoretical reflection. To respond in fear or welcome—as dramatized in the

celebrated paintings of Mary in the Annunciation or Jacob wrestling with the angel—already implies a movement of primary imagining. Indeed the act of faith—as belief in the possibility of the impossible, of a possibility beyond the impossible—would be inconceivable without this instantaneous response of imagination. As the Islamic sage, Ibn 'Arabi put it, the angels of God always appear to us, first and foremost, through the "imaginal"—the inner invisible meaning (*ma na*) becoming visible to us in the form of appearance (*sura*). And, as so many great mystics noted, when describing visions and visitations; the imagination is a "bride of God" serving as bridge between spiritual and corporeal worlds. "Revelation begins with imagination. . . . The angel imaginalizes (*takhayyul*) itself as a man, or as a person who is perceived. . . . The angel casts the words of his Lord in the prophet's hearing, and this is revelation."[1] If we have no imagination, we cannot open our eyes and ears to the Stranger who comes. Here speaks the divine suitor in Ibn 'Arabi's words:

Dearly beloved,
I have called you so often and you have not heard me.
I have shown myself to you so often and you have not seen me.
I have made myself fragrant so often, and you have not smelled
    me,
Savory food, and you have not tasted me.
Why can you not reach me through the object you touch
Or breathe me through sweet perfumes?
Why do you not see me? Why do you not hear me?
Why? Why? Why?

—Ibn 'Arabi, *The Book of Theophanies*

This inaugural moment of imagining—divine call and human response—is also poignantly captured by modern artists of epiphany from Hopkins and Rilke to Chagall and Rouault. Indeed most great works of religious art may be seen as responses to such an imaginative summons. And perhaps that is what Dostoyevsky meant, in *The Idiot*, when he said that "only beauty can save the world." I shall return to this question in my study of sacramental aesthetics in chapters 4 and 5.

The primal moment of imagination is also crucial to ethics. For without imagination there is no empathy between self and other. Imagining the other as other is what enables the self to become a host and the stranger a guest. Empathy, as Edith Stein reminds us, is the "experience of foreign consciousness." It is a "primordial experience of the nonprimordial" in that what is given to me by the other remains foreign to me in its very givenness. It never becomes fully myself, but only another in myself and for myself. A *gap* thus always remains and, as such, solicits imagination to respond to the irreducible transcendence and alterity of the stranger before me. In the process I am transformed into a host (oneself as another) who receives the visitor as guest (another as oneself). But always as an act of gracious imagining, for the stranger is never "really" translatable into my language of experience in any total or adequate sense. I greet the Other by imagining the Other "as" Other (metaphorically) or "as if" the Other were like me (fictively). Empathy can only work by analogy. For empathy to become sympathy—that is, feeling *with* the other as though one was the other—an act of imagination is called for. We can only murder strangers if we cannot imagine what it is like to be them. The "like" carries both similarity and difference. In imagination, in short, I both *am* and *am not* the stranger. And this in turn involves a double movement of action and passion: I actively imagine what it is to be like the stranger as I passively assume the stranger's summons and sufferings.[2] I will return to this point under our fifth heading, *hospitality*.

Humor

This second movement is sometimes overlooked in official religious doctrines where cheerless sanctimony can mask the essentially human response of the wager. By humor I mean here the ability to encounter and compose opposites: what I see as impossible and possible at one and the same time. So the barren Sarah, at the entrance of her tent, laughs when she hears she'll be with child; just as Mary, in the quiet of her boudoir, says "Amen"—meaning: let the inconceivable be conceived, let the uncontainable be contained in the fruit of the womb (*chora achoraton*). Humor, as Bergson reminds us, is a creative response to enigma, contradiction, and paradox. Humbly acknowledging the earthly and earthy limits of human experience, it makes our relationship to the ungraspable Other a divine comedy. As the Latin root *humus* reminds us, humor, humility, and humanity share a common source.

To focus first on the Christian Scriptures, we might recall Jesus's playful exchange with the Samaritan woman at the well (as he teases her about her five husbands and lying about the fifth); his conversion of water into wine to celebrate the marriage feast of Cana; his frequent riddling to his disciples about his identity—"Who do you say that I am?" echoing Exodus 3:15—or his posthumous visitation to his disciples on the shore of Lake Galilee as an unrecognizable cook! "Come and have breakfast" are not the first words the apostles expected to hear from their risen Messiah! Not to mention the multiple comic reversals, puns, and conundrums that recur throughout the Gospels: the last as first, the mountain moving, the kingdom as mustard seed, the rich man and the eye of a needle, etc.

The story of Jesus's own life is itself divinely comic, moreover, to the extent that it was largely lived, as Kierkegaard observed, "incognito." It is the drama of a Holy Fool disappearing in presence and reappearing in absence, at once there and not there (*Noli me tangere*). Jesus preexists his historical existence ("Before Abraham was I am") at the same time as he outlives it ("I must go so that the Paraclete can come"). And this comic sense of the Stranger, as both human and divine, as one who comes in the disguise of the least of these, masked and incognito, is also one playfully evoked by the great Sufi poets of Islam. Divine visitation as a game of hide and seek. Indeed one of Hafiz's most renowned ghazals is entitled "I Heard God Laughing,"[3] and his dazzling divans are replete with incidents where the poet banters and jokes with his divine lover. One might also note here the amusing Hasidic and rabbinical tales regarding messianic reversals and surprises—for example, the famous story of the beggar who approaches the Messiah at the gates of Rome and, tapping him on the shoulder, asks: "When will you come?" Messianic time, disrupting the familiar continuum of history and turning past and future on their heads, is divinely comic.

Humor, in this special sense, is deep *humility* before the excess of meaning the divine stranger carries like a halo round his head. The stranger surpasses the limits of accredited cognitions, calling us back to our terrestrial share as mortals in search of something "more." The highest as lowest, the master as servant; everything is upside down in the logic of sacred alterity. You either laugh or cry. Humor reminds us that we are deeply and invariably creatures of the earth (*humus*). Finite, mortal, natal. We laugh, like Sarah, when we see God because we are temporal beings facing divine surplus. True mystics and saints were, it is often said, noted for their humor. Recall Eckhart: "God told me a joke and seeing him laugh taught me more than all the Scriptures." But Chief High Executioners and Grand Inquisitors are incapable of laughing at the divine comedy of existence.

We laugh or weep when we do *not know*. This is the modesty of nescience illustrated by the fourth-century Egyptian monk who wrote in the *Apophthegmata of the Desert Fathers*: "Truly, Abbot Joseph has found the way, because he has said: 'I do not know.'"[4]

Commitment

The third movement of the wager is commitment. Our response to the stranger is already a decision. We choose, we commit, we say: Here I stand or do not stand. The openness of imagination and humor to contrary options is *simultaneously* accompanied by a moment of choice. (Even if that choice is to have no choice—to remain in indecision—it is still a choice: namely, the choice not to choose). This is the moment of "Here I am" (*Hinenee*) famously witnessed by Abraham, Moses, and the prophets in the conversion moments of their lives. It is the moment where Jesus, after the anxious equivocations of Gethsemane ("Let this chalice pass") and the loss of faith on the cross ("Why have You forsaken me?"), returns to the wager of second faith: "Unto Thee I commend my spirit." It is the instant when Muhammad, in the cave at Mecca, says yes to the voice of Islam that is bidding him open his lips and respond. We are speaking here, in sum, of a moment of truth—as *troth*—where we do not *know* the truth but *do* the truth. *Facere veritatem*, as Augustine put it. Orthopraxis precedes orthodoxy. Trust precedes theory. Action precedes abstraction.

Commitment, in this sense of betrothal, is the movement of the wager that makes truth primarily—though not exclusively—a matter of existential transformation (*metanoia*). Such performative truth as trust is inscribed in tactile and testimonial promise. (Though it is no less hermeneutic for that.) If God had truth in his right hand, as Lessing noted, and the striving for truth in the left, we should choose the left. In the anatheist wager, truth becomes possible as betrothal.

Discernment

This fourth aspect of the wager does not come *after* the other aspects but is simultaneous with them. There can be no commitment, for example, without discernment, and vice versa; though this wager of discernment may occur, I repeat, at the most basic affective and preconceptual levels. This is where we distinguish between a blind leap of faith and a wise one. The wager of response is not irrational. It is, as Ricoeur reminds us, hermeneutically vigilant and alert. And this means that every seeing is a *seeing as*, a reading of the Stranger *as* this or that other, as love or hate, life or death. Of course this is no easy matter, which is why Kierkegaard was right to say that faith is an experience of "fear and trembling" (if overhasty to add that it is absurd). Reading the face of the other is difficult, often disorienting and puzzling, but it is never completely impossible. If it were, every meeting with the divine would be a blind date. But an anatheist perspective suggests that even if the stranger shows up in the dark we receive him or her with eyes wide open. When we sense the holy we humbly open ourselves to the enigma of the Other and commit. That is why we are always already "discerning between spirits." We do not, as Ignatius knew, consent to just *any* kind of Other simply because they are other. And this is where we take issue not only with Kierkegaard and the fideists but also with Derrida and the deconstructionists for whom "every other is every other" (*tout autre est tout autre*).

Not every stranger is divine. There is the other who kills and the other who brings life. The other who loves and the other who lies. The knock on the door may be the Lord (qua host) inviting us to a feast or (qua guest) seeking entry to our home; but it may also be a psychotic murderer, a torturer come to inflict pain on innocents, a rapist bent on violating loved ones. (Derrida admits as much, but says we have no way of knowing the difference between one kind of other and another).[5] While some others bring peace, other others bring crusades, pogroms, and genocides, claiming to have God on their side. The examples are too legion to ignore. One cannot be naive in assuming that we, humans, are capable of unconditional or indiscriminate welcome to every other who approaches. (Perhaps that is the prerogative of God? And we are not gods.)

If Abraham, Jesus, and Muhammad listened to an Other who brought life, there are countless instances in history of people who did the opposite, namely, listened to voices that bade innocents be murdered in the Name of God. And even the most holy, as we saw, were not always exempt. Already with Abraham there was a voice that told him kill his son and a voice that bade him save him. He discerned and chose wisely, love over death; he received Isaac back as gift. Jesus heard a voice that bade him offer his life in service to Others and another voice (in the desert) that tempted him to become a Master God of spectacle (turning stone to bread) and triumph (possessing the cities of the world). He discerned and chose wisely, love over power; he healed the sick, washed his friends' feet and broke bread. And even when Jesus seemed tempted to compare the alien Phoenician woman to a dog waiting for crumbs, he, the Holy Stranger of Israel, learned from this most estranged of beings to recognize true faith in the humble foreigner become him: Jesus and the Phoenician outsider exchanged the roles of host and guest. Jesus was ready to learn from the "least of these." He was ever "watchful" as he in turn admonished Peter to be (Mark 14:39). The term *watchful* (*gregoresai*) means to be alert and vigilant. "Be watchful and prayerful" (*gregoreite kai proseuxesthe*), he urges. For prayer is attention to otherness.

And so on, down through the lives of holy ones, prophets, and saints. There is always a discernment to be made—often in the middle of the night, in the depth of a cave, in an instant of holy not-knowing—when the "thin small voice" whispers. And such discernments are often made in a moment, by the body, by the ear and eye, as in the Botticelli portrait of Mary that shows her move from withdrawal to consent. As noted previously, Mary was "troubled and pondered" (*dietarachte kai dielogizeto*) when she met Gabriel. Discernment is, to be sure, a matter of prereflective carnal response to the advent of the Other *before it* becomes a matter of reflective cognitive evaluation. The body already "ponders" in dia-logue with the stranger.

Hermeneutics goes all the way down. It begins in our nerve endings, organs, and sensations. Our most basic existential moods—fear and love, anxiety and wonder—are, as Heidegger and the phenomenologists noted, already modes of prepredicative interpretation: they follow the basic structure of *understanding-as*. Sartre recognized as much when he defined emotions as "structured means toward an end," as did Scheler when he characterized feelings as intentional responses to deep values. And Merleau-Ponty goes further still when he claims that "perception already stylizes" and that every bodily function has its own distinct *symbolique*. Even our unconscious dreams—unfolding in the darkest hours of night—are already ways of responding to our enigmatic world, as Freud demonstrated in *The Interpretation of Dreams*. To respond to the Other is always already to have chosen, to have interpreted, even if we are not yet cognitively aware of doing so. Which is why cognition of the stranger is always a matter of re-cognition.

But, I repeat: the matter is complex. As acknowledged earlier, history tells of many who did *not* choose wisely or well—those who invoked the voice of God to prosecute heinous atrocities. Even in our own so-called civilized time horrific acts have been carried out by crazed people who claim to hear a voice from God: Jim Jones, David Koresh, Charles Manson, Osama Bin Laden . . . the list goes on. And Schneider's famous psychotic accounts to Freud of how God penetrated his very being are not that different, at first blush, from countless popular descriptions of "alien abductions" or indeed, more intriguingly, from Teresa of Avila's personal testimony to mystical "transverberation." This is why so many of the great saints and mystics, who claimed to hear holy voices or receive holy visitations of divine eros, scrupulously insisted upon disciplined criteria of discernment, chief among them being the distinction between the divine visitor who brings compassion and counterfeits who bring confusion.[6] The drama of discernment involves an intense act of attention starting at the most basic carnal level and accompanying the movements of imagination, commitment, and humility (which includes the wisdom to learn from initial mistakes and misreadings). This multilayered hermeneutic drama—extending from embodied prereflection to critical reflection—is indispensable to the anatheist wager.

Hospitality

This final moment of the anatheist wager is in fact there from the beginning and coterminous with the other four. If discernment is integral to the anatheist wager, as argued, this does not mean that knowledge trumps love. Far from it. At best, love of the stranger is a form of "faith seeking knowledge" (*fides quarens intellectus*), knowing all the while that we never have absolute knowledge of the absolute. (To think otherwise, like Hegel or certain hyperrationalists is to risk totalizing knowledge and politics). The love of the host for the guest always precedes and exceeds knowledge. Indeed, as Scheler notes in *Love and Knowledge*, a frequent error of Western metaphysics has been to see love and eros as a means to knowledge rather than as the end of all knowledge.[7] Of course, the role of knowledge in hospitality is complex. When we discern—as we wager before the face of the stranger— we always run the risk of being mistaken, of getting it wrong. But such risk is not groundless. Love—as compassion and justice—is the watermark. There is a discernible difference between one who gives water to the thirsty and one who does not, between one who heals and one who maims, between one who hosts and one who shuts the door. Even if sometimes it is hard to fully understand the difference between hospitality and hostility. As with half-open doors.

The ability to serve as gracious host is not, however, only a matter of discerning between strangers; it is also a matter of discerning between selves. We might say, to borrow from Ricoeur, that the self that wagers is one "refigured" by opening itself to other possibilities of being. So doing it passes through a certain "nothingness," an act of self-dispossession from the familiar, habituated ego. This dying unto the ego, this caesura or rupture of ascesis, is not in itself *nothing* but the self "deprived of sameness."[8] It is the self defamiliarized, exposed to difference, alert to alternatives of alterity. Here the self becomes Other to itself as it encounters the Other beyond itself. Creative and chiasmic estrangment. *Moi* become *soi*. Ricoeur surmises that it is likely "the most dramatic transformations of personal identity pass through the crucible of this nothingness of identity," without which selfhood would be doomed to brute repetition.[9] And one might compare this motion of disowning oneself as ego (so as to become oneself-as-another) to the empty square of Lévi-Strauss's transformations. It is certainly integral to the movement of hospitality, for only in forgetting oneself as ego can one become host to the radically incoming Stranger.

The refiguration of ego into host is not limitless however. There are limits to hospitality, at least for finite beings. Only God, as Origen observed with his notion of "universal redemption," can love all beings indiscriminately, unconditionally, without why. Or the Buddha, for whom there are "no enemies." Even Christ had to ask his Father to forgive his enemies, the man in him appealing to the divine in him: "Father forgive them for they know not what they do." Unconditional hospitality is divine, not human. Which does not mean that we should not try to emulate the divine, while acknowledging our limits. But the divine is always a surplus, an excess beyond and beneath us, more than we can humanely manage: hence forever a stranger who beckons us toward the other always other than ourselves.

This hospitality applies not just *within* religions but *between* religions. And also, I would add, *beyond* religions (one cannot exclude the atheist as host and guest). To be truly hospitable one must be prepared to host not just those within one's faith culture, but those alien to it. Love of self and love of neighbor lead ineluctably to love of strangers, which is no doubt why the commandment says: "Love God [the Stranger] and love your neighbor as yourself." Here we touch on the important question of interreligious hospitality as a task of radical translation.

INTERRELIGIOUS TRANSLATION

Interreligious translation is, I suggest, at the heart of anatheism. It is a summons of imagination to transmigrate between one religion and another.

Ricoeur calls this "interconfessional hospitality," and he relates it, in turn, to the notions of 1. *linguistic hospitality* as an exchange between host and guest languages and 2. *eucharistic hospitality* as an exchange between selves and strangers (human and divine). Starting with the basic hermeneutic paradigm of translation, he writes:

> Bringing the reader to the author, bringing the author to the reader, at the risk of serving and of betraying two masters: this is to practice what I like to call linguistic hospitality. It is this which serves as a model for other forms of hospitality that I think resemble it: confessions, religions, are they not like languages that are foreign to one another, with their lexicon, their grammar, their rhetoric, their stylistics which we must learn in order to make our way into them. And is Eucharistic hospitality not to be taken up with the same risks of translation-betrayal, but also with the same renunciation of the perfect translation?[10]

I will return to a discussion of these "risks" in my conclusion. For now let us recall how the power of transreligious hospitality is evinced in certain breakthrough events of the wisdom traditions: Moses taking an African spouse, Solomon embracing the Shulammite woman, Jesus greeting the Samaritan woman at the well, or, to extend our range of reference, the Buddha welcoming those from alien and alienated castes, Sufi poets responding to the "uninvited guest," or the famous instance of Baucis and Philomen receiving Zeus and Hermes as disguised "strangers." Indeed, in classical texts, there is a common epithet attributed to Zeus—Zeus *Xenios*—meaning Zeus the protector of strangers. An offense against him, that is, against one's responsibilities for the stranger, was considered the worst sin. This ethic of hospitality is powerfully manifest in Homer's code of *filoxenia* in the Odyssey (think of how the Phaiakians welcome Oddyseus) and in his code of *xenia* in the Illiad (Glaucus and Diomedes refuse to kill each other in the sixth book when they acknowledge how they are bound by hospitality: "You are for me a guest [*xeinos*]," says Diomedes, "I am your host in the heart of Argolid and you are mine in Lycia . . . let us avoid each other's javelin and instead exchange our weapons so that everyone may know we are hereditary guests"). The ethic of hospitality is also witnessed in the Socratic welcome of the Eleatic Stranger and the outsider Gorgias.

But such examples are not confined to ancient epochs. In contemporary

times, we might invoke here the momentous impact of interreligious exchanges such as the Assisi gathering of world religions in 1986; the pilgrimages of Pope John Paul II to India and to the Wailing Wall in Jerusalem in
the 1990s; the meeting between the Grand Mufti and the Greek Patriarch
in Sarajevo in the midst of sectarian slaughter; the revolutionary addresses
by Eastern spiritual leaders like Vivekananda, Thich Nhat Hanh, and the
Dalai Lama to Western religious gatherings such as the World Parliament of
Religions or the World Council of Churches. Not to mention the ordinary
healing encounters across sectarian divides witnessed in recent decades in
places like Sarajevo, Hanoi, Warsaw, and Northern Ireland.

Regarding the famous Belfast Agreement, I am reminded especially of
the historic handshake between the Catholic (one-time seminarian) leader,
John Hume, and the arch-Protestant leaders, David Trimble and Ian Paisley, which led to the final peace settlement of 1998. The key to the breakthrough, as noted in our preface, was a simple act of reciprocal translation
captured in the formula: "Citizens of Northern Ireland may be British or
Irish or *both*." The exclusivist claims of a United Kingdom and a United Ireland (based on mutually incompatible sovereignty principles) were thus renounced in favor of a transnational compact of different peoples and faiths.
And, as is well known, this involved not just a translation of ideologies but
a "translation of hearts."[11]

Crossreading is a core principle of interreligious hermeneutics. It involves
an endless and reversible process of translation between one religion and
the next: a process whose aim is not some unitary fusion but mutual disclosure and enhancement. Interconfessional dialogue does not eliminate
differences but welcomes them, as the etymological root, *dia-legein* suggests. Here hospitality can only be an opening of self to stranger if the self
is a self and the stranger a stranger. As already observed, we welcome the
other as *other* not simply as the *same* as myself. Or, as Edith Stein put
it, genuine empathy with another is always a "primordial encounter" with
what escapes our immediate grasp or projection. Only through the shock of
affinity through alterity does something new emerge.

Let me now take some examples from transcriptural reading. What happens, for instance, if we read the text about Shiva's pillars of fire alongside
biblical passages on the Burning Bush or the Christian account of Pentecos-
tal flame? What new sparks of understanding and compassion fly up if we

read Hindu texts on the *guha* alongside Buddhist invocations of the "void" (in the Heart Sutra) or biblical references to Elijah or Muhammad in his cave, Jonah in the whale, Jesus in the tomb? What novel possibilities of semantic resonance are generated by juxtaposing the sacred bird (*hamsa*) of Vedanta alongside the dove of Noah's ark or of Christ's baptism in the Jordan? Not to mention the way in which the Islamic invocation of the Lote Tree (in Muhammad's *mi'raj* of ascent) may interanimate with such motifs as the tree of Paradise, the thorn bush of Exodus 3:15, Jesus's crown of thorns, or the famous *axis mundi* tree of Vedantin cosmogonies and Buddhist mandalas? We may wonder, finally, how sculpted images of the Hindu Trimurti (three-faced deity) might powerfully reinvigorate an understanding of Abraham's three strangers or the three persons of the Christian Trinity?

An initial hypothesis arising from such symbolic crossovers between Abrahamic and non-Abrahamic religions is that semantic exchange is at the heart of religious dialogue. Something new arises from multilateral transcriptions between the ancient imaginaries of diverse wisdom traditions. Out of the silent dark of the heart-cave—from which many religions originate and to which they often return—emerges a chorus of sounds, images, and gestures soliciting endless translation into different liturgies. This very translatability fosters the transversality of religions. It makes interspiritual conversation into a fertile crossroads where distinct paths traverse and intersect. And it lies, I submit, at the very core of anatheism as a return to God after God, that is, as an invitation to rediscover forgotten truths of one's own faith by traversing alien faiths. Just think, for instance, of how the Dalai Lama or Thich Nhat Hanh bring out new meanings in their reading of Christian Scriptures. Or how Christian translators like Thomas Merton, Bede Griffiths, or Henri Le Saux bring fresh perspectives to bear on certain holy Eastern texts? Not to mention the great Islamic translations of Vedantin classics by the likes of Buruni, Akbar, and Zafar. Certainly Indian figures like Vivekananda and Gandhi all acknowledged that their exposure to Western religions enabled them to better reclaim the precious emancipatory potentials of their own Hindu traditions. For, if Western religions can, for instance, learn from their Eastern counterparts how to recover a renewed sense of breath, body, and the holiness of all sentient beings, Eastern religions may learn from this dialogue a greater sense of personal selfhood, creative agency, and commitment to historical transformation.[12] If religions were the same rather than different, there would be no stranger to learn from, no alien to welcome to one's home. Genuine dialogue—as a welcoming of difference—would be impossible.

We will return to the question of interreligious hospitality in our concluding chapters. For now let me state my conviction that the mutual crossing of
religions does not lead to some spiritual Super Highway, but to a confluence
of multiple roads. The traversals proliferate in spiritual diversity just as fish
flourish where tides meet. The hermeneutics of hospitality finds rich hatching
grounds in the crosscurrents between different rivers. The wager here is that
it is precisely at the edges of *imagination*—before and after theory, ideology,
or dogma—that the aboriginal signs of the heart-well are first sounded and received. This is called *darshan* in Sanskrit, meaning sacred manifestation: the
becoming visible and audible of the divine in image, sound, or liturgy. The
wager of imagination invites one to attend to the primary scenes and stages of
embodying the ultimate, so finely celebrated by Mahayana Buddhism, Hindu
puja, or the great religious artworks of Jewish, Christian, and Islamic cultures.
These embodiments of the sacred I call epiphanies, and I will argue in chapters
4 and 5 that such epiphanies are not confined to official religions but are found
in both literary and everyday experiences of sacramental imagination.

In sum, I am wagering here on the possibility of a spiritual acoustics
capable of reinterpreting the oldest cries of the religious heart in both our
sacred and secular worlds. But to open oneself to such radical attention one
must, I suggest, abandon the old God of sovereignty and theodicy. That
Master God must die so that the God of interconfessional hospitality can be
born. And, insofar as religious dogma has often served as vehicle of infantile
fear and dependency, the interreligious God may be described as a postdogmatic God. That is why anatheism appreciates a rigorous atheistic critique
of the theistic perversions of religion. It sees it as a salutary estrangement
prior to a return to the genuinely sacred.

FROM SOVEREIGN TO SERVANT:
THE POWER OF THE POWERLESS

Another aspect of the fivefold wager worth emphasizing at this point is the
powerlessness of the divine. Here I take up again the idea of microeschatol-
ogy as a rediscovery of God in epiphanies of the everyday. Revisiting my
previous analyses in *After God* and *The God Who May Be*,[13] I wish to focus
especially on the notion of Incarnation as *kenosis*. By this I understand the
self-emptying of the omnipotent God, the surpassing of metaphysical categories of divinity as First Cause or Highest Being, the realization that God

is a promise, a call, a desire to love and be loved that can not *be* at all unless we allow God to be God. "You God cannot be God unless we create a
dwelling place for you in our hearts," Etty Hillesum wrote in a concentration camp shortly before her death. The greatest danger for religion is to
assume sovereign power. And this can mean both sacred sovereignty and
political sovereignty (as in the infamous conflation of spiritual and temporal powers in the hands of a territorial regent: *cuius regio eius religio*).[14]
The refusal of triumphal sovereignty is, I believe, firmly inscribed, if be no
means always observed, in the Abrahamic faiths: in the Hebraic command
to love the "widow the orphan and the stranger," in the Christian welcoming of Samaritan outcasts and in the Islamic message to accommodate the
uninvited Guest.

I shall offer a more extensive discussion of divine kenosis and nonsovereignty in chapters 6 and 7, so suffice it now to note that the concept of God as
absolute Monarch of the Universe stems from a literalist reading of the Bible
along with unfortunate misapplications of a metaphysics of causal omnipotence
and self-sufficiency. This has led to the ruinously influential notion of theodicy,
namely, the belief that God as Sovereign *causa sui*, as immutable Emperor of
the world, exercises arbitrary and unlimited powers over his creatures. Everything—even the worst horrors—could thus be justified as part of some divine
Will (the ultimate Will to Power). Max Scheler has a spirited riposte to the
God of theodicy in his essay on "The Meaning of Suffering," written during the
terrors of the First World War. Vehemently resisting any form of "teleological
theism" that seeks to legitimate events of human suffering in light of an overall
Divine Cause, he writes:

> If I had wanted to come to the idea of the existence of God by means
> of a cause-effect connection starting from nature and the existence
> of the world as known to me empirically, and not from an original,
> personal and experiential contact of the core of my personality with
> a divine goodness and wisdom as found in a religious act, then even
> if the rest of the world shines in peace, bliss, and harmony, the exis-
> tence of a single sensation of pain in a worm would completely suf-
> fice to destroy my belief in an "infinitely" good and almighty creator
> of the world.[15]

Theodicy and theocracy are miscreant offspring of theistic Sovereignty. The
alternative, I suggest, is anatheism of the stranger. Not as some final dialecti-

cal synthesis at the end of history, but as a timely repetition *forward* of the oldest story in the book. At least as old as the theism of sovereignty or the atheism of its negation.

The preferential option for hospitality over sovereignty affects our understanding of both being (ontology) and knowledge (epistemology). At the level of being, it privileges the may-be of the eschaton over the has-been of accomplished history. This calls for a "weak messianism" (Benjamin) that bids us redeem the forgotten voices of history by retrieving their "impeded possibilities," thereby emancipating the past into a future.[16] This eschatological giving of a future to the past is witnessed for example in Genesis 3:15 when Yahweh tells Moses he is not just a prerogative of ancestral memory but the *promise* that he "will be" with his people in their struggle for emancipation. "I am who will be with you." I am the God who may be, can be, shall be, if you listen to my summons and choose liberty over slavery, life over death, eros over thanatos. And this same eschatological paradox of past-as-future is at work in the Palestinian formula of the Passover that instructs us to remember the feast of the Passover "until he comes." It is reprised in the Christian invocation of "anticipatory memory" at the Last Supper (1 Cor. 11:25–26: "for as often as you eat this bread and drink the cup, you proclaim the death of the Lord until he comes"). And it finds additional echoes in John the Baptist's famous avowal of Jesus: "The one who is coming after me ranks ahead of me because he existed before me" (John 1:15).

The messianic exists before us ("before Abraham was I am") as the possibility that lies ahead of us. It heralds the one who comes *before* and *after* every "god" we presume to possess, the sacred stranger who is always in front of us, always to come. Which is surely why Jesus refuses the allure of self-possessed power, priority, and privilege, insisting that he be baptized by John rather than the contrary. "I need to be baptized by you," says John bemusedly, "and yet you are coming to me?" (Matt. 3:15). The washing of the apostles' feet (John 13) and subsequent enduring of death for others signals the conversion of sovereignty into hospitality. It epitomizes the anatheistic option for self-emptying service to strangers. Refusal of imperial power.

This reversal of Sovereign Being is echoed in the overturning of Sovereign Knowledge. Jesus does not *tell* his disciples who he is; he *asks* them "Who do they say that I am?" (Mark 8:27). And just as the voice in the burning bush refuses to impart some sacred name of magical power, replying instead with a riddling pun: "I am who I shall be"—so too Jesus resists all attempts to apprehend him in a categorical way. In fact it is only the "demons" who claim to *know* Jesus, as in the exchange with the unclean spirit at Capernaum who called out "I *know* who you are—the Holy One of God!" To which Jesus responds: "Be quiet! Come out of him" (Matt. 1:24). Even when Peter announces "You are the Christ," Jesus warns him to tell no one and actually denounces him as "Satan" for trying to dissuade him from going to his death (not a thing an omnipotent God would do! Mark 8:30–33).

Is it not significant, moreover, that whenever Jesus is pressed to reveal himself "as he is," he constantly refers to the Father or the Pentecost or the "least of these"? Is it not highly telling that he defers to *others* in a process of kenotic self-emptying? So that if he indeed admits he is the "Way the truth and the life," it is always a way that leads to others, a way that opens onto other ways. "You cannot reach the Father *except* through me," he boldly announces, calling for the radical exclusion of exclusion itself. For who cannot be counted among the "least of these"? Or among the "strangers" who hunger and thirst? (Though how often has this term *except* been invoked to support the opposite!). The messianic way leads from Sovereign Self to excluded stranger, breaching the highest in the name of the lowest, the first in the name of the last. Which is why I keep insisting that interconfessional hospitality toward other faiths is not just an option for Christians but an imperative. Christian *caritas*, as a refusal of exclusivist power, is a summons to endless *kenosis*.[17]

It is in a similar spirit, I suggest finally, that we may opt to read the frequent injunctions against idols and graven images in both Judaism and Islam. Namely, as a refusal to possess the sacredness of the wholly Other in anthropomorphic projections. In all three Abrahamic traditions we find evidence of a *via negativa* that safeguards the "strangeness" of the divine. This is why it is so important to constantly recall the anatheist moment of *not-knowing* at the very heart of spiritual experience: not as a threat to faith but as an integral part of the journey toward the Other. The anatheist wager is not some postmodern gloss on Descartes' doubt, but a movement of decision recognized as essential to genuine spiritual quest (viz. Anthony Steinbock's analysis of great mystics such as Ruzbiahn Baqli, Rabbi Dov Baer, and Teresa of Avila).[18] And one finds powerful instances of this wager in numerous other mystical texts from Gregory of Nyssa's notion of an unbridgeable gap (*diastema*) between human understanding and the irreducible strangeness of God to Bonaventure's famous definition of faith as a never-ending "pilgrim's progress" of many winding paths (*itinerarium mentis in Deum*). These all testify to an anatheist gesture of detachment from assumed faith that prizes open a possible return to second faith. That is why Teresa of Calcutta's diary confession of loss of belief should not have provoked worldwide scandal but been seen as a salutary maturation toward deeper belief. Her dark nights, lasting many years, were actually lived as special accompaniments to all those other strangers on this earth. "If ever I become a saint," she wrote, "I will surely be one of 'darknes'—I will continually be absent from Heaven, to light the light of those in darkness on earth." [19]

Perhaps there can be no anatheist wager without this moments of nonbelief? And, if this be so, I am tempted to compare such a cycle of faith to the ancient patristic figure of circumcession (*perichoresis*) where different persons move endlessly around an empty center (*chora*), always deferring one to the other, the familiar to the foreign, the resident to the alien. Without the *gap* in the middle there could be no leap, no love, no faith.

Anatheism cherishes the Siamese twins of theism and atheism and celebrates the fertile tension between them. The bracing oscillation between doubt and faith, withdrawal and consent is the aperture that precedes and follows each wager. It is the guarantee of human freedom before the summons of the stranger. The choice to believe or not believe is indispensable to the anatheist wager. And it is a choice made over and over, never once and for all.

IN THE NAME

AFTER AUSCHWITZ WHO CAN SAY GOD?

One has to free one's self inwardly of everything, of all existing representa-
tions, of all slogans, of all comforts. One has to have the courage to let go of
everything, of all standards and all conventional certainties. One has to dare
taking the giant leap . . . then life will be endlessly overflowing, even amidst
the deepest suffering.

—Etty Hillesum, notes from Westerbork Camp, July 7, 1942

What do we mean when we speak in the name of God? Do we mean an omnipotent God who will solve our problems, save and scold, condemn and
control? Or something very different? When we pray In the Name of the
Father do we regress to primitive rites of infantile dependency and projection (as Freud suggests)? Or is there more to it than that? Something beyond
childish superstition and fetishism? Something that gestures toward a divinity that may be in flesh and blood, here and now, if we allow it, responding
to the name that calls by creating a place where the one who comes can
arrive in our midst? If dogmatic theism often fostered the idea of primal attachment to a paternalist fetish, anatheism, having traversed the purges of
atheistic critique, endorses the counter idea of an advening God—God as
the *advena* who invites us to the feast of life in all its polyphony.

Strictly speaking then, ana-theism is neither antitheism nor antiatheism
but a form of post-theism that allows us to revisit the sacred in the midst of
the secular. It appreciates the candor of enlightened critiques of religion
and acknowledges Max Weber's diagnosis of the "disenchantment" (*Entzauberung*) of modernity. It says yes to all these no's and asks what, if anything,
comes after.

IN THE WAKE OF THE HOLOCAUST—PROPHETS
OF DARK TIMES

Let us begin with the no's. The pain of loss and the agony of protest. In what follows I rehearse the sentiments of certain post-Holocaust thinkers who, in my view, characterize an anatheist turn to God after God.

The biggest no to theism in our modern era was not Nietzsche's philosophical announcement of the death of "God" in 1882 but the actual disappearance of "God" from the world in the concentration camps of Europe in the 1940s. Elie Wiesel sounded the deathknell of conventional theism— namely, the belief in an omnipotent God—when he famously declared that "God" died on the hangman's rope at Auschwitz. I put God in inverted commas here because the God who died was the Omni-God of celestial Might: the divine grand master who sustained triumphalist notions of religion for millennia. There were, of course, already many reasons to doubt the logic of theodicy throughout Western history, from Holy Wars and Inquisitions to the slave trade, colonial genocides and countless natural disasters (like the Lisbon earthquake in Voltaire's famous rebuttal of Pangloss in *Candide*). But the Holocaust surely laid the ghost of any lingering belief in a divine Ruse of Reason. After Dachau, Sorbibor, and Treblinka, the notion that everything happens according to some Divine Plan was finally exposed as a cruel sham. The idea that God orchestrates good and evil alike was no longer tolerable.

Hillesum

The young Jewish writer Etty Hillesum recognized this when she wrote in her diary from the jaws of her Holocaust hell, "You [God] cannot help us, but we must help you and defend Your dwelling place inside us to the last." And this God—or post-God—of radical powerlessness was for Hillesum the only alternative to the tyranny of power (political or theological) that crushed the weak and persecuted strangers. The deity Hillesum discovered, after the demise of the stopgap God, was a summons to a second natality, to new life, a call to begin all over again in the midst of the most unspeakable horrors. Her God was a God of powerlessness who gave her the power to resist, to carry on, to dare to live in the face of death. Still, in her concentration camp at Westerbrook, she was able to confess, shortly before her death: "I have been feeling strong . . . so free of fears and anxieties. . . .

Perhaps I shall walk right across Russia one day, who knows? . . . [We] are lost permanently and for all time unless we provide an alternative, a dazzling and dynamic alternative with which to start afresh somewhere."[1] Thus Etty Hillesum offered herself as host to the divine guest who had nowhere else to go; she opened herself as a sanctuary to the stranger, knocking at the door of the moment, who could not enter until she responded. In this sense Hillesum could be said to echo Walter Benjamin's notion of the "weak Messiah," understood as a vulnerable migrant waiting to be received in each instant—if we open the door. Even in the darkest moments of history as a resistance to evil; God can *be* only if we let God be God.

Arendt

In one of her first essays after the war, Hannah Arendt, a Jewish thinker who managed to escape from her native Germany, though interned for a time in 1940, declared that the "problem of evil will be the fundamental question of post-war intellectual life in Europe."[2] Her own account of the Holocaust, *Eichmann in Jerusalem*, addressed this issue under the controversial title of "the banality of evil." Arendt does not dwell explicitly on the question of theism and atheism, but she is aware that after Auschwitz we have entered a period of deepest anxiety regarding fundamental issues of meaning. "Belief no less than non-belief" in the modern era is grounded in doubt, she writes. "Our world is a spiritually secular world precisely because it is a world of doubt."[3] Arendt considers the idea of a "religion without God" to be dangerous; but she does not seem to consider the possibility of a God without religion. She does agree, however, that the famous death of God should be understood in the sense of a specific kind of deity—namely, the God of metaphysics and theodicy. "It may be wise," she says, "to reflect upon what we really mean when we observe that theology, philosophy, metaphysics, have reached an end—certainly not that God has died, something about which we can know as little as about God's existence . . . but that the way God has been thought of for thousands of years is no longer convincing; if anything is dead, it can only be the traditional thought of God."[4]

Is the postwar rejection of a God of sovereign power, sustained by a metaphysics of necessary causality, an occasion to rethink divinity? This was an issue Arendt surely discussed with her fellow German Jew, Walter Benjamin, before his death at the hands of the fascists, or with her close friend W. H. Auden in New York years later—a poet obsessed with a God of neighborly love responsive to the darkness of our postwar world.[5] Arendt was philosophically discreet when it came to ultimate questions of the secular and the sacred, but she did acknowledge the need to counterbalance Kant's abstract universalism with an Aristotelian attention to particular action, practical wisdom (*phronesis*), and lived narratives of identity. Indeed she remarked in an interview with Gunter Gaus in 1933, that "if one is attacked as a Jew one must defend oneself as a Jew. Not as a German, not as a world-citizen, not as an upholder of the Rights of Man, or whatever."[6] It is probable, in my opinion, that her experience of being a Jew in Hitler's Germany profoundly informed her view of the human being as a stranger-guest on this earth. This, she held, is the specifically human way of being alive. It is, at the deepest level, our *human condition*: "for every single person needs to be reconciled to a world into which he was born a stranger and to which, to the extent of his distinct uniqueness, he always remains a stranger."[7] The question of how we reconcile evil—as manifest in Auschwitz—with our basic desire to "love the world" (*amor mundi* was key to her dissertation on Augustine) haunted Arendt throughout her career. She never resolved it but she never let it go.

Greenberg

What can you say about God when a child is tortured? This was Dostoyevsky's vexed question. But it acquired added urgency in the wake of the Holocaust, and by extension Hiroshima, the gulags, the killing fields of Cambodia, Rwanda, and other atrocities of the twentieth century. Rabbi Irving Greenberg, former chair of the U.S. Holocaust Memorial Council, put the matter boldly when he said that no theological statement should be made that could not be credible in the presence of burning children. For what could you say about an omnipotent God when an innocent infant is burning alive? Nothing.[8] Consequently those who lost their faith because of Auschwitz are to be respected. The line between belief and nonbelief becomes very thin indeed. Citing the famous Hasidic line that "no heart is so whole as a broken heart," Greenberg adds that "no faith is so whole as a broken faith." He could, he admits, admire those who responded to the Holocaust by forfeiting belief, "because their passion, their love of God and of people made it impossible to say empty words about God. I felt more sympathy for them than I did for people who went on praying as if nothing had ever changed, as if one could talk complacently and confidently about a God who exists self-evidently, as if that's true."[9] Moreover, a God who could will or condone suffering as punishment for the ill behavior of his people, or as expiation for their sins, is exposed as an egregious monster.

In the wake of the Holocaust we witness the option of a different kind of faith—a postfaith if you will—consonant with what I am calling anatheism. And for the likes of Greenberg such a faith is one capable of reconciling Jew and non-Jew around the basic recognition that the only God worthy of belief is a vulnerable and powerless one who suffers with us and is incapable of being relieved from this suffering unless we act against injustice. Greenberg speaks specifically of a compassion for the suffering God:

> This God had not stopped the Holocaust maybe because this God was suffering and wanted me to stop the Holocaust. As a Jew, I had hesitated to use language of God suffering, because it seems to be a Christian patent. But it's not so. I came to see this has been a central belief of the Jewish people—that God shares our pain. Indeed Christianity was never more Jewish than when it expressed it in those terms—that God suffers with humans.[10]

So where was God in Dachau and Treblinka? Suffering with his people. From an anatheist perspective, the covenant is to be understood as a divinity calling humans to full partnership, to co-creation, or, as the old Talmudic adage had it, to the completion of the seventh day of Creation. (Yahweh himself was unable to accomplish it without becoming a God of Totality. Anatheist faith is responsible for the ending of both human *and* divine suffering. It is about choosing God as an invitation to life and justice rather than a Moloch of murder and death. The God that died in Auschwitz was the God of theodicy. Post-Holocaust faith does not believe that God could have stopped the torture—and didn't. It believes that a Messiah will only come (or come back) "when we are able, ready and willing to bring the Messiah."[11] And here we return to Elie Wiesel's view that it would be a "moral monster" that could have come to save those burning children and did not. The only Messiah still credible after the death camps would be one who wanted to come but could not because humans failed to invite the sacred stranger into existence.

Levinas

Also writing in the shadow of the Holocaust, the Jewish philosopher Emmanuel Levinas, who lost many of his family in Dachau, speaks of the necessity to reject the infamous God of power who could allow such horrors.[12] In this sense he sees atheism as a salutary distancing from idolatrous fusion with the Totality of Being, a separation whereby each person discovers its own radical interiority as a self, an "I." This is the basis of freedom and responsibility: "One can call atheism this separation so complete that the separated being maintains itself in existence all by itself, without participating in the Being from which it is separated—eventually capable of adhering to it by belief. The break with participation is implied in this capability. One lives outside of God, at home with oneself; one is an I." And he goes on: "The soul, the dimension of the psychic, being an accomplishment of separation, is naturally atheist. By atheism we thus understand a position prior to both the negation and the affirmation of the divine, the breaking with participation by which the I posits itself as the same and as I."[13] Without this movement of atheistic separateness, the other as irreducibly alien cannot be recognized as *other*. And that, for Levinas, rules out the possibility of a genuinely religious relationship with God understood as absolute Other. We must, Levinas concludes accordingly, be *contre-dieu* before we can be *à-dieu*—in the double sense of taking leave from the old God as we turn to (*à*) a coming God and reopen our "home" to the radically alien. It is from an atheist moment of interiority within the self that we may open out toward the exteriority of the stranger: "Only if it starts from me as a separated being and goes as a host to the Other, welcoming the Other as guest, only in this manner can an eternal return within the interiority of the circle of being be escaped. For when I turn to the Other interiority turns into exteriority."[14] It is in this context that Levinas holds that the gift of Judaism to humanity is atheism—namely, separation from God so as to encounter the other as absolutely other.

Derrida

Jacques Derrida, a close colleague of Levinas in Paris, adds a further inflection to this contemporary debate. Though his early work does not address his own Jewish background, with the publication of the autobiographical *Circumfession* in 1993 Derrida spoke increasingly of this aspect of his thought, recalling how he had been expelled from school because of the anti-Semitic laws of the Vichy government in Algeria where he grew up. As the title of this testimonial work suggests, the mark of circumcision on his flesh is something that ultimately needed to be confessed rather than denied. A series of works alludes to Derrida's increased attention to the tragic implications of the Holocaust, notably *Cendres* (1991) and *Shibboleth: For Paul Celan* (1986), as well as his debt to the Levinasian notion of radical alterity recorded in his obituary work *Adieu* (1996).

But one of Derrida's most important contributions to the anatheist question comes, I think, in a late essay, *Sauf le Nom* (1993), where he speaks of how we may save the divine "name" by refusing to determine its content. This abstentionist gesture, this discretion about naming the divine, borders on a certain style of atheism, a way of saving the name of God by not naming God at all. But we are not dealing here with militant anti-God talk, anymore than we are dealing with subtle apologetics for apophatic theology (what we *cannot* say about God while believing in God). Derrida seems, in fact, to be excavating a space for what might be called "mystical atheism." And, while he does not use the term, he does point to a curious reversibility between mysticism and atheism. Avowing that he "rightly passes for an atheist," Derrida still calls our attention to a moment of radical receptivity that he terms messianic—a moment when one abandons all inherited certainties, assumptions, and expectations (including religious ones) in order to open oneself to the radical surprise, and shock, of the incoming Other.

In *Sauf Le Nom*—meaning both "saving and exempting the divine name"—Derrida goes so far as to suggest that a genuine desire for God presupposes a certain vacillation between atheism and theism. "The desire of God, God as the other name of desire," he writes, "deals in the desert with radical atheism." And he adds: "The most consequent forms of declared atheism will have always testified to the most intense desire for God. . . . Like mysticism, apophatic discourse has always been suspected of atheism. . . . If atheism, like apophatic theology, testifies to the desire of God . . . in the presence of *whom* does it do so?"[15] Derrida might be said to be offering here a post-Holocaust translation of Meister Eckhart's prayer to God to rid him of God. Unless we let go of God as property and possession, we cannot encounter the Other as radical stranger. Such a Derridean desire of God, as "desire beyond desire," is an important theo-erotic dimension of what we call anatheism. The felt absence of the old God (the God of death) ushers in a sense of emptiness that may provoke a new desire, a seasoned desire for the return of the Other God—the divine guest who brings life.

It must be admitted, however, that Derrida's deconstructive ascesis of traditional religions ultimately calls for a "religion beyond religion" that can scarcely give a name to God at all. At times, it seems as if Derrida is embracing a notion of "messianicity" beyond the concrete, historical "messianisms" of the Abrahamic tradition—a messianicity that serves less as a sacred, incarnate presence in the world than as an abstract structure for the condition of possibility of religion in general, that is, religion understood as an endless waiting with no sense of what kind of divine (or undivine) Other might appear. There is no room here for a "discernment of spirits." No real option of a hermeneutics of interpretation or commitment to holy rather than unholy ghosts. (For deconstructors all gods are ghosts.) There seems to be no possibility, in other words, of reading the face beyond or through the name. Faith in messianicity, for Derrida, seems at times to mean a radical absence of any historical instantiation of the divine—no epiphanies, songs, testimonies, no sacred embodiments or liturgies. In the name of a universal openness to any other at all (*tout autre est tout autre*), Derrida's "religion without religion" seems to have no visage to speak of, no embodied presence in space and time. "Ascesis strips the messianic hope of all biblical forms," as he says, "and even all determinable figures of the wait or expectation; it thus denudes itself in view of responding to that which must be absolute hospitality, the "yes" to the "arrivant(e)," the "come" to the future that cannot be anticipated. . . . This hospitality is absolute only if it keeps watch over its own universality."[16]

But such messianic universality is only guaranteed, it seems, at the cost of particularity; it forfeits the flesh-and-blood singularity of everyday epiphanies. "If one could 'count' on what is coming," says Derrida, "hope would be but the calculation of a program. One would have the prospect but one would no longer wait for anything or anyone."[17] The messianic, by contrast, is a waiting without any horizon of expectation. Ascesis without image or epiphany. Derrida refers to this abstention as an "epoché [bracketing] of the content" of faith; so much so, I think, that faith becomes an empty waiting, what he himself calls the "formality of a structural messianism, a messianism without religion, even a messianic without messianism."[18]

In sum, faith serves here as a purely transcendental move, a "formal structure of promise" that does not call for realization or incarnation in the world of particular beliefs. So that if—for mystical ascesis—the "epoché of the content" could be said to serve as a *provisional* moment before the return to the world of everyday belief and service, for Derrida this suspension of content seems to be a *nec plus ultra,* a point of no return. Here messian-icity becomes, arguably, so devoid of any kind of concrete faith in a person or presence (human or divine) that it loses any claim to historical reality. Which leaves me with this question: does deconstructive "faith" not risk becoming so empty that it loses faith in the here and now altogether?

I think this is something that could never be said of Walter Benjamin, for example, whose "weak messianism," mentioned earlier, promoted the idea of a mystical stranger—the weak Messiah—who may break open the continuum of history at any time: what Benjamin calls the irruption of a mystical "now" (*Jetztzeit*). Likewise, regardless of Derrida's profound debt to his mentor Levinas, his purely formal messianicity prevents him from embracing Levinas's ethical commitment to the "face" of the other—the widow, the orphan, and the stranger—as the trace of God. Unlike Benjamin and Levinas, therefore, Derrida's approach to the messianic hovers in the antechamber of messianism. He explores rather than embraces the anathe-ist option. His saving the Name does not entail a return to the Named. At best, it is an "endless waiting in the desert."[19] A waiting for Godot who never comes.

BONHOEFFER'S RELIGIONLESS FAITH

The anatheist response to World War II was not just a matter for Jewish think-ers and writers. This caesura in the history of Western religion, this ruptur-ing of the Grand Narrative of monotheism—which Lyotard identifies with the postmodern turn—is also attested to by several Christian philosophers. Foremost among these were two prisoners of war, one who died in captivity, Dietrich Bonhoeffer, the other who survived, Paul Ricoeur. Though there are other powerful Christian critiques of religion after Auschwitz, I will con-centrate here on these two pioneering "postreligious" writers.

Bonhoeffer was executed by the Nazis in a German prison camp in 1944. In the months leading up to his death he raised the possibility of a "nonreligious" faith. Such an option rejects the conventional notion of religion as a panacea where human weakness treats God as a stopgap so-lution to our woes, some magical *deus ex machina* in times of neediness. Bonhoeffer confirms the Nietzschean exposé of religious infantalism, intel-lectual dishonesty, and otherwordly flight. Religion in its Western Christian formulation was, Bonhoeffer argues, too often tainted by an unfortunate mix of metaphysics (God as Supreme Being) and interiority (man as disincarnate being). Such a dualist theology was predicated on the superiority of soul over body, the sacred over the secular, the timeless over time. It led to life-denying nihilism.

So what exactly did Bonhoeffer mean when he advocated an "irreligious Christianity"? Much of official Christian dogma, he claimed, was based on a religious a priori that was a historically conditioned and transient form of self-expression privileging "interiority" as personal salvation. But Bonhoeffer believed that by the middle of the twentieth century, for better or worse, Western civilization was moving toward a "religionless" time. "People as they are now," he wrote, "simply cannot be religious any more."[20] Religion was but a "garment" tailored to the needs of different historical epochs over two thousand years. So the real question for us today is What kind of God could be the Lord of a nonreligious Christianity? Moved by Karl Barth's statement in his *The Epistle to the Romans* (1923) that Christianity is the death of religion,[21] but rejecting what he considered to be Barth's "positivism of revelation," Bonhoeffer called for a reintegration of Christian faith in the secular world. He boldly posed the following questions, central to our discussion of anatheism:

> What do a church, a community, a sermon, a liturgy, a Christian life mean in a religionless world? How do we speak of God—without religion, i.e. without the temporally conditioned presuppositions of metaphysics, inwardness, and so on? How do we speak in a secular way about God? In what way are we religionless-secular Christians, in what way are we the *ex-klesia*, those who are called forth, not regarding ourselves from a religious point of view as specially favoured, but rather as belonging wholly to the world? In that case Christ is no longer an object of religion, but something quite different, really the Lord of the world. But what does that mean? What is the place of worship and prayer in a religionless situation?[22]

The first answer that Bonhoeffer gives to this is that a nonsovereign, nonmetaphysical God is one whose very powerlessness gives us power, making us capable of life, resistance, and rebirth. This involves a faith, coming after religion, that calls us out of the inwardness of private sentiment and secret guilt into a public world of shared action (what Arendt calls the political). It is a faith that signals a "simple brotherhood with men." Indeed, faced with the threats of Nazism and Stalinism, how could it be anything less? Against the modern individualist conception of private salvation, Bonhoeffer reminds us that the Bible did not distinguish inner from outer, but conceived the human heart in terms of an integral being in relation to God (hence the injunction to "love God with your *whole* heart").[23] We might thus say that Bonhoeffer's postreligious Christianity took the form of an atheistic rejection of the metaphysical God combined with a belief in the suffering God. The genuine Christian thus appears as a problematic seeker offering herself to others in a time of transition—mourning the old God and awaiting the new.

Bonhoeffer has no time for dogmatic religion separated from other citizens of the world. He holds that this nonreligious interpretation is discernible within the Gospels themselves in the central opposition between faith and law made explicit by Paul and retrieved by contemporary theologians like Bultmann and Ebeling. Faith is the summons to reach out to the nonreligious person, the stranger outside the law, the tribe, the nation, that the Scriptures refer to as the "lost sheep of the house of Israel."[24] In short, the opposition *law-spirit* for Paul and Luther becomes the opposition *religion-faith* for twentieth-century thinkers like Bonhoeffer and Bultmann. The Word of God is no longer invoked to explain away history but to liberate a space of shared life and communication. Thus after the demise of the "God" of power—rightly exposed by Nietzsche and his atheist peers—we find a reacknowledgment of God in all his weakness on the cross. The Word becomes that which transforms the defeat of the cross in human life into renewed life. Life *in spite of* death.

Bonhoeffer calls for a "secular" reading of the divine that affirms the life of the world in its darkest moments. Here, in a crucial but dense passage, the Protestant pastor writing in his Berlin prison echoes the sentiments of his Jewish sister, Etty Hillesum, at virtually the very same moment in her concentration camp. In both instances the call to a God after "God," to the power of a powerless divinity, is made in the face of Nazi barbarism. About to die, they appeal, in their different languages of faith, to a God (and a good) beyond the theism of omnipotence:

> The God who lets us live in the world without the working hypothesis of God is the God before whom we stand continually. Before God and with God we live without God. God is weak and powerless in the world and that is precisely the way, the only way, in which he is with us and helps us. Matt 8.17 makes it quite clear that Christ

helps us, not by virtue of his omnipotence, but by virtue of his weakness and suffering.

It is "religiosity," he says,

> which makes one look in one's distress to the power of God in the world: God (as) *deus ex machina*. The Bible directs man to God's powerlessness and suffering; only the suffering God can help. To that extent we may say that the development towards the world's coming of age, which has done away with a false conception of God, opens up a way of seeing the God of the Bible, who wins power and space in the world by his weakness. This will probably be the starting point of our "secular interpretation."[25]

It is noteworthy how a number of contemporary religious thinkers, most notably John Caputo and Catherine Keller, have developed this notion of divine weakness in the wake of the metaphysical God.[26]

In this double commitment 1. to the "suffering God" and 2. to "secular interpretation" the poles of atheism and faith converge in a curiously anatheist manner. The cultural process of nihilism, laid bare by Nietzsche and Freud, is a broad movement of "clearing" from which Bonhoeffer dares to speak of a new coalition of faith—namely, a realignment of the atheist refusal of a metaphysical God and the anatheist commitment to a suffering God. This involves a hope in spite of hopelessness that the estranged God may return in its empowering powerlessness. And, of course, as religious theism becomes problematic in this new constellation, so too does dogmatic atheism. From this double surpassing emerges an anatheistic alternative.

Here we witness a crucial moment of crisis exemplified by the demise of the God of "objective certainty" in the ashes of Nazi and Stalinist conflagrations:

> Ours is without doubt the time when humanity is connected to God by his silence and his absence. But is it not the Psalm that says: "How long will you remain silent Lord?" Is it not Jesus on the cross who cries, "My God, My God, why have you forsaken me?" If I assume all of this modern culture, and live—if I dare to say—out of the absence of God, then I can hear the word "God is dead" not as a triumphant thesis of atheism—because I will say that the word "God

is dead" has nothing to do with the word "God does not exist"—but as the modern expression, on the scale of an entire culture, of what the mystics had called "the night of understanding." "God is dead" is not the same thing as "God does not exist." It is even the total opposite. This means to say: The God of religion, of metaphysics and of subjectivity is dead; the place is vacant for the preaching of the cross and for the God of Jesus Christ.[27]

The anatheistic moment of returning to God after God—already experienced as a personal event by great mystics of Christianity (Eckhart, Julian of Norwich, Teresa, John of the Cross)—is experienced as a contemporary option in face of the nihilism of the death camps. Christianity thus becomes not an invitation to another world but a call back to this one, a robust and challenging "Christianity of this world," a secular faith that sees the weakness of God as precisely a summons to the rekindled strength of humanity. And, without such divine empowerment, Bonhoeffer asks, how are we to resist the evil of fascism and Stalinism? The God of anatheism is not some nihilist negation of profane existence, but the "affirmation of our affirmation," the one who comes to dwell in the fractures of our being in order to summon us back to life, to resistance, to action. Not a stopgap God then but a God of the gaps who, in all its radical powerlessness, solicits the fullness of our existential power.

In short, the death of God gives birth to the God of life. A God who resides at the "center of life" (and not only when death comes), a gift of healing and enabling rather than a Ghost who skulks in the gutters of guilt and sin.[28] Resurrection is to be understood accordingly as the event that returns us to the world, to the *secula seculorum*, so that we may live more abundantly. So we may say: to the weakness of the divine responds the strength of the human.

Anatheistically considered, the Christian adds no more to the human than God adds to the world. In this spirit, Bonhoeffer was committed more rather than less to the secular world because of his faith. A very short time before his execution, as the shadow of death crossed his prison walls, he wrote this poignant last testament:

I have come to understand more and more the profound this-worldliness of Christianity. The Christian is not a *homo religiosus*, but simply a man, as Jesus was a man. . . . I don't mean the shallow and banal this-worldliness of the enlightened, the busy, the comfortable, or the lascivious, but the profound this-worldliness, characterized by discipline and constant knowledge of death and resurrection. . . . It is only by living completely in this world that one learns to have faith. . . . By this-worldliness I mean living unreservedly in life's duties, problems, successes, experiences and perplexities. In so doing we throw ourselves completely into the arms of God, taking seriously, not our own sufferings, but those of God in the world—watching with Christ in Gethsemane.[29]

For, as Bonhoeffer observes, it is as he grieves in Gethsemane that Jesus asks us to "watch with him for one hour": the very opposite of what the religious man expects from God (namely, a supernatural answer to all our problems).

And so the task of anatheists like Hillesum and Bonhoeffer was to meditate on the weak and suffering God in the promise of the fullness of life. This is the very inverse, of course, of what Nietzsche hated about Christianity—a bellicose God opposed to weak humanity. By pushing the Nietzschean critique of God to its extreme, Bonhoeffer contrived to reverse it. He pushed Godlessness to the point of a return to Godliness. But this could only be done by abiding in the secular world to the bitter (or joyful) end. The true seeker of God today, he concluded, "must live a 'secular' life, and thereby share in God's sufferings. He *may* live a 'secular' life (as one who has been freed from false religious obligations and inhibitions). To be a Christian does not mean to be religious in a particular way . . . but to be a man—not a type of man, but the man that Christ creates in us. It is not the religious act that makes the Christian, but participation in the sufferings of God in the secular world."[30]

Let us note, finally, that Bonhoeffer was known by his fellow prisoners as someone who called for the "polyphony of life," for joy as well as sadness, the yes alongside the no, someone who exemplified this wager in his everyday gestures and actions right up to the end. Never a man of the *idée fixe* or single perspective, he lived by his dictum that "Jesus reclaims for himself and his kingdom, a full life in all of its manifestations and not only in the weakness and distress of man."[31] The presence of God was for him like a *cantus firmus*, the bass singing beneath the diversity of multiple experiences, the distant roar of a river in spate that accompanies every step of one's path. And this absent-present divinity called, he concluded, for a certain detached participation in every living moment, a wise compassion for all that is. Rejecting, in sum, the religiosity of condemnation and obligation, Bonhoeffer preferred a "church for others," a community open to strangers, wanderers, seekers, and protesters. Which is what he meant, I suspect, when he declared that "attending to the non-religious human being measures the faith of the church."[32]

RICOEUR'S POSTRELIGIOUS FAITH

Perhaps the contemporary philosopher who most consistently pursued Bonhoeffer's notion of postreligious faith was Paul Ricoeur. A fellow prisoner in a Nazi camp, but one who—unlike Bonhoeffer and Hillesum—managed to survive, Ricoeur spoke of faith as "the joy of yes in the sadness of no." He famously described his own Protestant faith as a "chance converted into destiny by a constant choice."[33] Nothing about God could be taken for granted. On the contrary, having lived for five years in German captivity during the war, Ricoeur knew there could be no return to faith that did not fully acknowledge the traversal of the abyss. He also recognized that the trenchant critiques of religion, delivered by atheists like Freud, Marx, and Nietzsche, had to be taken seriously.

In his postwar essay "Religion, Atheism, Faith" Ricoeur develops several points about postcritical faith that remained largely intimated in Bonhoeffer's prison writings. He speaks here of the "religious meaning of atheism," suggesting that an atheistic purging of the life-denying components of religion needs to be taken on board if a genuine form of faith is to emerge in our secular culture. Assuming the role of "philosopher" rather than "preacher," Ricoeur seeks to indicate certain possibilities of postatheistic faith, rather than fill in details of what such a faith might mean in a confessional or liturgical context. The discourse of the philosopher is always, he says, that of the perpetual beginner, a "preparatory discourse." And he adds that this is timely in our period of contemporary confusion "where the true consequences of the death of religion perhaps still remain concealed," requiring a "long, slow and indirect preparation."[34]

Two aspects of religion that call for radical critique, in this view, are *taboo* and *escape*. Under the first heading we have the archaic religious feeling of fear or, more particularly, fear of divine punishment and expiation. Under the second, we find the need for protection and consolation. Ricoeur defines religion, accordingly, as a "primitive structure of life which must always be overcome by faith and which is grounded in the fear of punishment and the desire for protection."[35] In this context, atheism discovers its true justification as both destructive and liberating. For as it exposes the dissimulating mechanisms of religious insecurity and infantile dependency—thereby destroying its destructiveness—it can also emancipate new possibilities of existing. And one of these possibilities, suggests Ricoeur, involves a faith situated beyond accusation and escapism. In this manner, atheism may be said to emancipate religion from itself, opening the promise of living faith curled within the shell of historical religion. That, at any rate, seems to be Ricoeur's wager regarding a "postreligious faith."

Under the first category of taboo Ricoeur invokes salutary critiques of both Freud and Nietzsche. Unlike other philosophers—e.g., British empiricists or Enlightenment positivists who attack religion on scientific grounds as unprovable—Freud and Nietzsche developed a new kind of atheism: namely, the claim that religion is a cultural representation of disguised symptoms of fear and need. In this way they did not bother with arguments for proving or disproving the existence of God but concentrated on deconstructing religious forms of prohibition and punishment. They thus advanced a critical "hermeneutics of suspicion" directed toward the *illusions* of religion, determined to unmask the *hidden* motivations of piety. This critical hermeneutics took the form of a genealogy resolved to expose religions as symptoms of a conflict of underlying forces that need to be laid bare. Nietzsche identified the main ulterior motive as a disguised "will to power," Freud as a perversion of libido resulting in "obsessive compulsion" and neurosis. The aim of Nietzsche's genealogical readings was to show that the so-called ideal realm of religion is in fact "nothing": a cover-up for a denial of life, an illusory projection of a supersensible world driven by the calumny of this earth. The aim of Freud's psychoanalytic exposé, for its part, was to show that religion operates on the basis of a delusional "phantasm of the primal Father" responding to our infantile dependency. The answer, Freud suggested in his book on Leonardo, was a "renunciation" of this illusory Father, constructed as a double fantasy of fear and power. Only by means of such a radical mourning of the divine superego, only by letting go of this phantasm of absolute authority and refuge, could the origin of values be restored to itself, that is, to Eros in its eternal struggle with Thanatos.[36]

So Nietzsche and Freud, in their respective voices, announce the death of God. But the question (once again) is: which God? Ricoeur suggests it is the God of ontotheology and that such a God deserves to die. The term *ontotheology* was given currency in our time by Heidegger to refer to the metaphysical concept of a highest and most general Being abstracted from the lived world. In Western intellectual history it often coincided with a moralizing deity of accusation and condemnation. Atheism set out to accuse the accusation and condemn the condemnation. It sought to unveil the nihilism at the core of the religious delusion, to reveal the superego's *lack* of power and the ideal world's collusion with nay-saying and death. Or as Nietzsche put it, when something is leaning give it a push. Atheism, in this sense, is a way in which the illusions of religion self-destruct, exposing themselves for what they truly are: *nothing*. And so dies the omnipotent God of ontotheology understood as Emperor of the World. So also dies the omniscient God of "self-sufficient knowledge" that places the "powerful over the good and law over love and humility that are superior to law."[37] And along with the omnipotent and omniscient God goes the omnipresent God who condones evil as well as good. So dies, in short, the Omni-God of theodicy, invoked to justify the worst atrocities as part of some Ultimate Design. This is the God rightly dismissed, in our day, by Richard Dawkins when he invites us to imagine a world with "no suicide bombers, no 9/11, no 7/7, no Crusades, no witch-hunts, no Gunpowder Plot, no Indian Partition, no Israeli/Palestinian wars, no Serb/Croat/Muslim massacres, no persecution of Jews as 'Christ-killers,' no Northern Ireland 'troubles,' no 'honor killings,' no shiny-suited bouffant-haired televangelists fleecing gullible people of their money ('God wants you to give till it hurts')." "Imagine," he surmises, "no Taliban to blow up ancient statues, no public beheadings of blasphemers, no flogging of female skin for the crime of showing some of it."[38]

After the hermeneutics of suspicion has done its work, it is no longer possible to return, in Ricoeur's words, to a moral life that would take the form of naive "submission to commandments or to an alien or supreme will, even if this will were represented as divine." That is why he urges that we acknowledge as a positive good the critique of ethics and religion undertaken by the school of suspicion. From it, he argues, we learn to understand that "the commandment that gives death, not life, is a product and projection of our own weakness."[39]

If atheism remains simply a negation, however, it runs the risk of being reactive rather than active. The rebel falls short of the prophet. The accusation of accusation, while necessary, may fail to return to a reaffirmation of life, that is, to a recognition that most things in our secular universe are in fact, already and always, sacred at heart. Nietzsche did, to be sure, speak of an "innocence of becoming" and embraced the "eternal recurrence of the same." And it is easy to forget that the "madman" who declared God dead began his declaration with the words "I seek God."[40] But by declaring the "will to power" to be the primary truth of existence, Nietzsche remained confined within a voluntarist universe: a world where even the celebration of life becomes a sort of personal mythology, a willful lyricism of animus, a fantasy of how things might be, albeit this time on the side of yea-sayers rather than nay-sayers.

Hence the option of anatheism. And I stress, again, the word *option* rather than *necessity*. Anatheism, I have been arguing, offers the possibility of belief after atheism. It allows for a return to a postreligious theism in the wake of Freud and Nietzsche. For Ricoeur, the philosopher as responsible thinker remains suspended between the secular and the sacred. But, as such, a critical hermeneutic opens up a space where the "prophetic preacher" may envisage a retrieval of a liberated faith within the great religious traditions. Ricoeur imagines in this context a "radical return to the origins of Jewish and Christian faith," a journey at once "originary and postreligious," that speaks to our time.[41] The philosopher dreams of a prophet who would realize today the liberating message of Exodus that exists prior to the law: "I am the Lord thy God who brought thee out of the land of Egypt, out of the house of bondage." Such faith speaks of freedom and proclaims the Cross and Resurrection as invitations to a more creative life; a belief that articulates the contemporary relevance of the Pauline distinction between Spirit and Law and interprets "sin" less as the breaking of taboo than as the refusal of life. In such a scenario, sin would be exposed as a life lived fearfully "in the infernal cycle of law, transgression, and guilt."

But the philosopher can only imagine such a faith. It is the business of postreligious believers to realize it. The philosopher occupies an "intermediate time" between mourning the gods who have died and invigilating the signs of a new return. While looking forward to a positive hermeneutics that would be a recreation of the biblical kerygma—the prophets and the primitive Christian community—the philosopher cannot, counsels Ricoeur, enter that promised land. For the philosopher's responsibility is to "think," that is, "to dig beneath the surface of the present antinomy until he has discovered the level of questioning that makes possible a mediation between religion and faith by way of atheism."[42]

. . .

I think Ricoeur's argument here is deeply anatheistic. It suggests that to think religiously is to think postreligiously. And it acknowledges that the best an anatheist philosopher can do is to disclose a site where the freedom of our will is rooted in a listening to a "word" of which one is neither source nor master. This attention to a primordial event of word and meaning is the fitting vocation of an anatheist who, at least when philosophizing, provisionally brackets out metaphysical questions of "God" and "religion." It is a form of existential hearkening to the coming and going of meaning prior to any institutional identification of the nature of that word. But, in attending to this landing site, this disposition to listen and receive (often in silence) from something beyond one's mastering will, the anatheist can prepare the ground for believers who may later wish to release the kerygma of their faith from the prison house of trepidation.

Listening philosophically to the word of existence may thus help us listen theologically to the word of God – without confounding the two. For existential listening, in Ricoeur's view, allows us to restore our originary affirmation of life, our primordial desire to be: a desire that preexists the many distortions that have made it a stranger to itself. Such harkening invites us to start all over again, from the beginning. Repetition. Recapitulation. *Anakaiphaleosis.* The word of existence—which affirms the goodness of being in spite of its multiple estrangements—speaks according to the grammar of *ana.* "This affirmation must be recovered and restored," insists Ricoeur, "because (and here the problem of evil emerges) it has been alienated in many ways. This is why it must be regrasped and reinstated. The task of ethics is thus the reappropriation of our effort to exist. Since our power has been alienated, however, this effort remains a desire, the *desire to be.*"[43] Without this ana-ethical turning and returning to existence, the option of ana-theist faith is not possible. There is, says Ricoeur, something that precedes the order of will and obligation, and this something is nothing else than "our existence in so far as it is capable of being modified by word."[44] In sum, ana-theism may be said to express both existential desire and eschatological faith.

A certain "gap" will always remain, nonetheless, between the philosopher's endless exploration of new beginnings and the practitioner's proclamation of a return to the word of God. But, in spite of this gap, a certain "correspondence" may appear between a theology that retrieves its own origins and a philosophy that embraces atheism's critique of religion.[45] Anatheism might be described as an attempt to respond to this correspondence. Ricoeur himself does not use this term, but I believe he prepares the ground for a recovery of God after God. This is how, with Bonhoeffer in mind, Ricoeur summarizes his dream of what such a recovery might entail:

> It would return to the roots of Judeo-Christian faith while also being a new beginning for our time. . . . It would be a faith that moves forward through the shadows, in a new "night of the soul"—to adopt the language of the mystics—before a God who would not have the attributes of "Providence," a God who would not protect me but would surrender me to the dangers of a life worthy of being called human. Is not this God the Crucified One, the God who, as Bonhoeffer says, only through his weakness is capable of helping me?

Ricoeur concludes his essay on religion and atheism thus: "The night of the soul means above all the overcoming . . . of fear, the overcoming of nostalgia for the protecting father figure. Beyond the night, and only beyond it, can we recover the true meaning of the God of consolation, the God of Resurrection."[46]

Nothing is lost in anatheism. Or rather what is lost, as possession, can be retrieved as gift, revisited after the salutary night of atheistic critique—just as Job received back all he lost, and Abraham received back Isaac, and Jesus received his life after death. Even the loving "father" of creation may be anatheistically retrieved as a symbol of life. For if biblical religion represented God as a Father and atheism bids us renounce the fetish of the father, anatheism suggests that, once overcome as idol, the image of the Father may be recovered as symbol. A symbol generous in its semantic and gender implications. This symbol, suggests Ricoeur, "is a parable of the foundation of love; it is the counterpart, within a theology of love, of the progression that leads from simple resignation to poetic life." Whence his summary of the religious meaning of atheism: "An idol must die so that a symbol of being may begin to speak."[47]

LAST TESTAMENTS

Almost forty years after this radical reflection, Ricoeur returns to the question of death and resurrection in his final testament, *Vivant jusqu'à la mort*

(2007). Written as he was dying, the author here blurs the distinction between the philosopher and the preacher and confides to his reader with unprecedented candor. His confidences, in my view, amount to the confessions of an anatheist. Speaking of a certain kind of "grace" accompanying the experience of death, Ricoeur notes that "it is not important for this moment of grace that the dying person identifies with a particular religion or confession. Indeed maybe it is only when faced with death that the religious becomes one with the Essential and that the barrier dividing religions (and non-religions like Buddhism) are transcended. Because dying is trans-cultural it is also trans-confessional and trans-religious."[48] Admitting his basic suspicion of "immediacy and fusion," Ricoeur makes one exception for "the grace of a certain dying" (45). Ricoeur talks about this grace as a "paradox of immanent transcendence," of an especially "intimate transcendence of the Essential which rips through the veils of confessional religious codes" (47). To encounter such authentic grace one must, Ricoeur writes, forgo the will for one's own personal salvation by transferring this hope onto others.

Here again we confront the basic scriptural paradox that "he who clings to his life loses it and he who lets it go gains it." Or, to put it in James Joyce's terms, "without sundering there is no reconciliation." In this context Ricoeur offers a startlingly refreshing reading of the Eucharist as a celebration of blood-as-wine, transubstantiation being taken as a sign of life and sharing rather than a token of sacrificial bloodletting (90). The eucharistic commemoration of the giving of one's life—"Do this in memory of me"—thus becomes an affirmation of the gift of life to and for the other rather than an anxiety about personal physical survival after death. In other words, when Christ said "it is finished," he meant it. He was offering up his own personal life, in a second gesture of kenotic emptying (the first being the descent of divinity into flesh), so as to give life to others, in *both* service *and* sacrament: the breaking of bread at Emmaus, the cooking of fish for his disciples in the form of the risen servant, and ever after, down through human history, in the guise of feeding the "least of these." Ricoeur concludes his testament with this remarkable note:

> The Son of Man came not to be served but to serve. Hence the link between *death-rebirth in the other* and *service as gift of life*. Hence also the link between feast and service. The Last Supper conjoins the moment of dying unto oneself and serving the other in the sharing of food and wine which joins the dying person to the multitude

of survivors reunited in community. And this is why it is remarkable that Jesus never theorized about this and never said *who* he was. Maybe he didn't *know*, for he *lived* the Eucharistic gesture, bridged the gap between the imminence of death and the community beyond. He marked a passage to glory (through suffering and death) without any sacrificial perspective. (91)

What Ricoeur is rejecting here, it seems to me, is the notion of Christ's death as a scapegoating ritual of periodic bloodletting to propitiate a divine bloodlust. He is *not* rejecting Christ's act of "sacrificing" his life out of love for others. Ricoeur's intention is, I believe, deeply anatheistic in its return to a postsacrificial Eucharist of sharing with the stranger, the other, the uninvited guest. We shall revisit the anatheistic approach to sacramental life in chapter 4.

The fact that Ricoeur calls himself a "Christian who writes philosophically" rather than a "Christian philosopher" seems to me significant here. For, so doing, he is acknowledging the importance of a gap that allows one to freely and imaginatively revisit, and at times retrieve, the often forgotten resources of one's traditional religion.

But there is one last question I wish to ask of Ricoeur: what exactly does he mean when he speaks of God as a *dieu capable*? Always one to oppose schismatic oppositions, Ricoeur suggests that the critical encounter between the categories of Greek ontology and biblical theology involved in the translation of Exodus 3:15 opens up new resources for understanding the nature of the divine as being-capable or enabling. (Indeed he might well agree with Derrida that, between the "tragic" being of Athens and the "messianic" alterity of Jerusalem, there is "philosophy").[49] Noting the traditional rendition of the Hebrew *ehyeh asher ehyeh* as "I am who am," Ricoeur is more interested in alternative renditions like "I am who may be" or "I am who will be with you." The latter acknowledges a certain "divine dynamism" in the Hebrew formulation that in Greek and Latin amplifies the existing range of understanding ontological categories of being and can-being.[50] Of particular interest here are the connotations of promise, becoming, and futurity contained in the exodic formula. Ricoeur is intrigued by the fertile tension emerging from the crossing-over of Greek ontology and biblical theology. "It is truly the verb 'to be,' but in none of the senses found in the Greek," he writes. "There is a sort of enlargement of the meaning of being as a being-with, or being-faithful, that is, the being as accompaniment of a people, another dimension of being."[51] When Aristotle says there is a variety of meanings of being, he had not, says Ricoeur, imagined the being of Exodus 3:14. Ricoeur endorses a mutual amplication of ontologies in the various translations between Greek and Hebrew.

Here, finally, we encounter what we might call an *eschatology of the possible* shared by philosophers and theologians alike. Eschatology is, by Ricoeur's own admission, his intellectual and spiritual "secret."[52] It usually arises at the end of certain hermeneutic analyses (e.g., *Freud and Philosophy*) in a relatively allusive fashion. The term *eschaton* serves as a limit-horizon for Ricoeur's work in both philosophy and theology, as suggested by his embrace—in his late work *Thinking Biblically*—of a medial position between "philosophical theology" and "theological philosophy."[53] This latter-day acknowledgment of an eschatological *posse* marks something of a departure from Ricoeur's earlier reservation—what he called his "methodological asceticism"—regarding the intermingling of philosophy and theology.[54]

In an intriguing essay on the Song of Songs in *Thinking Biblically*, entitled "The Nuptial Metaphor," Ricoeur pushes his eschatological secret to the point of rhapsodic avowal.[55] Here we find the eschatological potential of the divine responding to the liturgical power of the human in the form of a theo-erotic crossing. Commenting on verse 8:6 of the Song—where the allusion to God (*shalhevetyah*) appears as *yah*—Ricoeur notes that the famous "seal of alliance" inscribed on the human heart is to be understood as both wisdom and desire.

> Under the apple tree I awakened you
> There where your mother conceived you
> Set me as a seal upon your heart . . .
> For love is as strong as death . . .
> Its flame a flash of sacred fire (*shalhevetyah*).
>
> —Song of Songs 8:5–7

Here, suggests Ricoeur, we have a discreet eschaton that respects the incognito of an intimate *corps-à-corps* where human and divine desires traverse each other. In this nuptial traversal the "I can" of human being finds its correspondent in the "You can" of sacred love. *L'homme capable* and *le dieu capable* respond to each other in an act of daring complicity and co-creation. And it is no accident, I suspect, that Ricoeur chooses the term *metaphor* to describe this divine-human exchange, for metaphoricity is precisely the "tensive" power of language that comes alive in the crossing of ostensible opposites—immanent-transcendent, sensible-intelligible, finite-infinite. Reading this text, one realizes that for Ricoeur the divine is "capable" precisely because it is *eros* as well as *agape*: a dynamic potency (*dunamis, conatus, appetitus*) that expresses itself as a desire that is less lack than surplus: an eschatological desire to make human being more capable of new genesis and natality. *Désir à etre* rather than *manque à etre*. Desire beyond desire. Anatheist desire as a love that answers desire with more desire—and death with more life. And in such a process of mutual traversal, desire surely reveals "God" as another name for the "more," the "surplus," the "surprise" that humans seek.

So what are the implications of such a "capable God" for concrete questions of living and dying? Such an eschatological *posse*, for Ricoeur, implies a God of enabling service rather than of sacrificial bloodletting, a God who is willing to efface his own being for the sake of giving *more* being to his beloved creatures. In this sense we may speak of a God beyond religion (in the sense of confessional absolutism) or, at the very least, of an interreligious or transreligious God. I think Ricoeur comes close at this terminal juncture to his Paris friend, Stanislas Breton, who espoused a form of mystical kenosis whereby divinity becomes "nothing" in order that humanity can become more fully human.[56] The notion of divine *posse*—of an enabling God who says "You are able!"—repudiates all forms of theodicy and theocracy by returning power and responsibility to humans. And it is interesting that on this point Ricoeur specifically invokes the great Rhine mystics who "renounced themselves" for the sake of opening to the Essential, to the point of being, in their contemplative detachment, incredibly active in the creation of new orders, in teaching, in traveling and tending to the forgotten of this world. By being available like this to the Essential, they were motivated to "transfer the love of life onto others."[57]

God thus becomes a God *after* God, a God who no longer is but who *may be* again in the form of renewed life. Such a divinity is "capable" of making us "capable" of sacred life, and it does so by emptying divine being into nonbeing so as to allow for rebirth into more being: life more fully alive. In this option for natality over mortality, the dichotomy between before and after death may be refigured. The space of anatheism opens onto this "may be." But it is a space of free possibility—beyond impossibility— never a fait accompli. Nothing can be taken for granted. Wagers are called for, again and again.

{ TWO }

INTERLUDE

4

IN THE FLESH

SACRAMENTAL IMAGINATION

Only through singularities can we find the divine.

—Spinoza

There are three basic elements to anatheism: protest, prophecy, and sacrament. In chapter 3 we looked mainly at the first two, especially as they signal a challenge to the God of otherwordly omnipotence and invite retrievals of a God of service and natality. In this chapter I will focus on the third element—namely, a sacramental return to the holiness of the everyday. As the phenomenological analyses I explore in this and following chapters focus mainly on figures of eucharistand epiphany, I begin with some remarks on the Gospel tradition of embodiment. So doing, however, I by no means wish to confine the application of these analyses to Christianity.

From the beginning, and at its best, Christianity professed both a pilgrim and sacramental vocation. The first went out in search of aliens and strangers.[1] It was a quest of a kingdom still to come, which ran from early migrant missionaries to the bold thinkers of the Reform movements (including advocates of a "religionless faith" like Bonhoeffer and Ricoeur).[2] The second vocation—the sacramental—sought to welcome the stranger into the here and now: the kingdom already come. This hosting of the transcendent in the immanence of the present was epitomized by the great mystics of the monastic and mendicant orders (Carmelites, Beguines, Franciscans, Benedictines) as well as by numerous religious artists and saints.[3] Anatheism draws from these two vocations, seeking to combine the pilgrim commitment to protest and prophecy with a sacramental return to epiphanies of the everyday. It endeavors to balance the journey outward with a sojourning in the sacred here and now.

Sacramental return is a retrieval of the extraordinary in the ordinary. I am using "sacramental" here in a more general sense than that of ritual "sacraments" (though it may include these) to cover those special awakenings of the divine within the bread and wine of quotidian existence. Teresa of Avila argued that true mystical experience testifies to this sacramental movement from mystical meditation back to the ordinary universe. After the forgetfulness of self and detachment from possessions in silent contemplation, she speaks of returning to a life of service to others in the world, reminding us of the "sacred humanity" of Christ. The ultimate step in mystical abandonment is a sanctification of our mundane existence: "Know that the Lord walks among the pots and pans helping you both interiorly and exteriorly."[4] The Creator, she always insisted, "must be sought through creatures."[5] This sacramental return to a life of service in the secular world will be examined in more detail in our final chapters. For now, suffice it to say that this third element of anatheism signals a *via affirmativa* after the *via negativa* of disenchantment. Beyond the dark caesuras of history—whether the horrors of holocausts or the black nights of individual souls—anatheism promises a second consecration of the life-world. It embraces, in Ricoeur's phrase, *"la joie du oui dans la tristesse du fini."*[6]

Put another way: the sacramental invokes the power of yes in the wake of no. This is like the power of Zarathustra's "child" who can only reaffirm life after the lion has challenged the camel of conformity and the dragon of legalism ("Thou must"). It is a powerless power, yet ultimately more gracious and effective than the most powerful of powers. It is the possibility of a God after God (*ana-theos*) that signals the return of the sacred after its setting aside (*ana-thema*). And here anathema takes on the double sense not only of heretical condemnation—its colloquial connotation—but also of a setting apart as holy. Heresy as precondition of hallowing. Sundering as prelude to sanctity. Withdrawal as precursor to consent. We thus recover the original sense of *anathema* as a thing devoted to the divine.

In light of this *anathema-anatheos* paradox, I will be suggesting, in this chapter and the next, that sacramental return presupposes a certain "negative capability" that keeps us vigilant toward strange signs of the divine beyond the dichotomy between theism and atheism. In other words, the sacramental move, as I understand it, signals the possibility of a second God set apart from the first God of metaphysical sufficiency. It marks an opening toward a God whose descent into flesh depends on our response to the sacred summons of the moment. This calls for a special attentiveness to infinity embodying itself in daily acts of eucharistic love and sharing. An endless moving over and back between the infinite and infinitesimal. The highest deity becomes—kenotically—the "very least of these." The word made everyday flesh. Ongoing and interminable gift. Transubstantiation. In what follows I will trace a sacramental paradigm of sensibility explored by two continental thinkers, Maurice Merleau-Ponty and Julia Kristeva. In chapter 5 I will extend this investigation to a study of three modern novelists, Joyce, Proust, and Woolf. And, finally, in our last two chapters I will explore living examples of sacramental anatheism in the *vita activa* of modern ethics and politics.

A PHENOMENOLOGY OF THE FLESH

What can contemporary philosophy tell us about sacramental incarnation? What light, if any, can it cast on the everyday marvel of word becoming flesh?

Edmund Husserl blazed a path toward a phenomenology of the flesh when he broached the crucial theme of the living body (*Leib*).[7] In order to open up a space where neglected notions of embodiment might be revisited in a fresh experiential light, Husserl considered it essential to operate his famous "epoché." This involved the bracketing of all previous presuppositions—in this instance, everything we thought we knew about the flesh. This suspension of received opinion ran all the way down from the heights of metaphysics to the most basic prejudices of common sense; a whole gamut of assumptions that Husserl lumped together under the label of the *natural attitude*. In other words, the acquired mind that Husserl's phenomenology sought to put out of play covered a wide variety of views about what the "flesh" actually is, ranging from those of speculative systems (realist or idealist) to those of positive sciences like physics and chemistry or any number of cultural, social, and ideological attitudes. And the suspension also included all religious doctrines and dogmas about the body, sex, desire, and sin. Once all such presumptions were provisionally bracketed, Husserl wagered that the phenomena themselves would be allowed to speak for themselves in their simple, ordinary everydayness. The hypothesis was that *after* the "epoché" of accredited conventions, the things of experience would be invited, without censure, to show themselves forth from them-

selves as they are in themselves, that is, in all their multilayered *thereness*—
sensible, affective, intelligible, spiritual. In this manner, experiences of the
flesh, all too often neglected by Western mentalities, would be redescribed
in a new and unprejudiced light.[8]

Husserl himself, however, only pointed in this direction. He blazed the
trail and took some steps along the path. But he did not enter or occupy the
terrain. His own work, however pioneering, remained a matter of promissory notes, missionary manifestos, half-finished charts, logs, and maps. For
all his talk of returning to the "things themselves," Husserl remained caught
in the nets of transcendental idealism and never quite escaped the limits of
theoretical cognition. It would be for his followers to drop anchor and bring
the expeditionary flotilla to shore. Heidegger certainly advanced the project
of a phenomenology of flesh with his existential analytic of "moods" and
"facticity." But the fact remains that Heideggerian *Dasein* has no real sense
of a living body: Dasein does not eat, sleep or have sex. It too remains, despite all the talk of "being-in-the-world," captive of the transcendental lure.
Other disciples of Husserl went further; but while Max Scheler and Edith
Stein made sorties into a phenomenology of sympathy and Sartre offered
fine insights into shame and desire, it is, I believe, only with Merleau-Ponty
that we witness a fully fledged phenomenology of flesh. Here at last the
body is no longer treated as a mere project, cipher, or icon but as *flesh itself*
in all its ontological depth. The ghost of metaphysical idealism is laid to
rest. We return to the body in its unfathomable *thisness*.

MERLEAU-PONTY'S SACRAMENTAL VISION

It is significant, I think, that Merleau-Ponty chose to describe his phenomenology of the body in sacramental language. This terminological option
amounts to what I would call a eucharistics of profane perception. Let me
take some examples. In the *Phenomenology of Perception* (1945) we read:

> Just as the sacrament not only symbolizes, in sensible species, an
> operation of Grace, but *is* also the real presence of God, which it
> causes to occupy a fragment of space and communicates to those
> who eat of the consecrated bread, provided that they are inwardly
> prepared, in the same way the sensible has not only a motor and
> vital significance, but is nothing other than a certain way of being in
> the world suggested to us from some point in space, and seized and

acted upon by our body, provided that it is capable of doing so, so that sensation is literally a form of communion.[9]

What we have here is a basic analogy of proper proportionality: A is to B what C is to D. Namely, the sacrament of transubstantiation is to the responsive communicant what the sensible is to the capable perceiver.

This is a bold analogy for an existentialist writing in France in the 1940s, a time when close colleagues like Jean-Paul Sartre, Simone de Beauvoir, and Albert Camus considered militant atheism *de rigueur*. Merleau-Ponty goes on to delineate the eucharistic power of the sensible as follows: "I am brought into relation with an external being, whether it be in order to open myself to it or to shut myself off from it. If the qualities radiate around them a certain mode of existence, if they have the power to cast a spell and what we called just now a sacramental value, this is because the sentient subject does not posit them as objects, but enters into a sympathetic relation with them, makes them his own and finds in them his momentary law."[10] In other words, each sensory encounter with the strangeness of the world is an invitation to a "natal pact" where, through sympathy, the human self and the strange world give birth to one another. Sacramental sensation is a reversible rapport between myself and things, wherein the sensible gives birth to itself through me.

It is a curious paradox that, when Merleau-Ponty traces the "phenomenological return" all the way down to the lowest rung of experience (in the old metaphysical ladder, the *senses*), he discovers the most sacramental act of communion. This is intimately related to his notion of a chiasmatic crossing of ostensible contraries, the cognitive in the carnal, the outer in the inner, the invisible in the visible. Here we have a reversal of Platonism: a return to flesh as our most intimate "element," namely, that which enfolds us in the systole and diastole of being, the seeing and being-seen of vision. Phenomenology thus marks the surpassing of traditional dualisms between body and mind, real and ideal, subject and object. This is how Merleau-Ponty describes the enigma of flesh as mutual crossing-over in his posthumously published work, *The Visible and the Invisible* (1964): "The seer is caught up in what he sees . . . the vision he exercises, he also undergoes from the things, such that, as many painters have said, I feel myself looked at by the things, my activity is passivity." So much so that "the seer and the visible reciprocate one another and we no longer know which sees and which is seen. It is this Visibility, this anonymity innate to Myself that we have called flesh, and one knows there is no name in traditional philosophy to designate it."[11] It is here, I suggest, that Merleau-Ponty gets to the heart of this "nameless" matter and descends—in a final return, a last reduction that suspends all previous reductions—to the incarnate region of the "element": "The flesh is not matter, in the sense of corpuscles of Being that would add up or continue on one another to form beings. Nor is the visible (the thing as well as my body) some 'psychic' material that would be—God knows how—brought into being by the things factually existing and acting on my factual body. In general, it is not a fact or a sum of facts 'material' or 'spiritual.'" No, insists Merleau-Ponty, the matter is quite otherwise. "The flesh is not matter, is not mind, is not substance. To designate it, we would need the ancient term 'element,' in the sense it was used to speak of water, air, earth, and fire, that is, in the sense of a *general thing* midway between the spatio-temporal individual and the idea, a sort of incarnate principle that brings a style of Being wherever there is a fragment of Being. The flesh is in this sense an 'element' of Being."[12] The element of the flesh, in short, is the medial *entre-deux* between the whole of Being and each individual fragment. It signals, in pre-Socratic terms, the embodiment of "nascent logos" in everyday mundane things.

Returning to examples of painting—Cézanne and Klee—in *Eye and Mind* (1964), Merleau-Ponty expounds on the chiasmic model as a mutual transubstantiation of seer and seen. This he calls a "miracle" of flesh. He articulates his position in these ontological terms:

> There really is inspiration and expiration of Being, action and passion so slightly discernible that it becomes impossible to distinguish between what sees and what is seen, what paints and what is painted. . . . There is no break at all in this circuit; it is impossible to say that nature ends here and that man or expression starts here. It is mute Being which itself comes to show forth its own meaning.[13]

Already in *Signs* (1960), a collection of essays devoted to questions of language and art, Merleau-Ponty had explored the claim that the flesh of art is invariably indebted to the bread of life. There is nothing so insignificant in the life of the artist, he holds, that is ineligible for "consecration" in the painting or poem. But the "style" of the artist converts his/her corporeal situation into sacramental witness at a higher level of "repetition" and "recreation." The artwork still refers to the life-world from which it springs, but opens up a second order reference of creative possibility. Speaking specifically of Leonardo de Vinci, he writes:

> If we take the painter's point of view in order to be present at that decisive moment when what has been given to him to live as corporeal destiny, personal adventures or historical events, crystallizes into "the motive" (i.e., the style), we will recognize that his work, which is never an effect, is always a response to these data and that the body, the life, the landscapes, the schools, the mistresses, the creditors, the police and the revolutions which might suffocate painting are also *the bread his work consecrates*. To live in painting is still to breathe the air of this world.[14]

In sum, the bread of the world is the very stuff consecrated in the body of the work. Here once again we see how Merleau-Ponty's phenomenological accounts serve to revitalize theological and sacramental idioms in a post-metaphysical language. We will return to this aesthetic of transubstantiation in the discussion of our three novelists in chapter 5.

But let's be clear, Merleau-Ponty is no theologian—and he is certainly no Christian apologist. My point is that, from a philosophically agnostic viewpoint, he offers an intriguing phenomenological interpretation of eucharistic embodiment as recovery of the divine within the flesh, a kenotic emptying out of transcendence into the heart of the world's body, becoming a God beneath us rather than a God beyond us. This brings us to the heart of Merleau-Ponty's sacramental vision. These are his words, and, while ostensibly agnostic, they are not, I think, neutral. "The Christian God wants nothing to do with a vertical relation of subordination," he writes.

> He is not simply a principle of which we are the consequence, a will whose instruments we are, or even a model of which human values are the only reflection. There is a sort of impotence of God without us, and Christ attests that God would not be fully God without becoming fully man. Claudel goes so far as to say that God is not above but beneath us—meaning that we do not find Him as a suprasensible idea, but as another ourself which dwells in and authenticates our darkness. Transcendence no longer hangs over man; he becomes, strangely, its privileged bearer.[15]

When it comes to expressing love for another human being, Merleau-Ponty sees the presence of this "transcendence" in the promise we make to another beyond what we can know or realize in the present moment. The absolute the lover looks for *beyond* our experience is implied *within* it. Just as I grasp time by being present, I perceive others through my individual life, "in the tension of an experience which transcends itself." There is thus, Merleau-Ponty suggests,

> no destruction of the absolute . . . only of the absolute separated from existence. To tell the truth, Christianity consists in replacing the separated absolute by the absolute in men. Nietzsche's idea that God is dead is already contained in the Christian idea of the death of God. God ceases to be an external object in order to mingle in human life, and this life is not simply a return to a non-temporal conclusion.

And he adds: "God needs human history. As Malebranche said, the world is unfinished." Merleau-Ponty realizes that most official Christian churches of his day would not endorse this, but he suggests that "some Christians might agree that the other side of things must already be visible in the environment in which we live."[16] And he knows that, writing as a philosopher, not a theologian, he is free to experiment with phenomenological reappraisals of otherwise sacrosanct ideas. He needs no *nihil obstat*.

Finally, in his lectures on "Nature," delivered at the Collège de France between 1956 and 1960, Merleau-Ponty explores the possibility of rethinking God through Nature. He objects to any theism that takes God out of the world, a move he associates with a certain Christian "acosmism"—or antiworldliness—epitomized in the metaphysical equation of total being with a God beyond the world. Such a removal of divinity from the natural and human world threatens to plunge nature into a state of nothingness. Merleau-Ponty links this to a special "malaise of Judeo-Christian ontology," which he defines thus: "Such a monotheism carries along with it in all rigor the consequence that the world is not. "From the moment when we say that God is Being, it is clear that in a certain sense God alone is" [quoting Étienne Gilson]. Judeo-Christian thinking is haunted by the threat of acosmism."[17] But this acosmic expression of Judeo-Christian belief is, of course, historically specific; it is a particular metaphysical account of the divine, and its relationship to nature, which became dominant in Western

philosophy and theology. Like Nietzsche before him, Merleau-Ponty identifies this orthodox account with a disguised nihilism. And I think he is right.
For to equate God with a timeless, otherwordly Being that is sovereign cause
of itself and has no desire for nature or humanity—as Descartes and the
rationalists did   is to reject the sanctity of the flesh. "To posit God as Being
[in the metaphysical sense] is to bring about a negation of the world."[18] And
it is also, Merleau-Ponty hastens to add, a betrayal of the original message
of Incarnation—the logos becoming flesh and entering into the heart of
suffering and acting humanity.

In reaction to this version of metaphysical theism, Merleau-Ponty calls
for the recognition of a genuinely atheistic moment in the Christian story
of incarnation and crucifixion where Christ experiences a radical abandonment before the father. "My God My God why have you forsaken me?"
Merleau-Ponty concludes by contrasting acosmic theism with a certain, albeit neglected, Christian alternative that he identifies with the sacramental
engagement with the world—an engagement epitomized by the worker-
priest movement in France in the 1950s, which later found expression
in liberation theology and in the attention to what he calls "minorities,"
namely, the marginalized and rejected ones. This is his critical diagnosis of
acosmic theism: "God is beyond all Creation. Theism comes from this position, and moves toward that of no longer distinguishing the critique of false
Gods. . . . And, as Kierkegaard said, no one can be called Christian; faith
must become unfaith. There is an atheism in Christianity, religion of God
made man, where Christ dies, abandoned by God."[19] But Merleau-Ponty
does not end there. He appends the following prognosis: "It may be, says a
hymn, that the passion of Christ is not in vain. . . . See the adventure of the
priest-workers, as awareness that we cannot place God apart from humanity
suffering in history; hence, so that God may be realized, [we need] the sort-
ing out of humans who are the furthest from God . . . because minorities
are the salt of the Earth!"[20]

Merleau-Ponty appears to be implying here that we need a new, nondog-
matic relation to Nature (and to God) that opens on the minor, the different,
the embodied. Recognizing the radical consequences of incarnation for our
understanding of both God and Nature is, for Merleau-Ponty, an anatheist
alternative to the endless doctrinal disputes between theism and atheism.
In this sense, we might say that Merleau-Ponty would have agreed with the
proposal by Bonhoeffer and Ricoeur that we move beyond religious forms
disfigured by otherworldly metaphysics to a faith in the divine potential in-

herent in the everyday life of action and suffering, of attention and service to others. But where Merleau-Ponty seems to differ from Bonhoeffer and Ricoeur is in supplementing their "prophetic" voice of protest (informed by their war experience of imprisonment) with a "sacramental" acoustic of natural existence. In this he might be said to add a more "Catholic" style to the "Protestant" iconoclasm of Bonhoeffer and Ricoeur. Though in both cases we are speaking of a postreligious expression of these confessional cultures. By relocating transcendence in the immanence of nature, Merleau-Ponty is restoring logos to the flesh of the world. *Deus sive natura.*

SARTRE'S VALEDICTION

I think that Sartre captures the transcendence-immanence paradox of his friend's thought accurately in his obituary essay, "Merleau-Ponty Vivant." Sartre acknowledges that Merleau-Ponty had been drawn to the Catholic community in his youth but had left the Church at the age of twenty while "refusing to be considered an atheist in his last years."[21] Merleau-Ponty remained intrigued, says Sartre, by a certain "miracle" of existence, whereby "being invents man in order to make itself manifest through him."[22] Though his friend's ideas on this subject are alien to Sartre, he offers a startling description of the anonymous Stranger who incarnates the summons of transcendence in the most destitute beggar before us. One passage—penned by the atheist Sartre confronted with a resonant Merleau-Ponty "metaphor"— is remarkable for its echoes of Christian kenosis and the identification of the divine with the hungry, homeless *hospes* (Matt. 25). I quote it in full:

> Didn't Merleau, from time to time, think he perceived some sort of transcendent mandate "hidden in immanence" within us? In one of his articles, he congratulates a mystic for having written that God is below us, and Merleau added, in so many words, "why not?" He dreamed of this Almighty who would need men, who would still be called into question in each one's heart, and yet would remain total being, unceasingly, infinitely instituted by intersubjectivity, the only one who we shall lead to the fount of our being, and who will share with us the insecurity of the human adventure. Here we are obviously dealing only with a metaphorical indication. But the fact that he chose this metaphor is not without significance. Everything is there: the discovery and the risk of being is below us, a gigantic

beggar-woman clad in rags, we need only an imperceptible change for her to become *our task*. God, the task of man? . . . Nothing says that he may not, at times, have dreamed it. . . . He worked without haste. He was waiting.[23]

But this is not all. Merleau-Ponty resisted the Hegelian temptation to choose closure over divine fragility. Sartre's supplementary invocation of the kenotic trope in Merleau-Ponty's late ontology is as apt here as it is arresting:

Merleau had sought envelopment within immanence, and had collided against the transcendent. More than ever avoiding any recourse to Hegelian synthesis . . . he lets transcendence flow into immanence, there to be dissolved at the same time as it is protected against annihilation by its very impalpability. It will be only absence and supplication, deriving its all-encompassing power from its infinite weakness.[24]

But Merleau-Ponty, I repeat, is neither an apologist nor an historian of religion. He is a philosopher who deploys a specific phenomenological method to articulate the "nameless" experience of sacramental flesh. And it is to be noted that a number of recent phenomenologists have implicitly followed Merleau-Ponty's lead when seeking to inventory the sacred dimensions of the sensible and erotic. One thinks of Jean-Luc Marion in his writings on the "flesh" as saturated phenomenon or Jean-Louis Chrétien in his account of embodiment in sacred art.[25] But Merleau-Ponty differs from the theological hermeneutics of Marion and Chrétien in observing a methodological agnosticism with regard to the theistic/atheistic implications of sacramental sensation. An agnosticism that, I am suggesting, opens onto an anatheist option.

No crypto-evangelist then, Merleau-Ponty follows Husserl in suspending confessional truth claims. And this amounts, I think, to the philosophical equivalent of the poetic license enjoyed by artists when it comes to the marvel of transubstantiation in word, sound, or image. In this respect, we could say that the phenomenological method—which brackets given attitudes—is analogous to the literary suspending of belief and disbelief for the sake of inclusive entry to the "kingdom of as-if." This suspension, I will claim in our next chapter, allows for a specific negative capability regarding questions of doubt, proof, dogma, or doctrine, so as to better appreciate the "thing itself," the holy *thisness* of our flesh-and-blood existence. The attitude of pure attention that follows from such exposure to a "free variation of imagination" (the phrase is Husserl's) is not far removed, I believe, from what certain mystics have recognized to be a crucial preparatory moment for sacramental vision: a moment they have called by such various names as the "cloud of unknowing," the *docta ignorantia*, or in Eastern mysticism the *neti/neti*(neither this nor that)—experiences that pave the way for the deepest wisdom of reality.[26] True belief crosses nonbelief. In the free traversal of the imaginary, indispensable to the phenomenological method, everything is permissible. Nothing is excluded except exclusion. By allowing us to attend to the sacramental miracle of the everyday, without absolute claims, Merleau-Ponty offers fresh insights into the eucharistic character of the sensible.

This is not a last word. It is a cleared space to begin again.

KRISTEVA AND THE AESTHETICS OF SENSATION

Before moving on to a close reading of certain "sacramental" artworks, however, I wish to mention one other contemporary thinker—Julia Kristeva—who has insightful things to say about the aesthetics of "transubstantiation." As a linguist and psychoanalyst, Kristeva adds new perspectives to the phenomenological vision of Merleau-Ponty. In particular she ventures rich insights into the workings of unconscious tropes and associations in modernist writings about sense and sensibility. Brought up in the culture of Greek Orthodox Christianity and educated by Catholic nuns in Sofia, Kristeva has a keen sense of the sacramental in a religious context. But she, no less than Merleau-Ponty, rejects the God of metaphysical theism. She recommends, in *Strangers to Ourselves*, that we surmount the theocratic dualisms of pure and impure, saved and damned, native and stranger; for, she argues, such dualisms lead to sacrificial scapegoating and war. "The big work of our civilization," she says, "is to fight this hatred—without God."[27]

Once again, however, we are compelled to ask: what kind of "God" must we jettison if we are to become hospitable to the strangers in our midst? What sort of religious exclusivism do we need to combat if we are to accept not only the foreigner at our borders but also the foreigner in ourselves? And, if we can observe such an abstention from the "savage gods" of belligerent sovereignty, what kind of sacredness, if any, can we hope to reaffirm in the everyday secular universe? These anatheist questions are Kristeva's as they are ours.

Interestingly, Kristeva looks to a certain *sacramentality of the senses* that she locates in works of art and literature. Dostoyevsky and Novalis are key figures in her retrieval of the sacred after the death of God, but Proust is probably her most privileged subject. In *Time and Sense*, Kristeva identifies a certain grammar of "transubstantiation" at work in Proust's notion of involuntary memory. She offers this example, among others:

> A sensation from the past remains within us, and involuntary memory recaptures it when a related perception in the present is stimulated by the same desire as the prior sensation. A spatio-temporal association of sensations is thus established, relying on a link, a structure, and a reminiscence. Sensation takes refuge in this interwoven network and turns into an *impression*, which means that sensation loses its solitary specificity.

And as it does so, notes Kristeva, "a similarity emerges out of all these differences, eventually attaining the status of a general law in the manner of an idea or thought. The 'general law,' however, is no abstraction, for it is established because the sensation is *immanent in it*. . . . This process keeps the structure from losing its sensorial foundation. Music becomes word, and writing becomes a *transubstantiation* in those for whom it creates 'new powers.'"[28]

Kristeva links this aesthetic of transubstantiation—which she finds in Proust and Joyce—back to the writings of the late Merleau-Ponty. These she calls "mystically significant."[29] Indeed her notion of a "general law" of ideational sensation is surely not unrelated to Merleau-Ponty's reference to a "momentary law," previously cited. Most specifically, Kristeva relates the eucharistic aesthetic to the chiasmic liaison between the visible and invisible, the inner feeling and outer expression—a liaison that Merleau-Ponty described as a reversible interpenetration of *flesh*. Refusing the dualistic division of spirit and body into separate substances, Kristeva invites us, in line with Bachelard, to think flesh more phenomenologically as an *"element,"* that is, as the "concrete emblem of a general manner of being."[30] And, in this respect, Kristeva endorses Merleau-Ponty's claim that "no one has gone further than Proust in fixing the relations between the visible and the invisible,"[31] though she would want to add Joyce to the list. Indeed identifying Merleau-Ponty's model of reversibility with the notion of "transubstantiation" (she explicitly uses this term), Kristeva takes the miracle of the carnal as paradigmatic for both 1. therapeutic healing and 2. reading literary texts.

In both writing and healing, the reversible transubstantiation of word and flesh expresses itself as catharsis.[32] Kristeva goes on, rather boldly, to suggest that the aesthetic of transubstantiation not only helps to heal the wounded psyche but also releases writers like Proust and Joyce from the prison house of linguistic idealism. Their writings are sacramental as well as semiotic. Indeed, she notes that although Proust never stops "deciphering," his world does not consist primarily of "signs." At any rate, she insists, his world is not made of "sign-words or idea-signs, and certainly not of signifiers and signifieds."[33] Proust, Kristeva observes, was disappointed by "empty linguistic signs" and used words to evoke a teeming life-world of embodied existence—a fluidity of "atmospheric changes," a "rush of blood," a sudden silence, an "adverb springing from an involuntary connection made between two unformulated ideas" (252). Kristeva finds support for this aesthetic of "real presence" in the young Proust's aversion to "strict significations," and she points to the fact that Jean Santeuil (Marcel *avant la lettre*) conceives of art as a "work of feeling" that focuses on a "sort of obscure instinct of permanent brilliance" or "lava about to overflow"—as well as on "what is not yet ready to come forth" (252). The Proustian text, she avers, rises up "against the abyss between language and lived experience." It operates as a "vast array of impressions that the hero's sentence strives to communicate (despite his reservations about language) by associating weather, villages, roads, dust, grass and raindrops through a mass accumulation of metaphors and metonymies" (252).

All this, Kristeva surmises, paves the way in Proust "for the *impression*, which makes up for the weakness of linguistic signs" (252). And so words are only useful for Proust when they exert an "evocative power" over our "sensibility," displaying a kinship with a sort of "latent music" (the terms are Proust's; 252). Resisting the temptations of both nominalism and Platonism, Proust's eucharistic writing aims for a "lively physical expressiveness that resists the passivity of the civilized sign" (252). Instead it sketches a corporeal liturgy of the lived body: what Proust calls "the vigorous and expressive language of our muscles and our desires, of suffering, of the corruption or the flowering of the flesh."[34] What pertains to Proust, I will suggest, also pertains to Joyce and Woolf. And it is to a closer reading of these three novelists that I turn in my next chapter. My aim is to sketch a sacramental aesthetics that illustrates how dying to an acosmic God may allow a God of cosmic epiphanies to be reborn. Whether these authors are concerned more with an *aesthetic religion* or a *religious aesthetic* remains an open question.

The insight of "immanent transcendence" that characterizes sacramental aesthetics is not of course unique to Merleau-Ponty or Kristiva, or the novelists and poets whom I will cite to illustrate such an aesthetics. Down through the ages many Christian mystics—from John of the Cross to Hildegard of Bingen and Meister Eckhart—articulated similar things. As did Jewish sages like Rabbi Luria and Franz Rosenzweig or Sufi masters like Rumi and Ibn 'Arabi. Indeed I am also reminded here of the bold claim by Teilhard de Chardin that God does not direct the universe from above but underlies it and "prolongs himself" into it.

Nor should we forget Francis of Assisi's sacramental vision of the natural world. This represented a profound "heresy of the heart" that broke from previous metaphysical doctrines of Christianity as acosmic denial of the body. Max Scheler's Franciscan reading of embodiment is of special relevance here, given his close links with phenomenology. He argues that the sacrament of the Eucharist shows how Christian love may "acquire a footing in the living and organic, through its 'magical' identification with the body and blood of our Lord under the forms of bread and wine."[35] And he suggests that these came to be virtually the *only* natural substances, in a very ritualized setting of Holy Communion, that permitted a union with the cosmos—until, that is, mystics like Francis and Claire of Assisi came to embody this communion in their everyday lives, restoring sacramentality to the living universe of nature, animals and humans. Francis's bold heresy, in Scheler's view, was to have challenged the gulf between humans and nature introduced by traditional Christian doctrine, addressing—as Francis did—both fire and water, sun and moon, animals and plants as "brothers and sisters." Against the acosmic tendencies of mainstream metaphysical Christianity, Francis's intrepid achievement was to combine love of God with a sense of union with the life and being of Nature.[36] His greatness was to have expanded the specifically Christian emotion of love for God the Father to embrace "all the lower orders of nature," while at the same time uplifting Nature into the glory of the divine.[37] Some of Francis's contemporaries thought him unconventional. Others thought him mad. For here, after all, was a "mystic who dared conjoin transcendence and immanence, the sacred and the secular, by calling all creatures his brothers, and by looking with the heart's keen insight into the inmost being of every creature, just as though he had already entered into the freedom of glory of the children of God."[38]

This mystical panentheism—the view that God is in all beings—was condemned as blasphemy by many orthodox Christians before and after Francis. But for Francis, as Scheler recognizes, it was a way of restoring God to the world, of rediscovering a living God amidst the ashes of a dead one.

Though Merleau-Ponty and Kristeva do not invoke the mystical Francis in any explicit sense, their vision of sensible incarnation is, I believe, deeply Franciscan—or should I say ana-Franciscan—in spirit.

5

IN THE TEXT

JOYCE, PROUST, WOOLF

I would like a great lake of beer for the King of Kings.
I would like to be watching heaven's family drinking it
Through all eternity.

—St. Brigid of Kildare

In this chapter I look at how certain modern authors illustrate the anathe-istic paradigm. I will focus on three pioneers of modernist fiction who bore witness to the return of the sacred—Joyce, Proust, and Woolf. No one of these was a believer in any orthodox confessional sense. Each was deeply marked, to be sure, by their religious education and upbringing: Joyce as a Catholic, Woolf as a Protestant, and Proust as someone with a mixed Christian-Jewish background. But none of them advanced an overtly the-istic position. Conventional wisdom might even suggest the contrary: that Joyce was a rebel apostate, Proust a secular sensualist, and Woolf a humanist aesthete (how otherwise make sense of her response to the news that T. S. Eliot had converted in 1928: "there's something obscene in a living person sitting by the fire and believing in God")?

At first blush, therefore, it would seem that these three writers, like many of their literary contemporaries, chose aesthetics over religion. There is a notion among modern intellectuals that matters of existential profundity and ultimacy, previously considered the preserve of churches, are now, in Western culture at least, being transferred to the sanctuaries of art. While there is clearly some truth to this view of secular modernity, it often misses the degree to which many authors remained deeply committed to a sacra-mental imagination that defied the either/or division between theism and atheism. Agnosticism is often used as a fill-in term to cover this medial position. But such a neutral noun ultimately fails, I think, to capture the radically mystical character of much modern literature. Hence my suggestion, in what follows, that the term *anatheism*—the return to the sacred after the disappearance of God—more accurately conveys the complex paradoxes and ambivalences at play. For these three authors believe, along with Paul Eluard, that there is indeed another world, but that it is inside this one. A sense of transcendence is alive in their work, I will argue, but it is one inscribed in everyday immanence. Mystery is preserved, even celebrated, not as ecclesiastical dogma but as a mystical affirmation of incarnate existence: Word made Flesh in the ordinary universe.

I will be suggesting, in other words, that these three authors manage to eschew the received divisions between sacred and profane, religious and secular, transcendent and immanent, in favor of a retrieval of the sacramental in the sensible. The eucharistic imagination, described by Merleau-Ponty and Kristeva in the last chapter, is no longer the exclusive preserve of High Church liturgies, but is generously extended to acts of quotidian experience where the infinite traverses the infinitesimal. Whether this mutual traversal of the sacred and secular in modernist fiction is a matter of sacramentalizing the secular or of secularizing the sacred is, of course, central to our discussion. What I am wagering here is that the anatheist paradigm may allow it be *both at once*: religion as art *and* art as religion. Not one or the other. Though I am well aware that the relationship between faith and fiction remains, here again, a complex one.

I mentioned in my preface that my main hermeneutic model in this work is a *narrative* one. So it is fitting that my three chosen figures of "sacramental aesthetics" are novelists. Proust, Joyce, and Woolf epitomize, I will suggest, a sacramental imagination that celebrates the bread and wine of everyday existence. In Joyce's *Ulysses* this takes many forms throughout the novel, culminating in the passing of the seedcake from the mouth of Molly to Bloom on Howth Head in the last scene of the narrative. In Proust's great novel it assumes the guise of a sonata of epiphanies, most famously those that occur at a Parisian party, chez les Guermantes, in the final volume, *Time Regained*. In Virginia Woolf's *To the Lighthouse*, the eucharistic vision expresses itself in a magical feast of boeuf en daube, presided over by Mrs. Ramsay, as recalled in a painting created after her death by Lily Briscoe. The stories these novelists tell—as well as their telling—exemplify a return of the sacred.

In all three we witness the consecration of ordinary moments of flesh and blood *thisness* as something strange and enduring. These acts of transfiguration, which following Joyce I call epiphanies, transpire in an embodied space and time far from the otherworldliness of metaphysical forms. My hypothesis in what follows is that the anatheist hermeneutic of incarnation — adumbrated by Merleau-Ponty and Kristeva — may help discern a grammar of transubstantiation in these narratives of sacramental sense. To this end, I will concentrate on certain "eucharistic" events in each novel, suggesting how they signal anatheist recoveries of the holy in happenstance.

JOYCE

Joyce invokes explicit idioms of transubstantiation to describe the writing process. Already in the *Portrait* Stephen Dedalus describes himself as a "priest of the eternal imagination"; his aim, he says, is to transmute the "bread of daily experience" in the "womb" of art. This is more than irony. Taking his cue from the sacramental act of transubstantiation in its liturgical formulation, Joyce treats the transformative event of writing as the "advent of new signs and a new body."[1] Joyce's brother, Stanislas, reports the following conversation on the subject: "Don't you think, said he reflectively, choosing his words without haste, there is a certain resemblance between the mystery of the Mass and what I am trying to do? I mean that I am trying in my poems to give people some kind of intellectual pleasure or spiritual enjoyment by converting the bread of everyday life into something that has a permanent artistic life of its own."[2]

Such conversions of life into text are witnessed at several key junctures in Joyce's texts. They often go by the name of *epiphanies*, referring, as I have shown elsewhere, to acts of textual "repetition," whereby the author treats a remembered event as both past (separated by time) and present (regained miraculously in the epiphany of the moment).[3] And yet there is a deeply deconstructive lining to many of Joyce's sacramental allusions. Indeed *Ulysses* itself may be read as a series of anti-Eucharists or pseudo-Eucharists. But that is not all. Joyce's character, Stephen Dedalus, is a self-styled "heresiarch." But if he refuses to pray at his mother's deathbed or partake of the Catholic Eucharist he cherished in his youth, it is not to uncritically embrace the black masses ministered by his blaspheming alter ego, Buck Mulligan. (See the opening chapter and again in the Hollis St. Hospital and National Library scenes.) There is another space opening up for Stephen between the

Scylla of naive theism—his mother's faith—and the Charybdis of cynical atheism—Mulligan's antifaith. As the novel evolves, Stephen gestures falteringly toward a new openness to Eucharists of the everyday offered to him by Bloom and Molly; and this return movement culminates, I suggest, in the final eucharistic epiphany of Molly's soliloquy. But such a climax is in no mere reversion to the first theism of infantile belief. As signaled in different ways by both Bloom and Molly, the return of the sacramental is neither theist nor atheist. It is anatheist. It marks not closure but a new overture, not some totalizing synthesis but a sounding of new possibilities of incarnation, not some grand finale of triumphalist dogma but a deeper attention to the call of the stranger in "cries in the street." In sum, we are not concerned here with apologetics but an *apologia pro sua vita* that opens the solipsistic self to the summons of the strange. Molly's "yes" to secular-sacred existence epitomizes this anatheist move.

Let's start at the beginning. The novel opens, significantly, with Buck Mulligan's mimicry of Mass on the turret of the Martello tower. He is carrying a shaving bowl for a chalice and mockingly intoning the liturgical *Introibo ad altare Dei*. Holding up the sacrificial bowl, he addresses Stephen as a "Jesuit" before adopting a priestly tone: "For this, O dearly beloved, is the genuine Christine: body and blood and soul and ouns. Slow music please. Shut your eyes, gents. One moment. A little trouble with those white corpuscles. Silence all." Mulligan's parody of the Catholic Eucharist is followed in the next episode by Bloom's morning feast of fried kidneys, during the course of which, as Molly later recalls, Bloom delivers himself of "jawbreakers about the incarnation" before burning the bottom of the pan! Later again in the novel we witness Stephen's parodic Mass in nighttown and Bloom and Stephen's failed Mass over a cup of cocoa in the penultimate "Ithaca" chapter. Not to mention the multiple mock-allusions to transubstantiation in the Oxen of the Sun and Scylla and Charybdis episodes.

This series of pseudo-Eucharists may be read as a long *via negativa* that eventually opens up the space for the "kiss" of the seedcake on Howth Head in the final chapter. This "long kiss" between Molly and Bloom when they first courted—recalled by Molly in her soliloquy—is redolent with sacramental associations. It could be said, for instance, to reprise not only the "kisses of the mouth" celebrated by the Shulammite woman in the Song of Songs but also the Passover of Judeo-Christian promise. Molly's remembrance of the "long kiss," where she gave Bloom the "seedcake out of (her) mouth," might be thought of as a retrieval of a genuine eucharistic gift of love after the various debunkings of failed or parodied Eucharists—and loves—recurring throughout the narrative. And it is this kiss that triggers, in true kairological fashion, the earlier memory of Molly's first kiss as a young woman in Gibraltar: a first kiss that becomes the final kiss of the novel itself, climaxing in the famous lines: "how he kissed me under the Moorish wall . . . and then I asked him with my eyes to ask again yes and then he asked me would I yes to say yes my mountain flower and first I put my arms around him yes and drew him down to me so he could feel my breasts all perfume yes and his heart was going like mad and yes I said yes I will Yes."[4]

This remembered kiss may, of course, also be read as a epiphanic repetition of the moment on June 16, 1904, when Joyce first went out and found pleasure with Nora Barnacle: the same day on which Joyce decided to set his great novel and which is subsequently celebrated as Bloomsday. A palimpsest of Joycean memories. Nor should we forget that the closing episode in which Molly remembers times past (and future) is, according to Joyce's notes, dedicated to the "flesh." It crowns a narrative that Joyce described as his "epic of the body."

In repeating a past moment, epiphany gives a future to the past. It somehow transubstantiates the empirical *thisness* of a particular lived event into something sacred and eschatological.[5] So when Molly recalls her first kiss as a young woman she does so—tellingly—in the future tense! "Yes I *will* yes." And we might be tempted to suggest that Molly's promissory "yes" here inscribes Benjamin's notion of "messianic time" as an openness to the future. This is, in short, epiphany understood as a transfiguring instant: the conversion of an ordinary secular moment (*chronos*) into sacred time (*kairos*). Epiphany happens in the gaps, in the breaks of linear temporality when an eternal now—Benjamin's messianic *Jetztzeit*—explodes the continuum of history.

It is also worth noting that epiphany, in its original scriptural sense, involved witnesses who come as *strangers* from afar. I am referring of course to the three magi who traveled from foreign lands to see and hear the word made flesh in a fragile, naked being. This could be read, in terms of our sacramental hermeneutics, as an event of textual openness to new, strange, and unprecedented meanings through the textual encounter between *author*, *narrator*, and *reader*. Such a sacramental reading might be said to epitomize the "desire to open writing to unforeseeable effects, in other words, to the Other." And, as such, it serves as "a function of a responsibility for the Other—for managing in writing a place for the Other, saying *yes* to the call or demand of the Other, inviting a response."[6]

Paul Ricoeur provides an interesting gloss on this notion of sacramental hermeneutics when he writes, "the process of composition, of configuration, is not completed in the text but in the reader and, under this condition, makes possible the reconfiguration of life by narrative." He claims, more exactly, that the "sense or signification of a narrative stems from *the intersection of the world of the text and the world of the reader*" (which is already "prefigured" by the world of the author).[7] Ricoeur goes so far as to construe the double surrender of 1. the author to the implied author (or narrator), and of 2. the implied author to the reader, as an act of kenotic service to the other that ultimately amounts to a transubstantiation of author into reader: "Whereas the real author effaces himself in the implied author, the implied reader takes on substance in the real reader."[8] In short, the author agrees to die so that the reader may be born.

We might also recall here Derrida's invocation of Elijah—also a favorite of Leopold Bloom—as a messianic paradigm of the reader: the unpredictable Other par excellence who calls the text forth and is called forth by the text. This notion of *Ulysses* as an open textual invitation to "refiguration" in the reader finds confirmation, I believe, in Joyce's repeated appeal to the longed-for "reader" who might respond to his text. (A gesture akin, as we shall see, to Proust's appeal to his future readers who would discover in their work the book of their own lives.) Hence Joyce's telling refrain: "Is there one who understands me?" In other words, Joyce (like Proust) invokes the sacramental idiom of transubstantiation to convey the miracle of textual composition and reception. In both we are confronted with a miracle of *repetition* that *recalls the past forward*. An epiphany that explodes the chronology of time.[9]

But how are we to read these novelistic *repetitions?* First let me make clear that I use the term in Søren Kierkegaard's sense of *repeating forward* rather than recollecting backward.[10] This existential interpretation is, by Kierkegaard's own admission, a philosophical retrieval of the Pauline notion of *kairos* as that moment of grace where eternity breaks through and allows the chronological tenses of past and future to be traversed and reversed. And this notion is taken up again by numerous continental thinkers like Heidegger (in his notion of *Wiederholung* in *Being and Time*) and Derrida (in the reflections on *revenant*, messianism, and memory in *Specters of Marx*) and also in Giorgio Agamben's reading of the messianic instant in *The Time That Remains*. (Not to reinvoke Benjamin, who deeply influenced both Derrida and Agamben.)

But what, we may ask, is the particular *style* that performs such gestures? I suggest it is "comic," recalling our discussion of the anatheist wager in chapter 2. Or, to borrow a phrase from Joyce himself, we might call it "joko-serious"; for it is a uniquely humorous way of celebrating the eternal in a breach of time that brings us back to earth (*humus*). Molly, for example, is a mock-heroic parody of the elevated and aristocratic Penelope. She repeats her Homeric prototype forward by opening up new modes of reinscription. To grasp this one need only compare Molly's all-too-mundane musings with the following description of Penelope in the last scene of Homer's *Odyssey*: "So upright in disposition was Penelope the daughter of Icarius that she never forgot Odysseus the husband of her youth; and therefore shall the fame of her goodness be conserved in the splendid poem wherewith the Immortals shall celebrate the constancy of Penelope for all the dwellers upon earth." This is a far cry from Molly's final cry. Certainly Penelope could never say of her beloved Odysseus what Molly says of her lover—"as well him as another"! And yet it is typical of Joyce's irony that, in turning Homer's epic heroism on its head, his characters curiously retrieve a narrative truth by means of creative repetition. Bloom is strangely blessed with his wife (however unfaithful) and does manage to defy his rivals, Boylan and the Citizen (however indirectly); Molly does not forget Bloom, and her ultimate affirmation is "celebrated" by many "dwellers upon earth"! In short, transliterating Penelope and Odysseus into Molly and Bloom, Joyce performs a daring act of eucharistic comedy. He converts the epic into the everyday and rediscovers the sacred in the bread and wine of profane existence. So doing, he proves his conviction that the "structure of heroism is a damned lie and that there cannot be any substitute for individual passion."[11]

Molly's rewriting of Penelope conforms, I believe, to the basic features of comedy outlined by Aristotle and Bergson, namely: the combining of more with less, of the metaphysical with the physical, of the heroic with the demotic. Or, to put it in our sacramental idiom, the combining of Word with flesh. And we might also add, bearing in mind a central motif of comedy, the juxtaposing of death and love. (Recall that *Ulysses* features numerous allusions to deceased persons—Paddy Dignam, Stephen's mother, the Blooms' son Rudi—and that it ends with a call to love: eros defying the sting of thanatos.) Molly's ultimate passing from thanatos to eros is prefigured

several times during her last soliloquy, from fantasies of being buried—
"well when Im stretched out dead in my grave then I suppose I'll have some
peace. I want to get up a minute if Im let O Jesus. . . . O Jamsey let me up
out of this pooh sweets of sin"—to the climatic cry of eschatological bliss:
"Yes I will yes." And it is surely significant that Molly herself is "full with
seed" (not her husband's) as she records her fantasy of death and rebirth,
just as Bloom himself is described as a "manchild in the womb." Allusions
to second natality abound.

But, here again, there can be no ana-theistic moment of rebirth without
traversing the a-theistic moment of disillusionment. No second life without
forfeiture of first life. Stephen dies to his inflated literary illusions, epitomized by his alliance with Mulligan, discovering that "without sundering
there is no reconciliation." Bloom dies to his paternal illusions to replace
his lost son—his final attitude is described as "less envy than equanimity."
While Molly, for her part, dies to her compulsive need to be revered, rediscovering instead forgotten moments of ordinary love.

So we return, finally, to the kiss. In her climactic recall of the kiss, Molly
echoes the Shulammite woman's celebration of wild flora in the Song of
Songs as she affirms that "we are flowers all a womans body." Indeed the
culminating Moorish and Mediterranean idioms of sensory ecstasy and excess are deeply redolent of the Shulammite's Canticle—itself styled after
the Jewish-Babylonian nuptial poem or epithalamium. And this impression
is amplified, I think, by the multiple allusions to seeds, trees, waters, mountains, and irrepressible passions between men and women. "What else were
we given all those desires for?" Molly asks. If there is something deeply humorous in this replay of the Song of Songs, there is something serious too.
As always in Joyce, the scatological and the eschatological rub shoulders. As
do Greek and Jew, man and woman, death and life. And they do so, I submit, without ever succumbing to some totalizing synthesis. Joyce's comic
transubstantiations do not amount to Hegelian sublations (*Aufhebungen*),
in spite of Derrida's suspicions.[12] Joyce keeps the dialectic on its toes to
the end, refusing the temptation of metaphysical closure. The eucharistic
transformation of death and rebirth is carried out on earth. Word is always
made flesh of our flesh.

Elsewhere I have written about the importance of epiphany in Joyce.[13] And
epiphanies—as Joyce knew from his studies with the Jesuits in Clongowes,

especially Father Darlington—imply Magi. The three Magi who bear witness to the textual epiphany of meaning are, I am suggesting, Stephen, Bloom, and Molly (each of whom reincarnates a seminal moment in the author's life). But the Magi may also be interpreted more textually as *author, actor,* and *reader.* Thus we might say that while 1. the lived action of Joyce's world "prefigures" the text, and 2. the voice, style, and plot of the narrated agents (Stephen-Bloom-Molly) "configure" the text, it is 3. the reader who completes the narrative arc by serving as a third witness who "refigures" the world of the text in his return to lived experience. Our own world as readers is thus enlarged by new meanings proposed by the text.[14]

This triadic model of epiphany—celebrated in the sacrament of word-made-flesh—always implies rebirth. It constitutes an event of semantic reinvention where the *impossible* is transfigured into the newly *possible.* And here we might recall those famous biblical epiphanies where three strangers appear to Abraham to announce the birth of an "impossible" child, Isaac; or, in Christian literature, the moment where the three Magi bear witness to the "impossible" child Jesus; or, again, when the three persons of the Christian Trinity herald the birth of an "impossible" kingdom in Andrei Rublev's icon of the Trinity. Indeed Rublev's paradigmatic portrait of the three persons of the Trinity seated around a eucharistic chalice could be read, hermeneutically, as the creative encounter of author/narrator/reader around the aperture of the open text. This suggests, moreover, that the triadic model of epiphany implies a fourth dimension—the vacant space of advent for the new (Isaac, Jesus, Pleroma). Eucharistic epiphany might thus be said to signal a miracle of reversible semantic innovation: of flesh into word and of word into flesh. But here again I would insist that the anatheist moment of retrieval emerges out of the gaps and indeterminacies of an open text that invites us to fill in the empty spaces. *Ulysses* is such a text.

The witnessing of the three personas is invariably met with a celebratory "yes" (Sarah's "laugh" in Genesis 27, Mary's "Amen" in the Gospels, Molly Bloom's final "yes I will yes"). This is telling, I think, for it illustrates how *kairological* time cuts across conventional time and engenders a surplus of possible meaning hitherto unsuspected and unknown. The epiphanic event may be seen, accordingly, as one that testifies simultaneously to the *event* of meaning (it is *already* here) as an *advent* still to come (it is *not-yet* here). And in this manner it reenacts the Palestinian formula of the Passover/Eucharist that remembers a moment of saving while at the same time anticipating a future ("until he comes").[15]

So I repeat: Molly's final cry blends and balances past and future tenses in a typically kairological way—"I *said* yes I *will* yes." As she lies in her bed in Eccles Street with Bloom curled by her side, her scatological memories of all-too-human eros are repeated forward to the rhythm of eschatological time. *I said. I will. Yes.* Word becomes flesh as flesh becomes word. The secular and sacramental traverse each other.

At the beginning of *Ulysses* the question is asked: "What is God?" To which Stephen replies: "A cry in the street." Perhaps the cry is Molly's cry? Perhaps the street is Eccles Street?

PROUST

Sacramental idioms are also central to the work of Marcel Proust. Tropes of "transubstantiation," "resurrection" and "revelation" occur in several key passages of *In Search of Lost Time*. They generally signal a grammar for recovering the timeless in time, as in the famous madeleine episode. But they also refer to a process of artistic transformation, as in Marcel's final disquisition on the writing process in *Time Regained*. If food and taste are sensible idioms that produce the quintessential epiphany of the first kind, I would suggest it is another kind of epiphany, at the end of the labyrinthine narrative, that amplifies the second aspect of Proust's sacramental vision. I am thinking of the penultimate scene chez les Guermantes when Marcel is left waiting in the library as a preprandial music recital is being performed. Having arrived late, Marcel experiences a cluster of epiphanies just before entering the Guermantes' salon. In this antechamber of remaindered time certain achronic moments return to him. Here again we note how the anatheist retrieval of the sacred in the profane is preceded by an acute acceptance of disillusionment and death.

Marcel's first involuntary memory is of entering the San Marco Cathedral in Venice. This is a site of eucharistic celebration par excellence. The flash of memory is triggered by Marcel's stumbling on some uneven cobblestones as he traverses the Guermantes' courtyard in Paris. Though he had been unable to take in the sacramental quality of the experience at the time (when he first visited Venice with his mother), he relives it now many years later here in Paris. After the event, through the lens of a second event. The former "unexperienced" experience is finally reexperienced across the gap of time.

This "miracle of the courtyard" is followed by another involuntary memory brought on by the sound of a spoon striking a plate as a waiter in the dining room prepares the banquet table (for the feast to come). Then we have a third quasi-eucharistic epiphany as Marcel wipes his lips with a starched table napkin, the sensation suddenly recalling a luminous moment in his childhood when he sat in the dining room of the Grand Hotel at Balbec. And, lastly, Marcel experiences a very formative (if forgotten) moment in his childhood: fetching a volume of George Sands' novel, *François le Champi*, from the Guermantes' library shelves, he suddenly relives an evening when Maman read this same book to him at bedtime in Combray. And it was this nocturnal reading that coincided, as we know from the opening scene of the book, with the inaugural moment when his mother left the dinner table with Marcel's father and Swann to come kiss her son, Marcel, goodnight. Reading and feasting are thus intimately associated with the maternal kiss—the kiss that set Marcel on his search for lost time, eventually culminating in the novel of that name.[16]

Samuel Beckett has described this cluster of epiphanies as a "single annunciation," and I think this allusion to the miracle of incarnation is revealing. For in this scene Marcel comes back to the flesh. He is reminded, at the Guermantes' party, that most of his loved ones are dead (Robert de St. Loup, Grandmaman, Maman, Swann, Odette, Françoise), that Charlus is dying, and that he himself (Marcel) has just escaped a brush with death in a sanatorium. Marcel is brought back to earth again and sees behind the masks of Parisian show and snobbery to the throes of mortal flesh—vanity, transience, and passing away. It is only then, the author implies, that Marcel is ready, at last, to renounce the romantic pretensions of his youth and acknowledge that true art is an *art of flesh*—a literary transubstantiation of those contingent, fragile, carnal, and seemingly inconsequential moments that our conscious will consigns to oblivion. (One recalls Merleau-Ponty on Da Vinci). Marcel can thus finally assume his vision of "Combray and its surrounding world taking shape and solidity out of a cup of tea."[17] The aesthete must perish for the artist to flourish.

Julia Kristeva lays special emphasis on the San Marco epiphany, recalling an earlier chapter in the novel, and a former moment in Marcel's life, when he visits Venice with Maman. Kristeva interprets this pivotal episode as central to the understanding of Proust's eucharistic aesthetic, combining, as it does, the various epiphanies of Maman reading, the madeleine, and the stumbling stone. Examining various drafts of Proust's novels and a number of notebook entries on John Ruskin—whose "religious aesthetic" greatly influenced him—Kristeva traces Proust's growing fascination with liturgical terms of *transubstantiation, real presence,* and the incarnational mystery of *time embodied* and *time resurrected.*[18] She herself uses these terms of eucharistic ritual to describe the way in which Proust's characters relate to themselves, each other, and the textual style of the novel through a mystical crisscrossing of tenses: "As combinations of past and present impressions, the characters contaminate one another and fuse their contours; a *secret depth* attracts them. Like the madeleine soaked in tea, they allow themselves to be absorbed into Proust's style. These Proustian heroes and visions will eventually leave us with a singular and bizarre taste that is pungent and invigorating. It is the taste of the sense of time, of *writing as transubstantiation*" (23).

Though Kristeva deploys a psychoanalytic rather than theological perspective, I believe her readings of Proust are deeply relevant to our anatheist argument. Kristeva procedes to cite many scenes that elaborate on the sacramental process of transubstantiation in terms of *translation, incarnation, metaphor,* and *superimposition* (102, 106, 108, 133). She shows how Proust searched for an object in which "each hour of our life hides," and how he believed that literature could resuscitate those hidden moments in the form of epiphanies. In his writings on the aesthetics of Ruskin and Male, for example, Proust identified two particular such moments: a bit of toast that will become a "madeleine" and a Venetian paving stone—namely, two of the key epiphanies of *In Search of Times Past.* Commenting on the example of the paving stone in San Marco, Kristeva writes: "Tripping on the stone and then stumbling would thus be a way of having faith in the sacred. Indeed the sacred is made of stone: a 'living stone, rejected by men but in God's sight chosen and precious' (1 Pet. 2:4–5)." And she adds that the cornerstone, "along with its manifestations in Proust's writings, is presented as a sign of the cult of Jesus, as the real presence of essence. The cornerstone appears to have been Proust's underlying motif, for between the cathedrals and the Mass . . . Proust wished to fathom the mystery of *transubstantiation*" (my emphasis). He managed to do so, Kristeva surmises, "by clearing his own path through everyday sensations, and by acknowledging an eroticism that influenced and increasingly overwhelmed the future narrator's involuntary memory" (106). Or again, in contact with the "living stone," Marcel himself becomes a "stream of light," a participant in the sacred, in "transubstantiation" (108).[19]

Proust himself describes the coming together of different time scenes as *metaphor* and *resurrection*. And for Proust these terms are curiously allied if not identical. Both involve the translation of one thing in terms of another. True art, Marcel comes to realize, is not a matter of progressively depicting a series of objects or events ("describing one after another the innumerable objects which at a given moment were present at a particular place"); it occurs only when the writer "takes two different objects" and "states the connection between them.[20] And here we return to Merleau-Ponty's logic of sacramental perception. For it is the identification of "unique connections" and hidden liaisons between one thing and another that enables the writer to translate the book of life (that "exists already in each one of us") into the book of art.[21] This is how Marcel puts it: "truth—and life too—can be attained by us only when, by comparing a quality common to two sensations, we succeed in extracting their common essence and in reuniting them to each other, liberated from the contingencies of time, with a metaphor."[22] That Marcel privileges figures of resurrection and transubstantiation in this work of metaphor is once again a confirmation of what I am calling—in Proust no less than in Joyce—a sacramental aesthetic. And, in both cases, the textual deployment of metaphor as sacramental act articulates an artistic imagination that has lived through the agnostic "disenchantment of modernity" before daring to recover anew the sacred in the secular.

But let us take a closer look at "The Trip to Venice" episode. This follows immediately after the death of Albertine and opens with a golden angel on San Marco campanile "announcing" a certain "joy." Several themes are tightly woven into this short chapter, which reaffirms Proust's notion of "art as transubstantiation" (Kristeva, *Time and Sense*, 112). Combray and Venice, childhood and adulthood, France and Italy, and the two distinct temporal sensations of past and present "condensed into a metaphor." The scene plays out a dream of death and rebirth. "Death plays a role in this condensation. A reference to the grandmother's death echoes Albertine's more recent disappearance, which is now ready to be internalized and transformed into the innermost depths of writing" (112). Recalling the mother's presence under the window, the narrator confesses an impression of "getting closer and closer to the essence of something secret" (112). Kristeva reads this visit to San Marco as pivotal to the entire development of the novel. It is, she claims, a crucial station on the initiatory journey between "The Death of the Cathedrals" chapter and the concluding volume, *Time Regained*, comprising what she calls a "voyage toward a *living* meaning" (113). This is how she interprets the scene:

> The mystery of this incarnate Venice resides in the mother's presence . . . the incorporation of mother and city. . . . A strange fusion is established between the mother's body and Venice's body. Sitting and reading underneath the pointed arches of an ogival window, the mother inscribes herself in the beautiful stones of Saint Mark's. The window is identified with "a love which stopped only where there was no longer any corporeal matter to sustain it, on the surface of her impassioned gaze. . . . It says to me the thing that touches me more than anything else in the world: 'I remember your mother so well.'" Through the magic of this infiltration, the Venetian window becomes the matter sustaining maternal love—the window *is* the love for the mother. The same process applies to the baptistery, where we find devoted women who appear to have been taken right out of a Carpaccio painting: "She (the mother) has her place reserved there as immutably as a mosaic." (113)

The word *fusion* here is telling, I suspect, given the French association with brewing beverages, e.g., the *infusion* of Linden tea in the madeleine episode. So that we might say that mystical fusion and liquid fusion brush together across memory and time. Nor is it insignificant that Marcel's anamnetic retrieval of the Venice baptistery in the epiphany of the Guermantes' paving stone is contiguous with the related recall of Maman reading the story of François le Champi and his foster mother, *Madeleine* Blanchet: a mystical-maternal association, which Kristeva makes much of (3–22, 116).[23] Kristeva concludes her psychoanalytic reading by suggesting that the Venice scene is best understood as an "incarnation founded on the love between a son and his mother" (114). She is well aware of the Catholic Marian connotations of this Madonna and Child imagery and deems it highly significant that Proust redrafted the chapter several times and was revising it right up to his death, as witnessed in certain deathbed notes to Celeste Albaret—e.g., "cross out everything that occurs before my arrival with my mother in Venice." Hurried by his final illness, Proust concentrated on communicating his own aesthetic credo in this pivotal episode; a credo that involves "the integration of the spiritual theme with the sensual theme, which includes the love for the mother in the celebration of Venice" (115).

Proust chose ultimately to highlight the interanimation between his mother and Venice, between the body and the angel's light; and this choice endures into the final typescript, inviting us to consider the trip to Venice "as an apotheosis of the madeleine and paving-stone episodes" (115). For Kristeva, accordingly, Venice powerfully assumes the mystical role of a "sensual and symbolic Orient," a city that becomes "maternal and thus stresses its own incarnation" (116). (We shall return to such "Oriental" allusions in our discussion of Woolf.) This, concludes Kristeva, is the "cornerstone" of Proust's entire eucharistic act, treating Venice as a "world within a world" (Proust's words), the very character of "time embodied." In this manner the visit to Saint Mark's Baptistery may be read as the crucial link between the erotic *Bildungsroman*—running from Maman and Ghilberte to Albertine— and the annunciation of epiphanies in the final pages of the novel. But the all-important point is, once again, that Marcel can only experience the final epiphanies *after the event*, when the earlier sacramental moments—with Maman sitting in Venice or reading to him as a child in Combray—are retrieved across the gap of time. *Après coup. Nachträglich.* So that if Marcel's visit with Maman to the Venice cathedral and baptistery are as pivotal to the novel as Kristeva suggests, it is not because this was where Marcel achieves his epiphany and becomes at last a sacramental author. No. If that were so the novel would logically end with that chapter. And it does not. It is, rather, only after Marcel has experienced the "death of the cathedrals" and, by association and extension, the death of mothers (Maman, Madeleine Blanchet, and the surrogate imaginary love object Albertine), that he can prepare himself for his ultimate awakening: the recovery in kairological time of what had been irretrievably lost in chronological time. In short, the first sacred fusion must be abandoned so that a second epiphany can be regained. This time not in a triumphal basilica but on a buckled paving stone. Venice is recovered in a Parisian yard.

Venice, in other words, is not the last station on Marcel's journey; and Maman is not the last object of his affections. On the contrary, by the end of the novel it seems that Maman has been finally accepted as the "lost object," prompting Marcel to move from an aesthetic of melancholy to one of mourning. As the novel progresses, I believe that Marcel moves increasingly beyond the various transfers of amorous want and returns to the madonna of the ordinary universe: Françoise. The menial maid of the opening chapters now reappears as "the Michelangelo of our kitchen"[24] (she is a quotidian creature capable of transforming a farmyard chicken into a delicious family feast of *poulet rôti*). I would even suggest that, by the final volume of the novel, *Time Regained*, Françoise—as everyday cook and seamstress—has become Marcel's model for writing the novel. His mundane muse. The narrator now confesses, after all, that he "should work beside her almost as she worked herself."[25]

This conjecture is confirmed, I think, if we recall how Françoise is compared to Giotto's *Caritas* in her being as well as her appearance (*pace* Swann) in the opening volume.[26] Replacing the endless litany of elusive metonymic loved ones—from Maman and Ghilberte to Mlle de Guermantes and Albertine—Françoise reemerges in the end as mistress of the everyday microcosm. The ethereal Albertine transmigrates back, as it were, into the Françoise of flesh and blood. The death of Marcel's exotic fantasy lover is the occasion for the rebirth of the forgotten scullery maid. Curiously, it is Françoise's very qualities of patient craft and endurance, grounded in a sharp sense of mortality and earthiness, that Walter Benjamin celebrates in his famous vignette of Proust—"for the second time there rose a scaffold on which the artist, his head thrown back, painted the creation on the ceiling of the Sistine Chapel: the sickbed on which Marcel Proust consecrates the countless pages which he covered with his handwriting . . . to the creation of his microcosm."[27] Kitchens and cathedrals. Dying and creating. Earthly frailty as portal to art. Moreover, it is also Benjamin who would observe—whether thinking of the culinary seamstress Françoise or not—that "the eternal is in any case far more the ruffle on a dress than some idea."[28]

So where does this leave Maman? I suspect that by the time Marcel recalls Maman in the final Paris epiphanies—which trigger the involuntary memories of both Venice and the reading of *François le Champi*—it is less a question of *fusion* than of transfusion. Or of *transversal*, as Proust himself uses the term in Marcel's terminal musings on time regained. In other words, rather than embracing a form of immediate, magical union, Proust introduces the preposition *trans* to capture the sense of both identity and difference over time. Transfusion, transversal, translation, transferal, transubstantiation.

But a final word on Françoise. If Françoise is indeed Marcel's ultimate guide, it is perhaps no accident that the novel becomes fragmented in a number of different directions in *Time Regained*, just when it appeared to reach closure and become whole (in the manner of some Hegelian Idea).

Proust resists the Hegelian temptation. His book remains undecided as to whether Marcel's projected novel is actually the author's *In Search of Lost Time* or not. This is for the reader to decide. Indeed, it is curious how each philosophical reading of Proust—by Ricoeur, Deleuze, Levinas, Benjamin, Ginette, Beckett, De Man, Blanchot, Kristeva, Nussbaum, Murdoch, Girard—manages, in every case, to *translate* the novel into its own hermeneutic! The ultimate definition, perhaps, of an open text. Or what we might call—taking our cue from Merleau-Ponty's model of eucharistic reversibility—a sacramental text. For again it is a question of the author sacrificing herself to the text so that each reader can be returned—anatheistically—to a refigured existence.

So we might conclude that, just as the marginalized Molly eventually returns as Stephen's promissory mentor in *Ulysses*, the once mocked Françoise is restored as Marcel's most reliable guide. It was this housemaid, we recall, who pointed Marcel away from literature for literature's sake in the direction of literature for life. She was the earthy servant who, "like all unpretentious people," had a no-nonsense approach to literary vainglory and saw through Marcel's rivals as mere "copiators."[29] It was Françoise, Marcel now suddenly realizes, who had "a sort of instinctive comprehension of literary work" capable of "divining [Marcel's] happiness and respecting [his] toil" (509). And so Marcel ultimately resolves to labor as she did, stitching and threading from bits and pieces of cloth—"constructing my book, I dare not say ambitiously like a cathedral, but quite simply like a dress" (509). The fantasy persona of Albertine, the main source of Marcel's tormented jealousies and deceptions, is finally replaced by the seamstress of the real. Mystique is unmasked by a maid.

In this respect, Françoise—no less than Molly—might be seen as a refiguration of Penelope. For Proust too navigates a return from heroic wanderings to the weavings of the everyday. The marvels of literature are no longer to be sought in monumental basilicas of grandiose design but in the intricate weft and warp of ordinary existence. And in this embrace of writing as weaving we find the literary trope of "metaphor" being allied to that of "metonymy." The transformative and synthetic power of metaphor, which turns contingency to essence, is here supplemented by a second moment that returns essence to contingency—to metonymy as a process of displacement and replacement, humble stitching and restitching, one thing ceding itself to another in the quotidian play of existence. This double trope of metaphor-metonymy is what we have been calling transubstantiation. The reversible translation of word into flesh and flesh into word.

This understanding of writing as stitching—of webs, tapestries, textures, texts—leads Marcel to the insight that he is the "bearer" of a work that has been "entrusted" to him and that he will, in time, "deliver" into other hands (that of the reader). The connotations of pregnancy and parturition are pronounced here. Such recognition of the basic intertextuality of writing comes to Marcel as a sort of deliverance from his own long fear of death. Affirming that real literature is a form of messianic "repetition" or remembering forward—from natality to mortality and back to natality again—Marcel suddenly finds himself "indifferent to the idea of death" (509). Learning to perish is learning to relive. "By dint of repetition," as he says, "this fear had gradually been transformed into a calm confidence. So that if in those early days, as we have seen, the idea of death had cast a shadow over my loves . . . the remembrance of love had helped me not to fear death. For I realized that dying was not something new, but that on the contrary since my childhood I had already died many times" (509).[30] Invoking the classic scriptural passage about the seed dying in order to flourish, Marcel's authorial self now faces the possibility of being posthumously reborn again as another, as one of those many harbingers of new life, epitomized by Mlle de Saint-Loup or, more generally, by his future readers. A second natality thus reemerges from mortality. So that the final passages of the novel—recalling the dead Albertine and the dying Charlus—invoke an enveloping movement of Time that swings back and forth, up and down, carrying us toward vertiginous and terrifying summits, higher than the steeples of cathedrals, before eventually returning us to earth again, "descending to a great depth within."

In short, if time is all too wont to raise mortals "to an eminence from which suddenly they fall,"[31] might we not say that the acceptance of this fall back into the ordinary universe enables fear to become love and literary delusion to become true writing?

WOOLF

My third example of sacramental aesthetics is Virginia Woolf's *To the Lighthouse*. If Joyce and Proust were commonly considered apostates or agnostics, Woolf makes no bones about her atheism. Indeed a sophisticated form of brazen atheism was almost de rigueur in the Bloomsbury circle in which she moved and worked. But it was not her rejection of a traditional child-hood God that prevented Woolf from rediscovering a sense of the sacred in the very midst of secular life. *To the Lighthouse*, I will suggest, performs a passage from theism to atheism — the famous interlude of death and derelic-tion — before reopening, in the third part of the novel, an anatheist option: the possibility of a second yes to the "real" at the heart of nonbeing. Here, I submit, we witness a move from first belief to unbelief to a second kind of assent: an affirmation of what Woolf calls, simply and mysteriously, the "it."

The novel's main protagonist, Mrs. Ramsay, is another mistress of the feast. Like Françoise before her, though in somewhat more urbane attire, Mrs. Ramsay is introduced in the first part of the novel as both cook and seamstress. She nourishes and sews. She has a singular gift for "summoning together," for bringing couples into liaison, for holding her brood of eight children in maternal connection and her husband in marriage. On the day we meet her, she has two tasks: first, to give her son, James, some hope that he may sail to the lighthouse; second, to prepare a supper of boeuf en daube for her family and guests that evening.

But this is no ordinary boat trip and this is no ordinary meal. Mrs. Ram-say is frequently depicted by Woolf in mystical terms. Woolf's use of indirect discourse — *le style indirect libre* — to convey what is going on in her various characters' minds gives the reader the impression, from the outset, that Mrs. Ramsay's soul is somehow porously interconnected with the scattered souls of those around her. And this sense of mysterious interbeing is confirmed in the last part of the novel when we find her devoted painter friend, Lily Briscoe, recalling the same thoughts and qualities of Mrs. Ramsay herself (the term *unfathomably deep* for example, recurs in the minds of both, as do curiously sacred sentiments of *emptiness* as *fullness*, or the three *strokes* of the lighthouse beam that Mrs. Ramsay contemplates, repeated in the three *strokes* of Lily's brush on the white canvas). Woolf writes in her diary how she used this narrative voice as a "tunneling process" deep into the minds of her characters that might reach a point where they could all connect, have similar thoughts, and move to the same deep "rhythm."[32] This rhythm she describes as "resonant and porous, transmitting emotion without im-pediment . . . creative, incandescent and undivided."[33] Through the free indirect voice, Woolf experiments with a "multi-personal representation of consciousness" that has "synthesis as its aim."[34]

When dinner time eventually arrives, the tone is subtly sacramental. We read how the gong announced solemnly, authoritatively, that all those scattered about the house and garden should "assemble in the dining room for dinner."[35] The meal unfolds as a quasi-eucharistic ritual. Mrs. Ramsay takes her place at the head of the table and assigns each person their seat. She presides over the assembly with a quasi-mystical sense of "being past everything, through everything, out of everything" (83). The convened guests and family unite around the candle-lit table:

> Now all the candles were lit up, and the faces on both sides of the table were brought nearer by the candlelight, and composed, as they had not been in the twilight, into a party round a table, for the night was now shut off by panes of glass, which, far from giving any accurate view of the outside world, rippled it so strangely that here, inside the room, seemed to be order and dry land; there, outside, a reflection in which things wavered and vanished, waterily. Some change at once went through them all, as if this had really happened, and they were all conscious of making a party together in a hollow, on an island; had their common cause against that fluidity out there. (97)

There are many antagonisms and rivalries between different people at table; but Mrs. Ramsay contrives to negotiate and mollify these frictions, letting each one find a personal voice and making various marriage plans for various guests (Paul and Minta, Lily and Mr. Bankes). So, by the end of the meal, everyone seems united in eucharistic communion. The messianic Mrs. Ramsay has worked her gracious magic on the gathering. The eschatological feast, it appears, is at hand:

> Everything seemed possible. Everything seemed right . . . just now she had reached security; she hovered like a hawk suspended; like a flag floated in an element of joy which filled every nerve of her body fully and sweetly, not noisily, solemnly rather, for it arose, she thought, looking at them all eating there, from husband, children and friends; all of which rising in this profound stillness (she was helping William Bankes to one very small piece more, and peered into the depths of the earthenware pot) seemed now for no special reason to stay there like a smoke, like a fume rising upwards, holding them safe together. Nothing need be said; nothing could be said. There it was, all round them. It partook, she felt, carefully helping Mr. Bankes to a specially tender piece, of eternity. . . . There is a

coherence in things, a stability; something, she meant, is immune from change, and shines out . . . in the face of the flowing, the fleeting, the spectral, like a ruby; so that again tonight she had the feeling . . . of peace, of rest. Of such moments, she thought, the thing is made that endures. . . . The Boeuf en Daube was a perfect triumph. (104–105)

Mrs. Ramsay's credo—as Lily will remember it in the final section of the novel—was "of the nature of a revelation. In the midst of chaos there was shape. . . . Life stands still here, Mrs. Ramsay said."

But it didn't. Life moved on and many partaking of that meal would suffer terrible loss in the war years ahead. And so this inaugural scene of union is shrouded with irony. A sense of elegiac doom hovers over the proceedings. Indeed, already in the midst of her musing, Mrs. Ramsay is caught by the awareness that "this cannot be." She finds herself "dissociating herself from the moment" (104–105). And for us, readers, it is equally short-lived. Within pages Mrs. Ramsay is dead and the novel descends—in the middle section, "Time Passes"—into an unconsoling exposé of transience and collapse. We also learn that Mrs. Ramsay's ideal matchmaking has come to naught and that two of her most beautiful children have perished during the war. In retrospect, the "smoke" rising from the dinner table takes on connotations of a sacrificial offering. The paschal feast seems less a Passover than a passing away.

Yet this is not the end of the story. And we are still left asking, in the third part of the novel, what Mrs. Ramsay meant when she spoke of the "the thing is made that endures." Was she thinking of the "perfect" meal remembered, after the event, by those who live after her and finally make their way back to the lighthouse? Or was she thinking of the work of art wherein Lily would resurrect Mrs. Ramsay and enable her to endure in the "finished" portrait? Or of the novel itself, which invites us readers to revive Mrs. Ramsay's eucharistic achievement in the very act of reading? Reading as a feat of anatheistic repetition?

The connection between things *lived* and things *made* brings us to the heart of the matter—namely, the rapport between Mrs. Ramsay and Lily Briscoe. Here we encounter a complex set of traversals at work. Mystical affinities abound. The two souls intersignify in all sorts of ways. A key example: Lily's final brush "stroke" in part 3 is, as mentioned, a repetition of the "stroke" of the lighthouse with which Mrs. Ramsay intimately identifies. The latter scene occurs in the first part of the novel when Mrs. Ramsay sits down late one night while her children are in bed and, taking out her knitting, feels an uncanny peace as she unites with the world outside her window. A "wedge-shaped core of darkness" deep inside her, we are told, merges with the beam of light emitted by the lighthouse far out at sea. To the third stroke of light on water, her own "unfathomable deep" blends with the depths of the ocean. We read that "often she found herself sitting and looking, sitting and looking with her work in her hands until she became the thing she looked at—that light" (62).[36] Losing herself in the things she beheld, leaving behind the "fret, the hurry, the stir" of her anxious self, there rises to her lips "some exclamation of triumph over life when things came together in this peace, this rest, this eternity." And it is in this moment of quasi-mystical communion with the surrounding universe, as deep calls upon deep, that Mrs. Ramsay adds: "We are in the hands of the Lord."

No sooner has she uttered this prayer, however, than she revokes it: "But instantly she was annoyed with herself for saying that. Who had said that?" Who indeed? And why feel so ashamed to have fallen back into the fold of common prayer? Because, apparently, it is somehow unearned. Too easy, too quick, too cheap. "She had been trapped into saying something she did not mean." A "lie," Mrs. Ramsay calls it, referring no doubt to the lure of an otherwordly deity, some Supreme Omnipotent Cause aloof and detached from the world of flesh, adjudicating our destinies. Resisting the temptation to escape into the hands of such a convenient God, Mrs. Ramsay embraces, I suggest, another kind of mysticism, a deeper sense of sacred space and time where one is "alone with the alone" (as the Upanishads say) and where the natural universe of ordinary things is loved rather than abandoned:

> It was odd, she thought, how if one was alone, one leant to inanimate things; trees, streams, flowers; felt they expressed one; felt they became one; felt they knew one, in a sense were one; felt an irrational tenderness thus (she looked at that long steady light) as for oneself. There rose, and she looked and looked with her needles suspended, there curled up off the floor of the mind, rose from the lake of one's being, a mist, a bride to meet her lover.[37]

But what is this posttheistic mysticism that Mrs. Ramsay incarnates? In a curious admission shortly before her death, Virginia Woolf spoke of the sudden shocks and surprises of life as tokens of "some real thing behind appearances." She intimated that "behind the cotton wool is hidden a pattern" and all human beings are somehow "connected with this." In short, Woolf expressed the view that the "whole world is a work of art." But no sooner had she made this confession than she added, "But there is no Shakespeare, there is no Beethoven; certainly and emphatically there is no God."[38] In short, her atheism could not be more evident. But what kind of atheism are we talking about? What exactly does she mean by her triple denial, her three "no's"? It would seem that Woolf is implying that the "pattern," the "real thing," is not *made* but *given*. It is not the product of creators—human or divine—but an intimation of some deep unfathomable love that connects all beings behind and beneath the appearances of agency and artifice.

Here we confront the problematic role of art in the novel, especially as represented by Lily's attempt to capture Mrs. Ramsay in a painting. For how can art—be it Lily's painting, Mr. Carmichael's poem, or Woolf's own novel—ever hope to represent the miracle of ordinary life? How can the "made" record the "given," the imaginary reflect the real? Facing her canvas, Lily, we are told, is aware of something not herself, some "other thing" that is "truth" or "reality," something both there in the lampshade and also timelessly abstracted from it, a thing emerging "at the back of appearances." There is, Lily realizes, something suspect in art's attempt to reduce the contingency and transience of life to "beautiful pictures" and "beautiful phrases." What Lily needs to get hold of is the "jar on the nerves, the thing itself before it had been *made* anything." She seeks to achieve that "razor's edge of balance between two opposite forces," namely, art and life.[39] The problem thus arises: how can art imagine the mystery of flesh without betraying it? How can it achieve the "razor's edge" of equanimity recommended by the sacred Vedic texts that, her notebooks show, so fascinated Woolf? Are we on the threshold here of another kind of anatheist wager, this time nourished by Eastern sources?

Let's take a closer look at Lily's final gesture. In the closing sequence of the book, Lily is seeking a particular stroke of her paintbrush that will, in a "leap" into the gap between art and life, complete her quest. She is struggling to somehow bring art and life together, make the impossible possible. What Mrs. Ramsay found in that special "stroke of light," beamed from the lighthouse at night, Lily will find in a stroke of paint: something that connects in a moment of repetition. Lily eventually achieves her "vision." She renounces the goal of some pure, transcendental aesthetic for an art of ordinary things, an art that recognizes "traces" as living gestures of the absolute. It is, in fact, just as her portrait of Mrs. Ramsay is being completed—repeating in the third part of the novel the painting that she could not achieve in the first—it is at this very moment of re-creation, of anamnesis, of second epiphany, that Lily hits upon the marvel of the everyday: "One wanted, she thought, dipping her brush deliberately, to be on a level with ordinary experience, to feel simply that's a chair, that's a table, and yet at the same time, It's a miracle, it's an ecstasy. The problem might be solved after all."[40]

Everything, it seems, revolves on this reversibility of higher and lower case *It/it*. The miracle consists in the transubstantiation of higher into lower, extraordinary into ordinary, transcendence into immanence. And vice versa. It is a moment both kenotic (the emptying of Word into flesh) and eucharistic (the celebration of the infinite in the finite bread and wine of quotidian experience).

Woolf records experiencing this same "it" in February 1926—while she was composing this section of the novel—as she crossed Russell Square in London. Her diary entry reads, "I see the mountains in the sky: the great clouds; and the moon which has risen over Persia; I have a great and astonishing sense of something there, which is 'it.'"[41] This "it" is, as she puts it, something "out there," some "other thing" beyond one's will and personality. It is at once "frightening and exciting," for it refuses to be humanized by our subjective projections and names—including the anthropomorphic name of "God."[42] But for Lily Briscoe to achieve this aesthetic "vision," for her to effect the final brush stroke, draw "the line there in the centre" of her canvas so that she can finally say "It was done; it was finished," for Lily to do this she first has to acknowledge the reality of Mrs. Ramsay's death. She has to forego her ideal *imago*, accept the cut of mortality, and leap into the gap.[43]

In terms of the novel's characters, this means, among other things, allowing Mr. Ramsay's atheism to cut through Mrs. Ramsay's mysticism: a typically anatheist move. Lily has to admit what is "other" to her fused and nostalgic memory of Mrs. Ramsay, renouncing the icon whom she has been invoking for solace and reunion: "Oh Mrs. Ramsay, Mrs. Ramsay!" Mr. Ramsay is the "opposite force" that resists Lily's reappropriation of Mrs. Ramsay and compels her to take a leap from the "narrow plank, perfectly alone, over the sea . . . into the waters of annihilation." Before she can finish her painting Lily has to accept that Mrs. Ramsay is *gone*, passed away, irrevocably absent. For only then can she recall her, posthumously, through the gap of atheism, across the caesura of separation, in the final stroke that cuts, like a sword blade, even as it reconnects.

But reconnects what? Reconnects Lily's project to memory, her present to the past in a way that liberates into a future, repeating a lost moment forward. Or, to put it in other terms, Mrs. Ramsay is the "lost object," the deceased savior-friend whom Lily must relinquish if she is to move from obsessive melancholy to a mourning that accepts the real and liberates new life. For Lily it is Mr. Ramsay—atheist and empiricist, angular and exigent—who represents this cutting edge of the reality principle. Mr. Ramsay is the alien in her world, the stranger to her vision of things. As Martin Corner deftly observes: "Mr. Ramsay is an unwavering witness to the nonhumanity of the world; he therefore represents to Lily that otherness which must somehow be got into the picture if it is not to be false."[44] Mr. Ramsay, in short, exemplifies the "thing itself before it has been *made* anything" (by knitting, cooking, painting, dreaming, fictionalizing). And this thing, it transpires, is a no-thing. It is that emptiness, that void, that "unfathomable deep" which haunts the imaginations of both Mrs. Ramsay and Lily. It is the "wedge of darkness" that has to be faced and acknowledged before it can well up into fullness and Lily can say: "empty it was not but full to the brim."[45] But first the letting go. The renunciation of the illusion of Grand Revelations, be it of art, metaphysics, or religion. The refusal of any grandiose system that trumps the world of flesh and blood and denies the universe of little things. We read, significantly, "The great revelation perhaps never did come. Instead there were little daily miracles, illuminations, matches struck unexpectedly in the dark."[46]

Lily's attempt to incorporate otherness—the "jar on the nerves," the "wedge of darkness," the "marvel" of the singular—into her art finds interesting echoes in Georges Didi-Hubermann's account of a certain mystical aesthetic that insists on "making a representation that abjures its own powers of narrative and optical resolution": an aesthetic that attests to a "sacred ignorance" where "God's presence is felt and known in the failure of representation, not its success."[47] This testimonial deforming or problematizing of the image signals its unconscious and unassimilable "underside," a move that typifies sacramental rather than mimetic aesthetics. Didi-Hubermann links this to a particular iconography of Christian Incarnation that emphasizes immediate "real presence" rather than legible representation (symbolism, allegory, mediation, mirroring, etc). It calls, he says, for an art of self-negating and self-transcending images that, loyal to a certain "sacred nescience" or apophasis, function less as mimetic icons of the known visible world than as disruptive mystical indexes of the invisible in the visible. Paradoxically, what is lost (as absence) is regained (as presence beyond representation). The renunciation of inappropriate expectations allows for the unexpected return of the sacred.

In Lily's final letting go we encounter, I suggest, an instance of such mystical aesthetics. But this is a mysticism less of fusion than of equipoise, less of triumph than of that "razor edge" balance between opposites, celebrated by the sages of the Upanishads and certain Jewish and Christian mystics. In this regard, what we might call Lily's—and Woolf's—mystical anatheism takes on another valence, recalling as it does the Asiatic features of Lily's countenance (those "Chinese eyes" the narrator frequently refers to). For the letting go of Mrs. Ramsay—for example, the harmonious memory of the opening meal—is also a letting go of our notion of an all-powerful divinity who "saves us," namely, the anthropomorphic deity of Western myth and metaphysics. It is only in the letting go—in the kenosis of "truth" emptying itself of Godhead—that Lily can complete her painting at the very moment that Mr. Ramsay fulfills Mrs. Ramsay's dream of bringing their son James and daughter Cam to the lighthouse. This is the moment of anatheistic return. The passage is particularly telling: "He [Mr. Ramsay] rose and stood in the bow of the boat, very straight and tall, for all the world, James thought, as if he were saying, "There is no God," and Cam thought, as if he were leaping into space, and they both rose to follow him as he sprang, lightly like a young man, holding his parcel, on to the rock."[48] It is precisely at this instant of *grounding* that Lily, watching from the shore, draws her final stroke and says, like the suffering servant yielding up to death, "It is finished." *Consummatum est.* This is a moment of death and rebirth, of letting go and gaining back. A time when, at last, "empty flourishes form into shape."[49]

The mystical allusions of Woolf's closing paragraph are resonant and deep. And I believe they confirm Woolf's numerous allusions in her autobiographical writings to a reality that goes beyond God to achieve its epiphany of the ordinary. Such mentions recall Advaita and Buddhist mysticism, which refuse to think transcendence apart from immanence. A refusal echoed in Meister Eckart's notion of *Abgeschiedenheit*: the abandonment of God so as to recover a God beyond God. This mysticism *after God*, is, I suggest, an affirmation of a Eucharist of the everyday, of a sacrament of common "reality," of an epiphany of "It/it" residing at the core of Woolf's vision. Lily Brisco, it seems, eventually finds her miracle "on a level with ordinary experience," a world at once itself and yet simultaneously transfigured into what Woolf calls "a reality of a different order."[50] A world poised on a razor's edge where opposites balance without collapsing into sameness. A world of anatheism.

TEXTUAL TRAVERSALS

So is it significant that our three witnesses of sacramental imagination—Joyce, Proust, and Woolf—are all, on the surface at least, agnostics? And what does it mean that the three characters who best embody their sacramental aesthetic are all women (Molly, Françoise, and Lily)? Is this not a different kind of eucharistic language to the one that informs our traditional male dominated liturgies (where no women featured for centuries)? This is surely a sacramental vision of a new sort—or at least of the old revisited otherwise. It deploys the poetic license of fiction to suspend accredited doctrines in order to offer "free variations" of transubstantiation, namely, the reversible "miracle" of word-made-flesh and flesh-made-word.

Recalling the canonical definition of transubstantiation as "the transforming of one substance into another," we may say, in conclusion, that we have identified three main hermeneutic modalities in our readings: 1. *intratextual*, 2. *intertextual*, and 3. *trans-textual*.

As instances of the first kind we may cite the numerous examples of 1. one *character* being transfused into another (Mrs. Ramsay into Lily, Maman into Françoise, Penelope into Molly) or 2. one spatiotemporal *moment* translated into another (the madeleine epiphany, the involuntary memory of Maman reading in Combray and Venice recalled years later in the Guermantes' library).

As examples of the second mode of transubstantiation (*intertextual*), we might cite 1. the transmuting of one *narrative* into another (Homer's *Odyssey* into Joyce's *Ulysses*, the biblical stories of Elijah and St. Stephen into the tales of Bloom and Dedalus, Georges Sand's novel into Proust's) or 2. the transliteration of eucharistic liturgies into sacramental reenactments by Mrs. Ramsay, Molly, or Marcel in their respective epiphanies.

And, third, we might cite numerous examples of *transtextual* transubstantiation: the conversion of 1. author into implied narrator and fictional character(s) and 2. the conversion of these textual creations, in turn, into the implied and actual reader. This third mode—involving the very process of writing and reading, of configuring and refiguring—is the one highlighted in the phenomenological analyses of Merleau-Ponty, Kristeva, and Ricoeur. And it is with this final modality, I suggest, that we encounter an opening of the world of the text beyond itself—both forward to the posttextual world of the reader and backward (by way of implied regress from character to narrator to author) to the pretextual world of the writer. This acknowledgment, however tentative and mediated, of some *extratextual* element—intimating a life of action before and beyond the text—is in keeping with the sacramental paradigm of transubstantiation: a paradigm that, I have been suggesting, testifies to the unbreakable liaison between the body of the text and the text of the body, namely, the sanctified bread of life. Or, to deploy the language of epiphany, the liaison between Word and Flesh.

Our three novelists may well be agnostics, apostates, or atheists, but this does not, I hope to have shown, prevent them from being haunted by a singularly mystical vision of things. It may, in a paradoxical sense, even contribute to such insight by predisposing them to something beyond the reach of many official religious conventions. (The history of religions, as already noted, evinces a deep complicity between mysticism and so-called atheism). Each writer bears witness to a special sacredness at the heart of the profane. But, in each instance, the mutual transfiguring of material bread and mystical body is anything but "sacrificial"; it is not about expiatory victims sacrificed to redeem sins and appease an Omnipotent Father. The sacramental aesthetic of our three authors is far removed from an economy of penalty and compensation. On the contrary, it bears witness to literary epiphanies of radical kenosis and emptying where the sacred unhitches itself from the Master God ("equality with the Father," as Paul put it) in order to descend into the heart of finite flesh. Thus the birth of the child as incarnate being attests to the demise of the Immutable Monarch. Unless the divine seed dies there can be no eucharistic rebirth. Or to put it in the words of the young Jewish mystic, Etty Hillesum, "by excluding death from one's life we deny ourselves the possibility of a full life."

It is not adventitious, I hold, that the three novels under consideration feature a deep anatheist openness to the "stranger" as prelude to epiphany: in Joyce the meeting of Stephen with Bloom, in Proust the acknowledgment of Françoise by Marcel, in Woolf the reckoning with Mr. Ramsay by Lily. Without this basic hospitality to the uninvited guest there would be no transubstantiation between self and other.

In our three novelists we witness the abandoning of a *first naïveté* in order to recover a *second naiveté*. This offers a moment of anatheistic return, after the experience of death and nothingness, that signals a new kind of "miracle," "resurrection," "grace," this time in ordinary events ignored first time around. For Joyce and Proust these moments of sacramental remembrance occurred when their literary heroes—Stephen and Marcel— came to renounce their Great Expectations and ultimately acknowledged the muse of the everyday (Molly and Françoise respectively). For Woolf it occurred when Lily finally recalled the failed painting of the "purple triangle" (which sought to depict Mrs. Ramsay and James in the first part of the novel), as she belatedly applied the final stroke enabling her to represent Mrs. Ramsay, *après coup*; only then can she have her "vision" and declare the painting "finished."

The bread and wine of quotidian existence are thus celebrated as eucharistic epiphanies: the kiss of the seedcake between Molly and Bloom, the touch of a table napkin for Marcel, Mrs. Ramsay's empty glove (like empty burial clothes?). Hitherto ignored moments are "resurrected" out of passing time into a life that assumes and subsumes death, impossibly retrieved for a new generation of survivors (James and Cam, Mlle de SaintLoup, Stephen). Resurrected here and now, again and again, for each new reader or community of readers. Unless the seed dies . . . the wheat cannot grow and the bread cannot be shared.

I am not, of course, suggesting that our three novelists are religious apologists. They are by no means advocates of Christian liturgies and sacraments. There are certain confessional writers who might be said to fit this category—G. M. Hopkins, Claudel, Bernanos, Eliot, not to mention Dante and many other religious writers throughout the centuries. But my purpose here is not to engage in confessional apologetics or to proclaim our three authors cryptotheists *après la lettre*. No, my task is to explore the possibility of a certain anatheist aesthetic where the secular and sacred conjugate and cross. Thus, while by no means excluding confessional writers from adherence to such an aesthetic, I deem it valuable in this secular era to consider how certain nonconfessional authors deploy an art of transubstantiation to explore a mysticism of *God-after-God*.

I have been suggesting that this poetic faith-after-faith may be clarified by the application of a phenomenology of flesh advanced by thinkers like Merleau-Ponty and Kristeva. But, I repeat, the "after" of anatheism should not be read as privative but as an affirmative function of *ana*, that is, of retrieving what was lost as found in a new way, *après coup*.[51] As in *analogy, anagogy, ananmnesis, anakaphaleosis*. In short, I have no wish to endorse an empty secularism that merely aestheticizes religion by removing its faith content. In moving from religion to art we do indeed replace a first belief in God *qua* God with a *quasi* belief in a *quasi* God. But this suspension of primary belief, as we enter the world of fiction, is not the last word. It is rather the opening of a space of imagination where the anatheist option may be made anew. And it is such an option that allows us, readers of fiction, to freely recommit to faith if we choose, to return to a God beyond both the *qua* God and the *quasi* God. In other words, the anatheist analysis of modern fiction we are attempting here has little to do with secularist reductions of sacred moments to humanist equivalents: All Hallows to Halloween, St. Nicholas to Santa Claus or the Mass of Christ to the commercial holiday of Christmas.

For anatheism, the transition from religion to art is not a one-way street. As our repeated emphasis on the hermeneutic return from text to life implies, the anatheist wager involves a moment of refiguration from author to reader where the reader welcomes the "estrangement" of the fictional text in order to recover his or her sense of the sacramental in profane existence. Textual epiphanies might thus be said to point beyond the text in the life of each reader. The sacramental is not confined to a play of signifiers. For as flesh becomes word in the text the word becomes flesh in the reader. That is the marvel of *transubstantiation*—relating art to faith and faith to art. If the composition of fiction can serve to aesthetize the sacred, reading can serve to resacramentalize the aesthetic in our everyday world. But I emphasize the *can*; it is a matter of choice. The movement from life to text can always be supplemented by a return from text to life.

In sum, anatheism is not about evacuating the sacred from the secular but retrieving the sacred in the secular.

{ THREE }

POSTLUDE

6

IN THE WORLD

BETWEEN SECULAR AND SACRED?

After our hermeneutic detour through sacramental poetics we return, finally, to the question of sacramental ethics. Here we revisit a central concern of
the anatheist wager: namely, what does it mean to accept the sacred stranger
into the secular universe? What is involved in translating epiphanies of transcendence into the immanence of everyday action? What are the practical
implications of moving from sacred imagination to a sacred praxis of peace
and justice? Or, to put it in another way, how do anatheists in a secular age
respond to the question: what is to be done?

TOWARD AN ETHICS OF KENOSIS

As we saw in chapter 3, Bonhoeffer already hinted at an answer when he declared from his death cell in 1944 that "secular and sacred are not opposed
but find their unity in Christ. . . . That which is Christian is to be found only
in the natural, the holy only in the profane."[1] More recently, a number of
postreligious Christian thinkers have pushed this even further, to the point
where their work is sometimes accused of atheistic nihilism, when in fact it
proposes to pass through the death of God to a renewal of sacred love for the
world (*amor mundi*). Here I am thinking particularly of the anatheist interpretation of kenosis (divine self-emptying) offered by the French Passionist
Stanislas Breton and the Italian philosopher Gianni Vattimo. Both have

shown how a kenotic moment of "nothingness" and "emptiness" resides at the core of a postmetaphysical faith; but neither sees this as the last word. Abandonment leads back to action, surrender resurfaces as service.

Breton, like Bonhoeffer and Ricoeur, a prisoner of World War II, claims that faith "must inhabit the world and give back to God the being he has not." Speaking more specifically of Christian kenosis, he talks of a process that follows "the descent of the divine into a human form, obedience unto death, the ignominy of the Cross. But at the very moment that the paroxysm of abasement touches the depth of nothingness, the shock of the negative, in its paradoxical power, commands the exultant ascent toward the point of origin."[2] In Breton's case, this renascence from the ashes of the old God signaled a renewed commitment to eucharistic sharing with the neglected "nobodies" of society. A fervent supporter of the priest-worker and liberation theology movements, as well as the *sans papiers* immigrants, Breton could not separate his sense of sacramentality from a sociopolitical service to the "wretched of the earth." His commitment to a *vita contemplativa* was inseparable from his commitment to a *vita activa* of protest and struggle. The bread of the Eucharist was the bread of the hungry and downtrodden. God had emptied himself, in other words, so that life could be resurrected in the fullness of human flourishing. The cup of cold water given to the stranger (*hospes*) and the water of life given to the estranged Samaritan woman are, for Breton, the same water. And the message of kenotic self-giving is one that invites us to worship together "in spirit and truth" beyond the confines of our confessional ghettos.[3] For all his political radicalism—in matters of both church and state—Stanislas Breton remained a member of the Passionist Order in France and celebrated the sacraments daily. As if each day was a giving up of God in the morning and a return to God in the evening.

In the case of the contemporary thinker and activist Gianni Vattimo, kenosis entails a reading of 1 Corinthians 12 (on love) that treats the Incarnation as God's relinquishing of all power so as to turn everything over to the secular order: the hallowing of everyday existence. Vattimo considers "God's self-emptying and man's attempt to think of love as the only law" as two sides of the same coin. And the conclusion of his "fragile hermeneutic" (*pensiero debole*), startling to many traditional theists, is that secularization is the "constitutive trait of authentic religious experience."[4] On this account, Copernicus, Freud, and Nietzsche need no longer be considered enemies of the sacred but, as "carrying out works of love."[5] It is significant,

I think, that Vattimo, no less than Breton, saw the incarnational process of "self-emptying divinity" as pointing to emancipatory action. Becoming one of Italy's most prominent public intellectuals, Vattimo served as a leading activist in progressive political causes and an influential deputy in the European Parliament, invariably providing a voice for voiceless emigrantsand outsiders.

W. H. Auden, one might recall, sounded a similar note when he surmised that the kerygmas of Freud, Blake, and Marx were all "Christian heresies" in the sense that one cannot imagine "their coming into existence except in a civilization that claimed to be based, religiously, on belief that the Word was made flesh and dwelt among us, and that, in consequence, matter, the natural order, is real and redeemable, not a shadowy appearance or the cause of evil, and historical time is real and significant."[6] Auden actually held that the point of psychology and psychoanalysis was to "prove the Gospel." For the natural need to break from the authority of one's parents involves "liberation from the superego, obeyed like the parents whom Christ enjoined us to abandon." When asked once about Freud's influence on his work, he replied that it was the same as what he had learned from the Agony in the Garden (10). Auden believed that the best secular philosophers of liberation were in fact simply fleshing out the basic message that *agape* (love of God and neighbor) is not a refusal of *eros* but its continuous transformation; just as suffering and happiness are not inevitably opposed but bound together as soul and body are bound in Incarnation (82). "Thou shalt love God and thou shalt be happy mean the same thing," he wrote; which is not to deny suffering but to always be thankful for what is (16). Auden insisted on the radically embodied character of the Christian Eucharist: "At the last supper, [Christ] took eating, the most elementary act of all, the primary act of self-love, the only thing not only man but all living creatures must do irrespective of species, sex, race or belief, and made it the symbol of universal love" (27). Loving one's neighbor as oneself, he added, "is a bodily, blood relationship" (27). The Divine Law, Auden concluded, operates in the *here and now*, and genuine faith is the opposite of a denial of the world. "Jesus said My Kingdom is not of *this* world. He did not say of *the* world" (20–21).

Auden's own anatheist return to Christianity was brought about by two main things: 1. a mystical experience of solidarity with a group of relative strangers at a liturgical feast and 2. a conviction that the Nazi condemnation of the weak had to be opposed by a transcendent law of hospitality to strangers. "I wondered," he writes, "why I reacted as I did against the [Nazi] denial of every humanistic value. The answer brought me back to the Church" (22).

Other influential advocates of a kenotic faith include John Caputo, whose *The Weakness of God* (inspired by the Jewish messianicity of Levinas and Derrida) has mobilized a whole new debate on religion-beyond-religion, and René Girard, who critiques "sacrificial" religion as a "scapegoating of strangers" in the name of nonviolent Christianity. Caputo explores a hermeneutics of weak divinity, deeply informed by the deconstructive notion of *khora* (a radical alterity that precedes all metaphysical binaries) and issuing in an ethics of "quotidianism," similar to our own notion of sacramental praxis. For his part, Girard identifies the victimization of the "mendicant stranger"—in the foundational Greek myth of Oedipus and the biblical story of Job—as key to ritual victimization. And, in *The Scapegoat*, Girard argues that the only way to combat this is to put our natural violent instincts in check and welcome rather than kill the stranger. In other words, the antidote to the atavistic instinct for repetitive bloodletting is to acknowledge our guilt and make the radical choice for gracious hospitality over cyclical hostility.[7] I suspect that Gilles Deleuze is making a somewhat similar point when he declares that we must abandon the old sacrificial instinct for scapegoating aliens, which has so bedeviled triumphal Christendom, and instead identify with the emancipatory message of the lamb: "The God who, like a lion, was given blood sacrifice must be shoved into the background, and the sacrificed god must occupy the foreground. . . . God became the animal that was slain, instead of the animal that does the slaying."[8]

All these contemporary thinkers contribute, in their distinct ways, to the anatheist option of a sacredness beyond sacrifice. And it is interesting that in each case the understanding of kenosis leads inevitably to an option for the poor and oppressed. As if the recognition of God as a "nothing and nobody" (*ta me onta*) enables us to identify with the nothings and nobodies of this world in a movement of loving revolt. As Isaiah did when he identified the Messiah as a "broken reed" and called upon his people to practice hospitality toward the widow, the orphan, and the stranger. As Jesus did when he identified with strangers and opened his heart to Samaritans, lepers, and sinners, drawing them from exclusion to a more abundant life. Or as Francis did when he followed the kenotic way of Christ to the point of stigmatic identification with his death on the Cross before being reborn as a lover of all living things natural, animal, and human.[9]

Nothing human was alien to these holy ones for they bore witness, directly or indirectly, to the death of the God of death and the rebirth of a God of life. For what is God, as Irenaeus put it, if not us fully alive? This is not some anthropological reduction of the infinite to the finite, but a recognition that the infinite is to be found at the core of each finite now, that the divine word inhabits the flesh of the world, in suffering and action. This anatheist option of new life beyond death answers many of the objections, it seems to me, leveled against believers by recent militant atheists like Hitchens, Dennett, and Dawkins. But I shall return to this point in my conclusion.

The acknowledgment of divine kenosis, the appreciation of the mystical moment of nothingness that precedes the breakthrough to a mystical epiphany of renewal, is by no means confined to Christianity. Great Jewish mystics like Isaac Ben Solomon Luria and Dov Baer fully acknowledged the insight that divine withdrawal and emptying (as described in Rabbi Luria's notion of *zimzum*) is a crucial moment of new creation. As did Islamic mystics like Ibn 'Arabi and Hafiz who embraced the notion of sacred emptying out (*fan'fi'llah*) as prelude to sacred ultimacy. (One thinks again of Muhammad's nocturnal vision (*mi'raj*) or his receipt of the Qur'an in the emptiness of a cave). Sufi mystics were renowned for their poetic testimonies to a paradigm of self-annihilation (*fana*) followed by a return to the glorious "subsistence" (*baqa*) of everyday life.[10] And similar notions, I believe, are to be found in Hindu teachings on the mystical heart-cave (*guha*) and Buddhist teachings on sacred emptiness (*sunyata*) and nothingness (*nirvana*). But such an extension of the anatheist argument would take me beyond the limits of the present work, even though the spirit of anatheism does invite one to extend hospitality to foreign deities and sages beyond one's own tradition (in my case, Abrahamic). This is work for a subsequent volume.

FROM HOSTILITY TO HOSPITALITY

In what follows I propose to explore how anatheist attitudes might be put into actual practice. How may one keep open the space of hospitality when it is real strangers knocking at the door, real migrants seeking food and shelter, real adversaries challenging our way of life—and maybe even our lives? Here then we return to the ultimate, and unsurpassable dilemma: what is to be done?

Let me begin by saying what, in my opinion, is *not* to be done. To be avoided, at all costs, is the ruinous temptation to use religion to dominate politics. We have seen the consequences of this down through the centuries, in religious wars, crusades, and inquisitions against the evil enemy, in the scandal of religious slaughter *in hic signo*. Nor is this a thing of distant history. Stalinism and Nazism were, as Mircea Eliade recognized, examples of perverted messianism and the more recent examples of Northern Ireland, the Balkans, and the Middle East all bear out the sorry lesson of ongoing religious violence. In fact, it may well be that, for all our talk of a postenlightenment new world order, most wars in our time are still, at root, fueled by pathological religious passions, however vehemently denied at the official levels.

The most topical case of this is arguably Iraq, where Sunnis and Shiites have been engaged in a religious civil war. But pathological religion goes back to the very beginnings of that conflict. One too easily forgets how George Bush used explicitly evangelical language in his demonization of the "axis of evil," choosing loaded religious terms such as *crusade* and campaign of *infinite justice*, and even confiding that "God" was his guide and protector. This apocalyptic mentality was chillingly demonstrated in a major TV documentary (*Frontline*, April 2004) called "The Jesus Factor," which confirmed that Bush's view of Christianity was not just a matter of personal salvation but of a global millennial battle between Good and Evil. Indeed one of the leading figures in the Pentagon, Lieutenant General William G. Bodkin, went so far as to publicly assert the metaphysical superiority of America's Christian God over the God of the Muslim enemy: "I knew that my God was bigger than his. . . . My God was a real God, and his was an idol."[11] The rest was silence—until the bombs dropped.

Al Qaeda's attack on the Twin Towers and subsequent support of the jihad against the West was conducted in even more explicitly sectarian language. Allah and the Qur'an were invoked to legitimate the campaign against the "big Satan" of America and the "little Satan" of Israel. Holy War against the infidel West was declared, and the American fight against Al Qaeda and the Taliban denounced as a "Christian terrorist crusade." In other words, here at the beginning of the third millennium we found ourselves still in the middle of a religious war between God and the Evil One, between the Lord of the Elect and the abominable adversary.

So how does one chose between a faith that kills and a faith that gives life? Between a God of fear and a God of hospitality?

SACRED SECULARITY

I have been arguing for the introduction of the sacred into the secular, but this is a two-way process. The sacralization of the secular needs to be supplemented by the secularization of the sacred. The sacramental needs the critical and vice versa. In the secular-sacred chiasmus, word invokes flesh and flesh word. Otherwise it is hard to see how one avoids a fatal relapse to the cycles of religious hostility that, as atheists remind us, have maimed human history for as long as we can recall. The task is to reenvision the relationship between the holy and the profane such that we can pass from theophany to praxis while avoiding the traps of theocracy and theodicy.

But let me clarify further what I mean by secularity in an anatheist context. In its most conventional sense, secularism has come to be the dominant worldview in Western culture along with the emergence of the modern scientific attitude. It coincides with Max Weber's diagnosis of the "disenchantment" (*Entzauberung*) of contemporary society, brought about by a combination of factors: the industrial revolution, the rise of capitalism, the mechanical and technological mastery of nature, the rationalist Enlightenment, and the various bourgeois revolutions in Europe and the New World. From this positivist viewpoint, religion is considered a remainder of the primitive past, a form of institutionalized superstition sure to disappear in the age of secular reason.[12] As the authors of *The Future of Religion* put it: "At least since the Enlightenment, most Western intellectuals have anticipated the death of religion. . . . The most illustrious figures in sociology, anthropology, and psychology have unanimously expressed confidence that their children, or surely their grandchildren, would live to see the dawn of a new era in which, to paraphrase Freud, the infantile illusions of religion would be outgrown."[13] This secular philosophy has became the standard view of religion from Comte, Durkheim, and Weber right down to the more recent campaign against the backwardness of religion waged by intellectuals like Sam Harris and Anthony Grayling. And it supports the influential "functionalist" thesis, first proposed by Talcott Parsons, that we have evolved from religion as a holistic traditional life-form toward an increased differentiation of social functions rendering religion obsolete.

By this account, there is no longer any place for the sacred in our modern Western democracies. At best, it should be radically separated from the civic realm, as the private from the public sphere. C. Wright Mills offers this summary of the evolutionary progression from a sacred to a secular universe: "Once the world was filled with the sacred — in thought, practice and institutional form. After the Reformation and the Renaissance, the forces of modernization swept across the globe and secularization, a corollary historical process, loosened the dominance of the sacred. In due course, the sacred shall disappear altogether except, perhaps, in the private realm."[14] The notion of "laicism" (*laïcité*) in the modern French Republic is a good case of how this secularist attitude translates into a politics of radical opposition to any inclusion of the sacred in the neutral space of public affairs. It corresponds to what Charles Taylor critically calls a secularism of "exclusive humanism" in *The Age of the Secular*.[15] But I shall return to this debate in our conclusion.

For now let me consider two different understandings of the secular: one privative, the other affirmative. The privative, called secularism by John Mayer, involves a negative concept that determines what should *not* inform the functioning of any public institution. The affirmative, called secularization, entails a more positive acknowledgment of the original Latin term, *saeculum*, designating a particular century or timescale. This signals a form of temporalization or turning toward the temporal world, which need not exclude the experience of a mature faith but only those modes of religion that imply a denial of time. In this later sense, secularity carries the much more inclusive meaning of what turns toward the world. A secular attitude, therefore, need not deny the possibility of a faith attentive to the realm of action and suffering but only a faith withdrawn from lived experience into a sphere of private interiority or otherworldly abstraction. Secularization thus has no difficulty, in principle, acknowledging the existence of the sacred *in* the world of the here and now. So, in this more affirmative view, secularity and sacramentality need not be adversaries.

Raimon Panikkar is a contemporary philosopher who proposes the option of a creative relationship between the secular and the sacred. His position is something like this: only secularization can prevent the sacred from becoming life denying, while only sacralization can prevent the secular from becoming banal. Once we interpret the secular in the original sense of *saeculum* or *aion*—that is, the "epoché" that directs our attention to particular time—we are actually in a privileged position to save religion from itself by liberating it into a fidelity to the sacredness of this life. Our own time, Panikkar believes, offers a unique opportunity to discover the sacred quality of the secular: "what seems to be unique in the human constellation of the present *kairos* is the disruption of the equation sacred-nontemporal with the positive value so far attached to it. The temporal is seen today as positive and, in a way, sacred."[16]

This is not to say the secular and the sacred are identical. The secular involves the human order of finite time, while the sacred denotes an order of infinity, otherness, and transcendence that promises to come and dwell in our midst—if we are willing to host it. The anatheist task, I submit, is to avoid both 1. a dualism that opposes secular and sacred and 2. a monism that collapses them into one. Anatheism is the attempt to acknowledge the fertile tension between the two, fostering creative cobelonging and "loving combat" (to borrow Karl Jaspers's phrase). For anatheism, the sacred is *in* the secular but it is not *of* the secular per se. It is a matter of reciprocal interdependency rather than one-dimensional conflation. And this chiasmic coexistence may itself serve as model for the interanimation of democratic politics and mature faith: "God and the world are not two realities, nor are they one and the same. Moreover . . . politics and religion are not two independent activities, nor are they one indiscriminate thing. . . . The divine tabernacle is to be found among men; the earthly city is a divine happening."[17] To collapse politics and religion into one leads, as history shows, to holy war, theocracy, and ecclesial imperialism. Whence the need to preserve the fecund tension between the secular self and the sacred stranger, whose crossing (without fusion) yields a hybrid—anatheism.

This secular-sacred offspring is, Panikkar suggests, recognizable in new forms of alliance between a politics of transformation and a religion of incarnation. An alliance where we may discover "the sacred character of secular engagement and the political aspect of religious life" (195). In such an anatheist constellation, the secular and the sacred are recognized as distinct but not opposite, different but not contrary. Panikkar speaks accordingly of a "sacred secularity" that allows us to reinterpret the secular in such a way that faith becomes a commitment not to some transcendental otherworld but to a deep temporality in which the divine dwells as a seed of possibility calling to be made ever more incarnate in the human and natural world. Here Panikkar coins the word *cosmotheandrism* to connote the creative cohabiting of the human (*anthropos*) and divine (*theos*) in the lived ecological world (*cosmos*). And he sees this, rightly, in my view, as an alternative "middle" voice to both 1. an autonomy that deprives the secular of the sacred and 2. a heteronomy that drives a dualist wedge between them. He thus hopes to avoid the twin dangers of reductive humanism (extreme autonomy) and dogmatic fundamentalism (extreme heteronomy).

In an essay entitled "The Future of Religion," Panikkar adverts to a major crisis occasioned by the fact that official religion is increasingly lagging behind people's actual practice of faith. For people today, he notes, are bringing God back into the world as faith migrates from "the temple to the street, from institutional obedience to the initiative of conscience" (199). Ignoring the doctrinal disputes between the churches and the world, most people see the pressing problems of faith to be "hunger, injustice, the exploitation of man and the earth, intolerance, totalitarian movements, war, the denial of human rights, colonialism and neo-colonialism" (199). Panikkar encourages traditional denominations to overcome their sectarian exclusivism and enter into dialogue with other faiths and nonfaiths. Arguing for the importance of interreligious cross-fertilization, he makes an urgent plea for "a mutual fecundation among the different human traditions of the world—including the secular and modern traditions," without lapsing into bland eclecticism or New Age syncretism. Such an understanding of "sacred secularity" should lead to the conciliation, without uniformity, of different peoples in our globally interconnected age. It is not, he concludes, "a matter of speaking the same language nor of practicing the same religion, but of remaining with an awake consciousness, aware that we are intoning different notes in the same symphony, and that we are walking on different paths toward the same peak. This then is faith: the experience of the symphony, of catching a glimpse of the summit, while being attentive to the path we follow, and trying not to stumble on the way" (200, n. 20).

Here again, then, we encounter the anatheist paradox: namely, that we can only return to God after we have abandoned 'God'. The secular entails a radical reorienting of our attention away from the old God of death and fear, for without such con-version we could not rediscover the God of life at the heart of our incarnate temporal existence. This means, I submit, re-inserting the hyphen between secular and sacred where it always belonged. Such reconfiguring of the secular-sacred is the catchcry of anatheism.

ISLAMIC QUESTIONING

Since our consideration of the secular-sacred debate thus far has focused mainly on the Judeo-Christian experience, it is time to reconsider some voices from Islamic intellectual culture. Not only is Islam the third sibling of the Abrahamic heritage discussed in this book, it is also the one most dramatically cited in "secularist" polemics against the tyranny of religion.

The dilemma is often posed by non-Muslims like this: is Islam compatible with modern secular democracy? Or, put differently, if we understand secular democracy to be a civic space where no principles of government or power are beyond free and reasonable debate, then is the historical leaning of dominant forms of Islam toward theocracy not problematic? In short, is Islam *intrinsically* belligerent and intolerant? As noted in our opening chapter, there are leading thinkers within Muslim intellectual culture who claim otherwise, and I now revisit some of their arguments.

The Iranian political thinker, Abdolkarim Soroush, describes the situation thus: whereas the "presecular age is marked by the hegemony of metaphysical thought in political, economic, and social realism," the modern secular age unsettles these presecular holistic premises in favor of regimes in which "no value and rules are beyond human appraisal and verification." This means everything is open to critique.[18] And so here again we have to ask what *kind* of God is Islam talking about such that to believe in its existence would prove compatible or incompatible with modern secular democracy? Against a common anti-Islamic prejudice, Soroush argues that at the heart of Islam we find a "Lord of the oppressed" (*al-Rahman, al-Rahim, and Raab al-mustaz 'afin)*), a divinity in whose name the prospect of democratic socio-economic development and freedom of expression are not only to be sanctioned but vigorously embraced. In light of the God who comes to "black and white" peoples and posits the equality of natives and strangers alike, democratic emancipation is to be considered "beneficial not only for the pursuit of spiritual goals, but also for the fostering of an uncoerced public life and political praxis."[19] In fact, the God of the estranged and dispossessed, invoked in the Qur'an, should be seen as a guarantor of such liberty against despotism of any kind, theocratic or totalitarian. Soroush interprets democracy accordingly as both procedural (a neutral legal method) and substantive (a commitment to goods like justice and truth).

But again we may ask: what *kind* of truth? And whose truth are we talking about? If we are prepared to include the truth of a sacred "outsider," then, argues Soroush, it should always be a critical truth that puts the powers that be in question. This would suggest, for example, that democracy is not necessarily tied to unfettered liberal capitalism or to a blind belief in the inevitability of technological progress. A critical voice of protest asks: What about disabled citizens who cannot earn a living? What about nature and the environment in the face of corporate industrial greed? In other words, one invokes the sacredness of the stranger not to put the governmental in power but in question; and this means protecting the civic space of *all* beings, rich and poor, human and natural, religious and irreligious alike. Such a view "from the outside," as it were, shows how the sacred may safeguard the secular by preventing it from succumbing to a purely utilitarian calculus of means and ends, profit and loss. Here, in short, the divine becomes the guarantor of the humane. The stranger, from beyond the limits of our familiar nation or state, comes to remind us that there is always *more* to justice than meets our present legal code. Our laws can always be *more* just, and democracy—though already present in parts of the world—is always in part still to come. This particular view is, of course, one promoted by Jewish and Christian thinkers of "messianic justice"—such as Benjamin, Derrida, and Caputo—as much as by Islamic thinkers like Soroush.

Soroush calls, ultimately, for an uncoupling of democracy from a morally neutral and purely technocratic liberalism. And he even goes so far as to suggest the possibility of a "democratic religious society." This requires, he hastens to add, that we separate religion from dogmatism and democracy from amoral indifference. And it also means sharply distinguishing government from civil society in order to prevent the manipulation of public power by any religious movement in violation of open democratic contestation and deliberation. Understood in this anatheist sense, religion might become a bolster for human rights, pluralist debate, and moral sensibility toward the needs of the excluded. Legal protections, Soroush argues, need to be supported by ethical compassion and spiritual commitment. Indeed, a democracy that claimed to be totally neutral on questions of substantive moral goodness could not presume to defend the rights of others, not to mention the right of the majority. For such a defense requires a sense of real justice toward the stranger, real sympathy toward the disenfranchised, real trust toward the outsider. A secular sense of duty, in this context, would be aided, not hindered, by a sacred sense of virtue. For, if secular democracy prides itself on care for the needs and rights of all citizens, including the most vulnerable, it is timely to recall that one of the most venerable traditions of Sufi Islam speaks of encountering "the face" of the divine in inter-personal experience—a space where we can each become a sacred friend (*wali*) and servant to each other.[20]

But the sacred can only serve as guarantor of democracy if one avoids the disastrous conflation of religion with absolutism. And here a rigorous hermeneutics of divine texts and teachings must be ready to submit every scriptural doctrine to "continuous scrutiny, that is, to the cauldron of inter-pretation and reinterpretation (*ijtihad*)."[21] As Soroush reminds his Islamic interlocutors, "Tolerance in the domain of beliefs is the correlative of a fallibility in the domain of cognition that has encroached upon traditional dogmas" (189, n. 18). Democratic tolerance does not, therefore, demand a total repudiation of beliefs, Islamic or otherwise, but a modest willingness to expose one's beliefs to constant examination (in dialogue with others). This, as Fred Dallmayr reminds us, is not relativism but relationism. It means living the sacred in relation to a plurality of perspectives that prevail in any democracy worthy of the name. The sacred *in relation* to the secular, in other words. But never fully identical with it. For such identification would mean collapsing the stranger into the same, the other into the self, "you" into "me."

The sacred, by contrast, has the potential to keep the secular on its toes, never content with itself, always compelled to imagine and reimagine new modes of living democracy, more just, more creative, more hospitable. And the secular, for its part, can serve the salutary role of keeping the sacred from being hijacked by theistic fundamentalists. To secularize the sacred is to bring it back into the body of time where living beings act and suffer. To sacralize the secular is to remind liberal democracies that there are always neglected strangers not only at their gates but in their midst.

Soroush concludes that genuine tolerance is not some amoral open-ness to anything that goes (for example intolerance); it is the readiness to overcome "infantile and immature" attachments to a sense of one's own infallibility. And the advantage of bringing religion into relation with the public realm of democratic life is, he wagers, that it exposes belief to reason-able open-minded discussion, thereby fostering a dialogue between genuine reason (*aql*) and divine revelation (*shar'*). Secular democracies do not need to turn their back on religion altogether. They only need to engage it in open public debate with nonreligious views of reason, respect, and com-mon sense. A religiously informed democracy would, Soroush suggests, be one freed from the lure of theocratic power and radically committed to a pluralism of beliefs, religious or otherwise. Indeed it would be a democracy more pluralist than a narrowly liberal-secularist model that prefers to banish religious voices from the public sphere altogether.

But Saroush is not naive. Well aware of the undemocratic spirit abroad in many Muslim societies today—especially informed by the spread of Wahhabism—Soroush addresses the guardians of Islamic conformism and purism thus: "You respect uniformity, emulation and obedience to religious jurists . . . [but] I implore you to appreciate the complexity and colorfulness of belief, the subtlety and the agility of faiths and volitions." For, he insists, the plurality of beliefs is itself a symbol of the "elusive plurality of souls" (181). To this end, Soroush pleads for a sacred-secular democracy inspired by an enlightened Sufi faith in the "heterogeneity of souls and the wandering of hearts." Invoking a God beyond dogmatism, he concludes: "Belief is a hundred times more diverse and colorful than disbelief. If the pluralism of secularism makes it suitable for democracy, the faithful community is a thousand times more suitable for it" (181).

Soroush is not, of course, alone in his views. Other Muslim intellectuals who have discussed ways in which Islam can be accommodated with modern democracy include thinkers like Mohammed Al-Jabri, Muhammed Arkoun, and Hasan Hanafi. And it is noteworthy, I think, that their reinterpetations of the relation between faith and reason are invariably indebted to a noble legacy of hermeneutic thought going back, as noted in chapter 1, to philosophers like the Andalusian Ibn Rushd (Averroes), who questioned the absolutist notion of a sovereign God and called for a critical interpretation of religious texts.

To understand God as sovereign rather than stranger is to render divine power all too easily transferable to theocratic power. Hence the perfidious conflation of church and nation. In pleading for latitude in intellectual debates against the fundamentalists of his time, Ibn Rushd challenged their absolutist cult of God's unlimited power removed from any kind of critical interrogation. He accused the fundamentalists of projecting an anthropomorphic view of God as Supreme Ruler of the World, thereby justifying all forms of despotic theocracy. In other words, by first projecting then reimporting this model of arbitrary divine power back to the political level, the fundamentalists became "allies and pacemakers of political despotism and tyranny—a despotism sharply at odds with the Prophet's own benevolent and fair-minded rule" (115). But this transfer of absolute divine sovereignty back onto unbridled human sovereignty, in the form of a political potentate on earth, betrayed the basic Islamic belief in the equality of all Muslims, as stated in the Prophet's claim that he was "sent to the white and the black," that is, to all people alike (135, n. 21). Every political leader, like every human person, has need of other people to acquire virtue and so cannot consider himself as sovereignly self-sufficient. Likewise, the teachings of political rulers, no less than those of God, are never to be taken blindly. They are subject to discussion, with critical appreciation for the distinction between different discursive genres such as metaphorical speech (*bayan*) and argumentative reasoning (*burhan*).

Philosophically speaking, Ibn Rushd played philosophic and Islamic perspectives off against each other in creative ways, insisting on the importance of applying reason to Islamic revelation on the one hand, while invoking Islamic equality to challenge the Greek segregation between "citizens" and "barbarians" (the strangers of the time) on the other (136–137).

The great proponent of Islamic hermeneutics did not hesitate, on occasion, to cite both reason and the Prophet's compassion to argue against clerics who sought to absolutize divine rule as a matter of arbitrary and willful fiat. Such a God—anticipating Hobbes's *Leviathan*—does anything he wills simply because he has the power to, unchecked by considerations of love and justice. Ibn Rushd opposed any such voluntarist-absolutist notion of God, claiming that it contravened the Prophet's principle of just rule as well as Aristotle's teachings on practical wisdom and judgment (*phronesis*). Despotic theology, he knew, leads directly to despotic theocracy. Tyrannical Gods breed tyrannical humans. And vice versa.

By attempting to steer a medial path between reason and faith, Ibn Rushd anticipated many of his followers in exploring a critical hermeneutic that might reconcile "God and the world." He was, not surprisingly, bitterly opposed by many of his Muslim contemporaries in Cordoba and further afield. But, as Fred Dallmayr has shown, there is a whole new generation of contemporary Muslim intellectuals, from Hasan Hanafi and Al-Jabri to Soroush and others, who are committed to a genuine retrieval of the Islamic *Umma* in the emancipatory light of Ibn Rushd's hermeneutic thinking (145f).[22] Such a creative reappropriation of the Muslim intellectual tradition requires an exposure of Islamic religion to a public space of pluralist discourse, in the hope of finding accommodation with the modern democratic world. Ibn Rushd's name and legacy can thus be taken as a stand-in for an age-old Islamic "yearning for a tolerantly open, yet morally responsible society, a society in which reason and faith, respect for humans and for the divine, are balanced (not collapsed) in a carefully calibrated way."[23]

In sum, if we heed the old adage that "Sovereigns are mirrors of the sovereignty of God," then it follows that the absolutist model of God as abstract bearer of rights devoid of duties to human beings legitimates human rulers behaving likewise. The equation of power with this model of authority leads to tyranny. Whence the sorry fact that the defenders of theocratic rule denounce the evils of secular freedom but never the evils of absolute power.[24] And it was for this reason that Hannah Arendt called for the suspension of "sovereignty" from our political discourse and practice, in both Western and non-Western societies, because it led, all too easily, to intolerance and war. "As long as national independence and the sovereignty of the state, namely the claim to unchecked and unlimited power in foreign affairs, are equated," wrote Arendt, "not even a theoretical solution of the problem of war is conceivable, and a guaranteed peace on earth is as utopian as the squaring of the circle."[25]

One of the advantages of Western democracies, however, is that, while not totally dispensing with all notions of sovereignty, they have at least dispensed with the idea that government is a translation of divine authority into human society. The Divine Right of Kings happily disappeared with the advent of modern revolutions and republics from the eighteenth century onward. Modern democracy is quintessentially opposed to the idea of an elected leader behaving as godlike emperor with unlimited powers. This is one of its most cherished virtues.

Such secular gains of democracy are, I have been suggesting, by no means incompatible with a certain tradition of Islamic faith that sees God as protector of the stranger and guarantor of equality for all. This venerable tradition has been ill-served in the postcolonial history of ideological Islam. And it is because of this unfortunate recent history (with some notable exceptions) that a Muslim theorist like Lahouari Adi argues that Islamic religion needs to be "depoliticized." But, when he speaks of depoliticizing Islam, Adi does not mean abolishing religion altogether or consigning it to a purely private realm. He means removing it from theocratic politics and reassigning it a more appropriate place—in practice as in theory—within the public sphere of civil society.[26] If it is possible to deabsolutize the notion of God (from God as Sovereign to God as Stranger) in the modern realm of democratic debate, there is no reason why an anatheist reconfiguring of the secular and the sacred might not occur in Islamic as well as Western culture. "Such a creation of modernism by way of Arab Islamic culture is theoretically possi ble," writes Adi, "for there is no reason why democracy should be inherently Western and Absolutism inherently Muslim."[27] In other words, anatheist Islam is no less conceivable, in principle, than anatheist Judaism or Christianity. Anatheism is an integral option of all Abrahamic faiths. For it begins and ends with the epiphany of the divine in the face of the stranger.

EXTENDING THE CIRCLE

What then of non-Abrahamic religions? Can one really speak of openness to the stranger in the Abrahamic tradition if one is not open to the stranger Gods of other religions? The Other is not a prerogative of biblical monotheism. Indeed, as I argued in our opening chapters, to be truly hospitable one must be attentive to the *other Others* who fall outside the family of the three testaments (Jewish, Christian, Islamic). Central to anatheism is the freedom to converse with those who remain alien to one's own faith. (And this includes both members of other religions as well as atheists with none.) This question of inclusive hospitality to "other Others" seems to be particularly crucial in an age when we are increasingly aware, through global communications, of just how many others there are in the world. We are all interdependent, as the postmodern phrase goes. But are we all really in dialogue with others *as* others (as opposed to merely "others *like* ourselves")? This question of religious difference, on a global scale, cannot be avoided if anatheism is to be true to its intentions of radical hospitality. And I say this for practical as well as theoretical concerns: the wager of welcoming or refusing the stranger is often a matter of war or peace.

The interreligious imperative is, I have suggested, an indispensable dimension of anatheism. It is not simply a categorical imperative of moral reason (à la Kant), but a summons of cultural imagination to translate between one's own religion and that of others. This means, in the context of our argument, not just between one Abrahamic tradition and another but between Abrahamic and non-Abrahamic religions. In other words, a translation that includes both West-East and North-South directions.[28] Most who engage in such interreligious conversing aspire to a set of shared principles in all wisdom traditions. These would constitute what Hans Kung and other ecumenists call a global ethic of compassion, a sort of universal ethic that gravitates around a Golden Rule of hospitality toward the Stranger. In addition to the examples from the Abrahamic tradition discussed in our opening chapter, here is a sample of typical formulations concerning compassion for the other adduced in a wide variety of religions:

Zoroastrianism: "Do not do unto others whatever is injurious to yourself" (Sahyast-na-Shayast, 13:29).

Buddhism: "Treat not others in ways that you yourself would find hurtful" (Udana-Varga 5:18).

Jainism: "One should treat all creatures in the world as one would like to be treated" (Mahavira, Sutrakrtanga).

Sihkism: "I am a stranger to no one; and no one is a stranger to me. Indeed I am a friend to all" (Guru Granth Sahib, 1299).

Confucianism: "One word that sums up the basis of all good conduct . . . loving kindness. Do not do to others what you do not want done to yourself" (Confucius, Analects 15:23).

Hinduism: "This is the sum of duty: do not do to others what would cause pain if done to you" (Mahabharata 5:1517).

Taoism: "Regard your neigbor's gain as your own gain, and your neighbor's loss as your own loss" (T'ai Shang Kan Ying P'ien, 213–218).

And one could, I am sure, add similar sayings about an ethics of compassion between self and others (human, natural, or divine) found in most other religions of the world.[29]

Such exchangeability between different spiritual traditions of the planet captures one of the essential points of interreligious dialogue: namely, the commonality of all religions across confessional differences. Hence the claim that when you reach through creedal distinctions to a shared praxis and mystical communion, you realize, as the ancients say, that "we are all one."[30] This stance can, I believe, make a crucial contribution toward world peace, given how many wars are caused by perverse sectarian passions. But anatheistic hospitality toward the stranger is, as noted, not just the recognition of the other *as the same as ourselves* (though this is crucial to any global ethic of peace). It also entails recognizing the other *as different to ourselves*, as radically strange and irreducible to our familiar horizons. Here lies the real challenge of anatheism. The host exposing him/herself to the guest.

The guest exposing her/himself to the host. For if all religions may be said to be equal in their right to claim truth they are not all the same. Here hospitality requires that we distinguish between equality and sameness. Which is not to deny for a moment that they may be the same in some crucial respects (like the Golden Rule), while remaining diverse in others.

Such mutual exposure marks, as we have seen, the wager of abandoning familiar deities in order to expose ourselves, however provisionally, to the exteriority of unfamiliar ones. The anatheistic wager is that after such exposure to the alterity of the other, suspending ourselves in the cloud of nonknowing, we come to see that others-than-ourselves are sacred and, by extension, have diverse ways of living this spiritually. That is the anatheistic supplement: the acknowledgment of difference as well as commonness. Thus in addition to seeking a new global ethics—above all religious and nonreligious differences—it is necessary to equally acknowledge the singular uniqueness of each faith, appreciating that this singularity may be quite as divine as the universality of Golden Rules. Anatheism demands no less from a hermeneutics of self and stranger. But I shall return to this point in my conclusion when considering the debate between Paul Ricoeur and Hans Kung on a "planetary ethic."

Suffice it for now to say that what applies to an ethics of interconfessional hospitality also applies to concrete exchanges between diverse cultures, nations, and communities: exchanges that are central to a contemporary politics of self and stranger (including atheists and humanists). The readiness to translate back and forth between ourselves and strangers—without collapsing the distinction between host and guest languages—is, I submit, one of the best recipes to promote nonviolence and prevent war.

7

IN THE ACT

BETWEEN WORD AND FLESH

If you have an eye for it, the world itself is a sacrament.

—Augustine

The three arcs of anatheism—the iconoclastic, the prophetic, and the sacramental—attest to ways in which the sacred is *in* the world but not *of* the
world. While the sacred inhabits the secular, it is not identical with it. They
are not the same, though for anatheism they need each other as self needs
stranger. If the sacred stranger were identical with the self, she would be
neither sacred nor strange. The stranger is sacred in that she always embod-
ies something *else*, something *more*, something *other* than what the self can
grasp or contain. This point has been recognized, in Western culture, from
the beginning: from Abraham's welcome to the wanderers in the desert and
Socrates' dialogue with the Stranger in *The Sophist* about the relationship
between Same and Other. From these biblical and Greek inaugurations,
the stranger is recognized as one who can make the impossible possible,
who brings sameness and alterity into fertile congress. And similar points
may doubtless be made regarding non-Western cultures.

In the modern epoch iconoclastic voices have been heard in the indig
nant critiques of religion that go under the heading of a "hermeneutics of
suspicion." Such protests signal, I have conceded, a welcome deconstruction of the false idols that every religion has carried on its back at some
time or other. Although salutary, such a move is not sufficient to account
for the integral life of faith. It concentrates on the "negative" aspects (quite
reasonably), but often ignores the "positive" *surplus* of meaning that exceeds

the sociohistorical perversions of religion. Extreme secularism tends to ignore God as Stranger in its exclusive focus on God as Sovereign (*suprema potestas*). In this sense, secular atheism, taken to militant extremes, risks becoming fixated on negation. Now while we have acknowledged at several junctures in our argument that the "negation of negation" has its necessary place in the demystifying of religious illusions, it is not enough. Secular exclusivism does not do full justice to the sacred. It does not attend to the deep and subtle complexity of human-divine relations.

That is why I have been suggesting that the initial moment of iconoclasm, which unmasks mendacious and illusory idols, needs to be supplemented with a second anatheist moment—the moment of prophecy. This second moment lets symbols speak of new things still to come. It recuperates stories of healing and emancipation from Exodus and Isaiah to the Sermon on the Mount or the ecstatic songs of Mirabai and Kabir. Such prophetic moments, as we saw in chapter 3, are also powerfully attested to in the European philosophies of Levinas, Bonhoeffer, and Ricoeur where they mark a step beyond the hermeneutics of suspicion to a hermeneutics of affirmation or, perhaps we should say, a hermeneutics of *reaffirmation*, for we are concerned here with gaining back a living God after forsaking an illusory one. Nay-saying, however salutary, needs to be answered by a yea-saying once again.

But there is, I have tried to show, still another moment to the anatheist journey—a third step fueled by both protest and prophecy as it goes forward to recover a second faith: namely, the recovery of the sacramental in the lived world of suffering and action. This, I have been suggesting, complements a prophecy of promise with concrete attention to embodied divinity. It combines a messsianicity of waiting with an engagement with the incarnate stranger standing before us. This is what I call the anatheistic return to the Eucharist of the everyday. It involves sharing bread with others and aliens surrounding us and (as Julia Kristeva reminds us) within us.[1] For if others are strangers to us we are equally strangers to others and to ourselves.

The sacramental moment of anatheism is when we finally restore the hyphen between the sacred and the secular. It is also the moment we return from text to action, from the realm of critical interpretation to the world of quotidian praxis and transformation. This ultimate transition from word to flesh is witnessed daily wherever someone gives a cup of cold water to a thirsting stranger. For in such situations one's faith in God as stranger is not a matter of theories or ideas but of living witness to the word made flesh. There are countless examples of this at every border, street corner, or threshold where a native meets a foreigner and opens the door to the messiah in our midst. In what follows I consider three modern cases of sacramental action.

DOROTHY DAY

Dorothy Day was a Christian who believed that God inhabited the homeless of inner-city slums. She worked with them daily. She gave them bread and water, shelter and care. She was political, but not in the sense of manipulating government (like the Christian coalition in the Bush years) or running government (as in church-state collusion known as Christian-Caesarism). Day's politics was that of the suffering and acting body. It pertained to everyday acts of love and justice in a secular world, transfiguring misery into care, hostility into hospitality. In this she resembled the politics of emancipation promoted by the famous theologians of liberation in Latin America, a politics not of state power or party ideology but of sacramental living in the here and now. Her New York friends included the rebel Berrigan brothers, civil rights activists, and the unhoused of Harlem. In *The Long Loneliness* and other writings, we witness a Christian woman committed to the reality of emancipation in the lives of the poor over against what she saw as the death principle promoted by limitless capitalist greed.

Dorothy Day loved the world and was determined to improve it. At an early age she earned the ire of her conservative family by joining the International Workers of the World and the Anti-Conscription League. She was imprisoned with suffragists, prostitutes, and pacifists. She protested constantly and went on hunger strike for justice's sake. She vigorously opposed nuclear arming and McCarthyism with fasts and pickets. She also wrote a novel and two autobiographies. She loved the literary life of the Village and admired her friend and playwright, Eugene O'Neill, for his mysticism of the sea. She had several lovers in New York and wrote lovingly of their bodies—this is how she described her one-time partner, Forster Batterham, who fathered her daughter, Tamar: "He stayed out late on the pier fishing, and came in smelling of seaweed and salt air. . . . I loved him for the odds and ends I had to fish out his pockets and for the sand and shells he brought in with his fishing. I loved his lean cold body as he got into bed smelling of the sea, and I loved his integrity and stubborn pride."[2]

Dorothy Day embodied the sacramental message of the Christian Gospel. Without standing with the officialdom of her pre–Vatican II Catholic

Church, she devoted most of her life to an intellectual and political renewal of Christianity through a worker's publication—*The Catholic Worker*—and the establishment of dozens of Hospitality Houses throughout the country. (Both newspaper and houses are still extant.) Day made a point about using the term *hospitality* instead of what she considered to be the condescending term *charity* for performing "duties" to the poor. And she knew suffering at first hand—the San Francisco earthquake, the Great Depression, imprisonment, the casualties of two world wars, racist oppression, dire urban poverty, and, at a more personal level, an abortion. Her pioneering workers newspaper first took shape on her kitchen table as she labored to establish her first hospitality houses in Harlem and Little Italy. Day saw these radical activities as vehicles of compassion and her protest campaigns as "underminings through love." Within years over a dozen U.S. cities had set up similar houses to shelter and feed the homeless.

Day always saw her role in the church as a "guest" and so, in turn, wished to provide sacred spaces in the secular world to house other "guests"—offering them both soup and prayer. But she was not naive. She knew, up close, the risks of keeping an open house when some who entered were drunkards, addicts, thieves, and perverts. As she put it: how does one know when the guest is Jesus or Jackie the predator? She knew it was all very well to hate the sin and love the sinner in theory, but another thing in practice. Yet she always struggled to do so. As Gary Wills put it, "this was a woman who fed the poor, not with a handout, but by handing over her life to them. . . . She was more radical than anyone in the way she asked for and gave love."[3]

Day's motto was eucharistic and simple: "We cannot love God unless we love each other, and to love we must know each other. We know God in the breaking of bread, and we are not alone any more. Heaven is a banquet, too, even with a crust, where there is companionship."[4] Here Day echoes the radically incarnational words of John 6:51: "the bread that I will give is my Flesh for the life of the world"—flesh here being understood as the gift of bodily care and nourishment for those who hunger and thirst. She also reiterates the sacramental wager of anatheism that God is known, like the stranger at Emmaus, in the breaking of bread. And this mutual transfiguration of sacred body and material nourishment is itself accompanied by a mutual transfiguration of God as both host (the one who gives us bread) and guest (the stranger who receives bread from us). It is telling that the word *host* in the *Shorter Oxford English Dictionary* means both the one who gives hospitality (our normal meaning of *host* or *hostess*) *and* the one who receives it. "Host: to give or to receive as a guest."[5] In short, host can mean guest and vice versa. And the eucharistic term *host* (*hostia*) itself carries this double meaning: the consecrated bread as body of Christ where the human and divine exchange roles as givers and receivers.

This double eucharistic epiphany, so central to Day's sacramental ethos, is one echoed in the words of Teresa of Calcutta when she writes that "in each of our lives Jesus comes as the bread of life—to be eaten, to be consumed by us. Then Jesus comes in our human life as the hungry one, the other, hoping to be fed with the bread of our life."[6] It is a motif beautifully captured in the famous paschal hymn *Pange Lingua*, which ends with the resonant and reversible locution of word and flesh: *Verbum caro, panem verum verbo carnem efficit* ("Word made flesh, the bread of nature by his word to flesh returns"). For Dorothy Day, as for Merleau-Ponty, this reversibility of word and flesh is the "subtle knot" that makes us hosts *and* guests. It is not confined to High Church liturgies but extends to moments of everyday sensibility and service in the world. Day takes Christ totally to heart when he says "I come not to be served but to serve" (Matt. 20:28).

This is not new, of course. The divine stranger who dwells in flesh and nature was already celebrated by revolutionary saints like Francis and Clare and by Church fathers like John of Damascus, who praised matter as the substance through which the divine is manifest to us. "I worship the Creator of matter who became matter for my sake, who worked out my salvation through matter," writes John. "Never will I cease honoring the matter which wrought my salvation."[7] Day's sacramental ethic may also be seen as a radical development of the Second Council of Nicea (787), which held that the divine could be present in the Eucharist "substantially" or in icons "hypostatically." For Christ could thus be incarnate as a "symbol that renders present what it *materially* signifies"—i.e., in material like water, bread, and wine united to the materiality of words and as a sign "in which signified and signifier are assumed to cohere."[8]

To this, of course, Day adds the eucharistic icon of the human person who gives (as host) or receives (as guest) the bread of life. For her, human hospitality, like eucharistic and iconic worship, is a process of "offering to God but also God's descent into our midst." Hospitality bears witness to the meeting of grace with nature and eternity with time. And this, in turn, can be read through the lens of Philippians 2:5–11: the crucial kenosis text that celebrates the Incarnation of Christ as one who, "though he was in the form of God, did not regard equality with God as something to be exploited but emptied himself, taking the form of a slave, being born in human likeness (*en homoiomati anthropon*)." Here we find a terminological reference to Genesis 1:26, which speaks of the first man made in the "likeness [*homoiosin*] of God." The suggestion being that God becomes "man fully alive."

Through kenosis, in other words, God ceases to be some omnipotent Patriarchal Cause over and above humanity and takes the form of a loving Gift that empties itself in and as the Son of Man who in turn empties himself out of love for the least of human beings. As though God as Master must pass away so that God as servant may be born—a servant who in turn passes away so that humans may be reborn in his "image and likeness." In this fashion, Dorothy Day's eucharistic practice of living with the poor was a daring reenactment of the kenotic indwelling in John 14: "I am in the Father and the Father is in me. The Father who dwells in me is doing his works. Whoever believes in me will do the works that I do and will do greater ones than these." The message here, so robustly witnessed by Day, is that just as the Son hosts the Father on earth so too we may host the Son in every act of care toward the "least of these." Kenotic descent from Father and Son to humanity invites a return journey whereby humans may ascend and flourish through eucharistic hospitality.

Expressed in more political terms, Day's sacramental praxis testified to what Fred Dallmayr calls sacred nonsovereignty. It involved a politics of the flesh based not on competition with power politics but on fundamental transformation. Day took her inspiration from Christ as healing servant; and she saw the ministry of the holy stranger as aiming "not to trump the world (by establishing a worldly superpower), nor to destroy or eradicate this world (along millenarian lines)" but to transfigure the world through grace. Such ministry "involved neither a anti-politics nor an super-politics but rather an *other* kind of politics"—what Dallmayr calls a "politics of sacred or redemptive non-sovereignty."[9] This "other" politics—observed by Christ as guest-host and by followers through the centuries down to Dorothy Day— challenges a prevalent modern view that faith is an entirely subjective matter: "Believe what you like as long as it doesn't affect life in society." For Day, faith is more than idiosyncrasy. It is more than an individual journey into the privacy of one's soul. It entails, as it did for the prophets and Jesus, a public ministry. For as Jesus said to the high priest, "I have spoken openly to the world . . . and have said nothing in secret" (John 18:20). Indeed, Day is well aware that one of Jesus's most contentious public statements was to teach his disciples the message of nonsovereign service to others. So that when two of his disciples sought to be assured that they would sit on the right hand of their Lord, he responded with an altogether different model of social existence: one of sacramental service: "You know that those who are supposed to rule over the gentiles lord it over them, and their great men exercise power over them. But it shall not be so among you . . . whoever would be great among you must be your servant, and whoever would be first among you must be slave of all" (Mark 10:37–44).

For Dorothy Day, as for Dallmayr, one of the greatest tragedies of Christianity was that Christ's teaching about nonsovereignty went largely unheeded. Still today, the addiction to ecclesial sovereignty has not abated. Indeed, it is highly ironic that a common complaint leveled by religious "fundamentalists" against democracy is that it challenges the absolute "sovereignty of God."[10] Day refused the dualism that opposes a supernatural realm inhabited by a Master God to a fallen world governed by political sinners. She deplored the Manichaean polarity that preached the necessary destruction of "this" evil world in a final Armageddon where a "pure" post-world would prevail. This apocalyptic scenario has not, alas, disappeared from our geopolitical landscape, as the rhetoric following 9/11 has shown (with Bush and Bin Laden claiming "divine" endorsement). By contrast, the sacramental politics practiced by Day entailed concrete acts of service that bring the sacred and the secular back into contact, translating transcendence into body and blood.

I think it is crucial, however, to distinguish sacramental politics from religious politics as such. And here we might usefully invoke Charles Taylor's argument, in *The Secular Age*, that after the sixteenth century no religion has a right to impose itself on the political sphere. One of the most positive benefits of secularity is to prevent any further recourse to political theocracy. Christendom, as the conflation of divinity with emperors and nations, is gone. And this salutary separation of church and state (which Taylor calls *secularism 1*) should be honored. Further discriminations are required, however, as this secular space opens up different interpretations. On one hand, we have an "exclusive humanism" that denies any meaning or transcendence beyond the purely human order (what Taylor calls *secularism 2*). On the other hand, we have a tolerant pluralism that fosters the coexistence of different views and beliefs, religious and otherwise (what Taylor calls *secularism 3*).[11] The sacramental politics of Dorothy Day presupposes the first secularism, defies the second, and embraces the third. But most important, in my view, it testifies to the message of divine in-*carnation* in the least of these, fostering the bodily well-being of fellow humans in opposition to the growing tendency toward *ex-carnation* in our world of neo-capitalist simulation.[12] Day's commitment to sacramental action was a powerful reminder that contemporary materialism neglects the glory of matter.

JEAN VANIER

My second example of sacramental action is Jean Vanier. A Canadian philosopher who experienced the fallout of World War II as a young man, Vanier later gave up a university career to devote his life to the service of discarded people—those he called the wounded of the earth. Opening a house in a small village, Trosly-Breuil, north of Paris, Vanier invited a group of disabled people to join him. He called it L'Arche—an open-door ark for the estranged and rejected. L'Arche housed people normally treated with fear and suspicion or locked away in asylums. From its genesis in a group of so-called normal and abnormal people sharing life together, L'Arche has spread throughout the world. In 2008 there were over 130 communities in 33 countries on 6 continents.

In opening the gates of "secure society" to the "estranged," Vanier believes we learn to grow by accepting not only the wounds of others but of ourselves. Exposing ourselves to insecurity, we are instructed by the strangers we set out to teach. In this process of welcoming the sacred stranger in our midst, the dominant paradigms of sovereign power and atomic selfhood are reversed into a counterparadigm of sacramental host and guest. We thus move from what Vanier terms the vision of the hierachical *pyramid* to that of the shared *body*. "Sharing our lives in community with the weak and the poor," he says, "we come in touch with our own limits, pain and brokenness. We realize that we too have our handicaps which are often around our need for power and the feeling that our value lies in being powerful—a power that frequently involves crushing other people." We are thus confronted with two visions of society: "a vision of the *pyramid*, where you have to have more and more power in order to get to the top, or a vision of a *body* where every person has a place."[13] It is often through the moment of breakdown, loss, and nothingness—the kenotic moment of abandonment—that we find ourselves returning to God after God. Stripped of our pretensions to mastery, we are liberated at last, by encountering the alienated guest, to care for others. For it is frequently when life as we know it forfeits its meaning that we find ourselves estranged until we befriend that strangeness and, overcoming fear and dread, rediscover new depths to life: sacramental depths. So letting go of familiar existence we find ourselves "called to give life and help people discover who they are, so that they in turn can give life to others."[14]

The advent of the stranger thus turns us from sovereignty to service, from will-to-power to wonderment at the endless rebirth of life: that inexhaustible surplus of natality over mortality in speech and action. In L'Arche the welcoming of the estranged (traditionally confined to *des asiles d'aliénés*) challenges us to forego our defense mechanisms and become incarnate selves in the face of incarnate others. And this act of sacramental hospitality, solicited by the living presence of an embodied other without mask or subterfuge—*face-à-face*—creates a togetherness "in which weak people have an important gift because they call us together into a gradual birth of a body." Together with them, says Vanier, "we can let down the barriers and turn our backs on the need for power. We discover a life where the weak and strong can dance together."[15]

Teresa of Calcutta has something similar in mind, I suspect, when she speaks of moving from recoil to welcome when confronted with suffering. When you meet someone in pain or dying, she observes, "your first reaction is often one of repulsion. But if you get close to the person and take care of his or her body in pain, you touch compassion . . . and if you go a little bit further in the relationship, you enter into wonderment."[16] Vanier, like Teresa, recommends that we live our anxiety before the strangeness of existence not in denial or compensation but by responding to breakdown as a breakthrough to new life. This moment is what Vanier calls "a cry for the infinite and for presence." And it is his bold belief that this cry is at the very heart of incarnation as sacrament of corporeal presence: "we yearn to discover and know a God who became flesh, not a God who came to manifest the power of God but rather to manifest God's love and togetherness and tenderness."[17] (Perhaps James Joyce's "cry in the street" is not unrelated?)

Here again, I would argue, we encounter the anatheist choice between hospitality and hostility. A wager that we witness daily as one part of humanity strives for more dominion, while another opts for sacramental care of the nonsovereign stranger. This is not part of some dialectical destiny, but a decision for each one. The Yes or No to the estranged in our midst. The opening or closing of the door to uninvited guests. And it is within each one of us—as well as on the broader stage of history—that the anatheist wager is made.

With these contemporary examples of Vanier and Teresa we rejoin, I believe, a long tradition of hospitality going back to those biblical stories of caring for the stranger, cited in our opening chapters, and extending right down to the *frères hospitaliers* of the famous pilgrimages through Europe—hostelers who cared for the sick and wounded migrants from other lands as they made their way to some sacred place: St. Jacques de Compostella, Rome, Jerusalem. This tradition gave rise, in turn, to the subsequent notion of hostels, hotels, and hospices where hosts received traveling guests in need of alms or healings. Indeed there is a story of how the celebrated hospital in Paris, Le Val de Grâce, came to be. The nuns at one of the many convents in Paris threatened with destruction by the revolutionary guards in 1789 decided to open their doors and care for the wounded "adversary" who had originally come to execute them. At one stroke, the enemy became a guest, the besieged incumbent a host. An enclosed priory was transformed into an open public hospital for wounded soldiers: Val de Grâce—a gracious opening to the alien. The hospice movements for the dying in our own day, pioneered by the likes of Cecily Saunders and Therese Vanier, not to mention the various volunteer hospitals for famine, genocide, or disaster victims, are, I believe, inspired by a similar spirit of hospitality to the stranger. They epitomize the transfiguring of fear into care.

GANDHI

The final figure I propose to exemplify the sacramental moment of anatheism is Mahatma Gandhi. Here again we witness a movement from protest and prophecy to a life of sacramental witness in suffering and action. In Gandhi we find a compelling instance of that "other" kind of sociopolitical engagement I have been calling sacramental, and which I locate at the heart of the anatheist return. My choice of someone from outside the Abrahamic tradition is not insignificant.

Gandhi himself returned to a life of political action in India after many years in exile in Europe and Africa. He could, in fact, be said to have traversed a double estrangement before finally committing himself to a life of service and struggle for his people. First, his encounter as émigré scholar with the Western rule of imperial politics exposed Gandhi to what he called the rational principles of secular society—at once disillusioning him and instructing him in the ways of political modernity. But, within his own spiritual journey, integral to his Hinduism, Gandhi experienced a second and very different kind of estrangement—the estrangement from his own ego-self as he underwent the Vedantin ascesis of detachment and renunciation (*brahmacharya*). This double exposure to the unfamiliar, both external and internal, helped Gandhi to embrace *karma yoga* as a "self-transcending or non-attached praxis." It was to become his passageway to liberation.

Having retreated from anthropomorphic notions of God—as he withdrew to the heart-cave (*guha*) of inner darkness—Gandhi eventually returned to the world of action. Henceforth he declared that his vision of personal and political freedom rested on a "philosophical-cum-religious assumption," namely, that each individual "existed in God" and was to be treated as a sacred wayfarer on the path to emancipation (*moksha*): a path to self-realization that transgressed the familiar self to discover the divine stranger within (*Atman*). Human beings who suffered and acted were indeed "makers of their own destiny"—something he learned from modern democratic politics. But this need not lead, Gandhi believed, to a self-centered individualism or nationalism at variance with the "sacred relationality of all beings."[18]

Gandhi sought a delicate balance between secularity and sacredness. He was critical of what he saw as a reductive materialism in Western civilization (which, he declared, was a civilization only "in name"). When it came to India, he advocated instead for a conjoining of the sacred and the secular in a new form of liberated self-rule (*swaraj*). In his manifesto, "Hind Swaraj," Gandhi proved quite an iconoclast in his portrait of Western secularism. "This civilization takes note neither of morality (*niti*) nor of religion (*dharma*)," he wrote. "Its votaries calmly state that their business is not to teach religion. Some even consider it to be a superstitious growth. . . . Civilisation seeks to increase bodily comforts, and it fails miserably even in doing so. This civilization is irreligion [*adharma*], and it has taken such a hold on the people in Europe that those who are in it appear to be half mad."[19] Gandhi returns to the subject later in his work, candidly adding: "I do not consider England or America as free countries. . . . They are [ignorant] of that freedom their poets and teachers have described."[20] Gandhi was thinking here of writers like Thoreau who sought, as Gandhi himself did, to combine a sense of individual liberty with a keen commitment to public action. Feeling an outcast in the West, on his return to India Gandhi sought to embrace the outcasts of the East—namely untouchables from the lower castes.

Gandhi charted a middle way. If traditional Indian culture was too sacred at the expense of the secular, modern Western society was too secular at the expense of the sacred. The aim was to find a median path that would reintroduce the hyphen between secularity and sacredness. Only thus could one obviate the twin extremes of modern materialism in the West and regressive spiritualism in the East, which Gandhi had experienced firsthand. True civilization, for Gandhi, presupposed a sense of spiritual and moral rightness (central to dharma) that endowed one's public actions with a sense of sacramental love (*bhakti*). This was a key teaching of karma yoga that Gandhi retained from the Bhagavad Gita. Genuine religion, he insisted, could not be confined to some private realm of interiority, as liberal modernity suggested. Swaraj required both inner self-rule and outer self-rule, both transcendental contemplation and public action in the world. This is what Gandhi meant when he said that those "who say that religion has nothing to do with politics do not know what religion means."[21] For religion, as he understood it, is no more a matter of private faith cut off from the world than it is a theocracy ruling people in the name of God.

When it came to religion, Gandhi was bravely interreligious. He held that each of the wisdom traditions pointed to a life of service to others. He saw all spiritual paths as "different roads converging on the same point."[22] And, with this in mind, he had no difficulty declaring that while a Hindu he was also "a Muslim, Christian, Jew, and Sikh." This was not perhaps surprising given his devotion to the multiple religions of India so generously accommodated by his own "open source Hinduism."[23] The life of service he espoused was fundamentally a life of "sacrifice," understood not in the sense of expiatory blooodletting, but in the sense of a sacred duty, a sacramental engagement in the life-world of action. Sacrifice here meant *sacer-facere*, a making holy, a consecration of ordinary events as sacred and special. It meant acknowledging things as gifts beyond the normal economy of production and consumption, as *something more* than the logic of profit, utility, and exchange.[24] For Gandhi, in short, the spiritual path of *karma yoga* was a path of everyday sanctification; it equated "action with *yajna* (sacrifice), namely, the performance of action as a sacred duty." And in this light Gandhi held that one's "sacred duty lies in exerting oneself to the benefit of others, that is, service."[25]

A central aim of Gandhi's career was to combat the dichotomy between the spiritual and the social. His key notion of swaraj entailed both 1. personal practice of self-restraint ("experienced by each one for himself")[26] and 2. public commitment to political emancipation ("a complete independence through truth and non-violence . . . without distinction of race, color or creed").[27] Swaraj was thus understood as "freedom of self-actualisation in a transcendental sense" that must also be "realised in this world."[28] Without this double and simultaneous fidelity to both inner and outer liberation, the independence movement in India threatened to collapse into narrow nationalism—or else, as bad, relapse into the atavisms of the caste system where the life of the spirit was divorced from human rights and justice. Gandhi advocated, accordingly, for a "free play of mutual forces" between the journey toward spiritual freedom *and* the journey toward social trans-formation. "Man is not born to live in isolation," he famously declared, "but is essentially a social animal independent and interdependent. No one should ride on another's back." [29] Gandhi's politics of sacred action was thus conceived as a sacramental conjoining of the human (*dehin*) and the divine (*atman*). It was a pathway of loving devotion (*bhakti*) conceived by a sincere follower of Vaishnava *bhakta*. And Gandhi believed that this way involved a special kind of soul-force or love-force (*satyagraha*) exemplified by the holy ones of the great wisdom traditions: Christ in the Sermon on the Mount no less than Krishna in the Gita. This was at the basis of Gandhi's radical op-tion for nonviolence over war. And, I repeat, it was always conceived as an odyssey rather than a fait accompli, a pilgrimage rather than an ideology, a venture rather than a dogma.

Service to strangers—across caste, color, or creed—required a sacra-mental transfiguration of everyday life. It meant a practical living out of the old Hindu dictum, *aditi devo bhavah* ("The guest is God"). Swaraj was not an abstract idea or utopia but something that began on the ground, on the street, in the local village or community hall, only later spreading outward, by human witness and association, into larger communities through a series of "oceanic circles." This is precisely how Gandhi interpreted the ancient Hindu teaching of karma yoga. Combining Western notions of Christian charity and secular justice with indigenous Indian notions of dharma and swaraj, Gandhi allowed these two culturally and historically opposed phi-losophies to traverse each other. And, by means of such intercultural hos-pitality, Gandhi wagered that traditional strangers might became allies— anatheistically—on a common path to freedom.

Freedom, Gandhi concluded, involved the whole life of a person in both its sacred and secular dimensions. Prayers to Brahman at *puja* could not be separated from the dharma of feeding the hungry or welcoming alien castes. The holy had to be exemplified in the everyday world of concrete praxis—or it was not holy. Swaraj was much more than a doctrine; it was a testimony of engaged living. Politics could not be left to politicians any more than religion could be left to Brahmins. The secular needed the sacred as much as the sacred needed the secular. For, in Gandhi's view, social life *was* sacramental life.

Our three exemplars of the sacramental—Day, Vanier, and Gandhi— shared the option for a God of hospitality over a God of power. Following a hermeneutics of narrative, I have tried to tell their stories as epitomes of an anatheism of action. I have endeavored to show how they each restored, in specific ways, the bond between the sacred and the secular, challenging the tendency to oppose inner and outer, private and public, human and divine. These pioneers did not, I submit, deny a difference between the two poles but lived the productive tension in between. Their lives bore testimony to the incarnation of divinity in the flesh of the world. And, so doing, they resisted God as sovereign in favor of God as guest. For Day this guest was the oppressed urban poor, for Vanier the disabled and wounded, for Gandhi the struggling multitudes of India.

This final step in the anatheist journey—from protest to prophecy to sacrament—is, I have been suggesting, a return to a God of life after the death of God. (Death meaning here the dissolution of a counterfeit divine.) But, if it is indeed a return journey, it is one without end. A pilgrim's path, a road of multiple twists and turns, to be taken again and again.

CONCLUSION

WELCOMING STRANGE GODS

The feeling remains that God is on the journey too.

—Teresa of Avila

Anatheism, I have argued, is not an end but a way. It is a third way that precedes and exceeds the extremes of dogmatic theism and militant atheism. It is not some new religion, but attention to the divine in the stranger who stands before us in the midst of the world. It is a call for a new acoustic attuned to the presence of the sacred in flesh and blood. It is *amor mundi*, love of the life-world as embodiment of infinity in the finite, of transcendence in immanence, of eschatology in the now.

|

Anatheism is not an atheism that wishes to rid the world of God, rejecting the sacred in favor of the secular. Nor is it a theism that seeks to rid God of the world, rejecting the secular in favor of the sacred. Nor, finally, is it a pantheism (ancient or New Age) that collapses the secular and the sacred into one, denying any distinction between the transcendent and the immanent. Anatheism does not say the sacred *is* the secular; it says it is *in* the secular, *through* the secular, *toward* the secular. I would even go so far as to say the sacred is inseparable from the secular, while remaining distinct. Anatheism speaks of "interanimation" between the sacred and secular but not of fusion or confusion. They are inextricably interconnected but never the *same* thing.

This is why anatheism should not be confounded with Hegelian dialectic. It refuses the temptation of subsuming singular persons and events into some Grand Finale. But, if it resists the lure of totality, it also resists a teleology of ineluctable progress. I am not suggesting that faith is only genuine if it has passed through the grids of Western liberal secularism. Far from it: the faith that anatheism gestures toward has always been there, in past ages, and in non-Western cultures and societies too. It was there wherever a person suspended her certainty about a familiar God and opened the door to the stranger. And, we may ask, was there any religion anywhere on earth that did not witness such gestures of hospitality? Anatheism is not something that comes only at the end of history, as dialectical teleologies might suggest. It marks the eternal crossing of time. It was there from the beginning and recurs at every moment that the stranger trumps the sovereign.

Anatheism is not atheism then, but it does agree with enlightened atheism that the God of theodicy is dead. To return again to the specifically Western context, anatheism embraces the Enlightenment critique of the triumphal deity who rules over his creatures and metes out punishment and plaudits. It concurs, as we saw in chapter 3, with the demythification of religion carried out by Nietzsche, Freud, and the postwar advocates of religionless faith. And as noted in chapter 4, it endorses the spirit of the phenomenological epoché—the provisional suspension of inherited confessions and assumptions—not to enter some positivistic value-free zone but to attend more faithfully to the sacred "things themselves" in the midst of life. For, as phenomenologists remind us, what we leave outside the brackets of suspension we can gain back again a hundredfold after we return.

Anatheism does not propose a new God, a new belief, a new religion. It simply invites us to see what has always been there *a second time around— ana*. Here it is important to clarify our embrace of a salutary atheist moment in the anatheist odyssey. We conceive of this as a necessary purging of the perversions of religious power, following the adage (oft cited by Ivan Illich) that *corruptio optimi est pessima*: the corruption of the best is the worst. To justify torture, conquest, and domination "in the name of God" is, I believe, the worst sin of all.

Here it is important to take seriously the recent campaign against religion waged by liberal critics like Hitchens, Dawkins, and Dennett. Much of their indignation is aimed at the deleterious delusions of theism, and these have been many. The litanies of deception and domination carried out in the cause of religion are legion. And I agree with Dawkins that the idea of

God as a superterrestrial "superintendent" of the universe, who controls and determines our actions, needs summary debunking. It is essential to say "no" to these aberrations of religion. But it is not enough. If one never gets beyond accusing the accusers and negating the negators, one remains at the level of nay-saying. Ricoeur noted how Nietzsche became ensnared in the very spirit of nihilism he sought to expose, how he fell victim to the resentment he resolved to combat—and neglected the yea-saying. And Max Scheler makes a similar point about the militant apostate who becomes contaminated by the very ills he endeavors to repudiate. "He is motivated by the struggle against the old belief and lives only for its negation. . . . He does not affirm his new convictions for their own sake" but is "engaged in a continuous chain of acts of revenge against his own spiritual past."[1] Scheler goes on to argue that "a secret *ressentiment* underlies every way of think-ing which attributes creative power to mere *negation* and *criticism*."[2] For whenever convictions are arrived at, not by direct contact with the objects themselves but indirectly "through a critique of the opinions of others, the processes of thinking are impregnated with *ressentiment*."[3]

II

This point is worth bearing in mind when considering recent writings by the so-called anti-God squad. Dawkins, Dennett, and Hitchens spend much of their time denouncing the diseases of believers without acknowledging the complexity of belief. They invoke the certainties of science against the falsities of faith, not appreciating that genuine faith has never expressed it-self with certainty, but always through a cloud of unknowing. The wise per-son, as Socrates taught, is one who seeks truth precisely because he "knows he does not know"; a teaching that, we noted, finds its anatheist equivalent in the famous *docta ignorantia* of Nicholas of Cusa. But in addition to the practice of scientific negation, adopted by critics of religion, one sometimes finds the dubious use of bias to attack bias. The deployment of a biological term like *virus* to indiscriminately describe all theists is, I think, disingenu-ous, especially if you consider how this might sound if one replaced *theist* with *black* or *Jew* or *immigrant*. To dismiss roughly 90 percent of the world's population as disease carriers in the name of some indubitable empirical standpoint is to decline serious dialogue. Prejudicial language is no way to combat prejudice. Indeed the reduction of faith to the abuses of faith is, arguably, yet another form of abuse—a violence of interpretation that does a disservice to the generosity and rigor of science.[4]

It is curious to note how Daniel Dennett takes the very terms *host* and *guest*, so central to our anatheist account, to characterize the pathology of religion. He makes an analogy between religion and certain parasites that "cause their hosts to behave in unlikely—even suicidal—ways, all for the benefit of the guest, not the host."[5] To be more exact, Dennett compares the "Word of God" that "invades a human brain" to a "parisitic worm (a lancet fluke) invading an ant's brain." The parasitic invasion leads to absurd behavior: the ant climbs up and down blades of grass, just as the believer climbs up and down sacred mountains—for no reason.[6] Thus where anatheism sees the sacred as a life-giving guest to be received by a host, Dennett sees it as a death-dealing invader.

All a matter of interpretation of course. But which is the more violent? We are dealing with hermeneutic wagers in both cases—anatheist or antitheist. And such a hermeneutic conflict surely merits civilized debate. Not denunciation. Scientific reason and religious faith may be separate language games, as Wittgenstein says, but that does not mean they cannot afford each other a respectful hearing or aim at some "reasonable" common ground. Are not advocates of both science and faith, for example, capable of translating between their guest and host languages so as to agree that whatever leads to tolerance, justice, and love in this world is commendable?[7] Do they not share this noble aim?

For antitheists to view Scripture as a single seamless "book," which pretends to explain the world in the manner of a scientific treatise, is to miss the point. The Bible, like most spiritual texts, is an assembly of fables, histories, chronicles, polemics, letters, and moral teachings as well as some inevitably primitive prejudices and errors. This is what hermeneutics realizes from the outset. For, we repeat, if the Word was in the beginning, so was hermeneutics. There is no word that is not interpreted. Something well known by the Talmudists who taught that there are ten meanings to every line of the Torah—a view shared by other gifted hermeneuts like Ibn Rushd and Augustine. So when militant atheists like Hitchens accuse believers of "picking and choosing," they are actually accusing them of being *responsible* believers. That is what faith is about: making a choice, venturing a wager, discriminating between rival interpretations in order to make the best decision regarding love and hate, justice and injustice. Anatheist faith, to borrow from Ignatius, is about "discerning between spirits" of hospitality and hostility. And this is why we have been arguing throughout that anatheism adheres to a second belief *after* first belief. (Dawkins has a point when he says there is no such thing as a Christian child, only Christian parents.) It is when our inherited conditionings have been shed in favor of genuine not-knowing that we can return to faith anew (*ana*). For faith means knowing you don't know anything absolutely about absolutes. That is why we have to read sacred Scriptures as carefully as we greet strangers who come to us out of the night. So we may discern wisely. And, where possible, such discernment solicits, philosophically, what Charles Taylor calls "the best account available"—an endless exercise in practical reason.

Anatheism welcomes robust critiques of religion wherever religion makes the "category mistake" of trying to explain the world scientifically (e.g., creationism). There is a difference between history and story, and to read sacred texts as if they were records of verifiable or falsifiable "facts" is to misread them. Abraham's followers told stories—as Thomas Mann brilliantly illustrated in *Joseph and His Brothers*—and these holy narratives were never meant to be treated as literal, scientific accounts. Theistic fundamentalists are as guilty of this error as atheistic fundamentalists. For both refuse the hermeneutic complexity of truth claims. But to say that holy Scriptures are made up of stories is not to say they are just made up! That is what antitheists hold when they denounce religion for its fabrication of facts. Stories, as Aristotle stated in the *Poetics*, can often reveal more essential and profound truths than histories that chronicle a mere sequence of events. And one should not forget that certain so-called histories have in fact produced some of the worst ideological distortions: Stalin and Hitler both considered themselves great historians.

In sum, to bundle all spiritual beliefs into the single bag of fanaticism is itself fanatical. It is as unfair as claiming that all science is dangerous because of nuclear armaments or that all psychiatry is bad because mentally ill people were once given bromides. The misuse of something is not a sound basis for judging right use. This is why militant antitheists would do well to recall that, in addition to right-wing fundamentalists, dogmatic creationists, sectarian puritans, or reactionary moralists, believers also include millions of decent people—as well as nuanced philosophers like Ricoeur, Bonhoeffer, and Levinas—thinkers for whom the symbolic and linguistic character of holy Scripture was never in doubt. In their zealous faith in an absolute ideology of science, antitheists sometimes mirror those with an equally zealous faith in the absolute ideology of religion. But genuine science makes no more claim to absolute knowledge than genuine faith. It takes one straw man to know another. Removing the straw helps us realize that science and faith are living processes that need not be opposed.

Anatheism tries to introduce reasonable hermeneutic considerations to the theist-atheist debate. Duly admitting the multiple horrors committed in the name of religion, anatheism does not stop there. It goes on to consider how religion, guided by authentic faith, hope, and love, is much more than the sum of its perversions. So, after the hermeneutic detour through atheistic critique, anatheism offers an opportunity to reinterpret religion. To this end, we might cite, in conclusion, a number of redefinitions of religion in the wake of dogmatic religion. We already noted, for example, Levinas's contemporary retrieval of the Jewish God, Soroush's of the Islamic God, and Bonhoeffer's of the Christian God. But we might also add here Christopher Lasch's recent description of post-Enlightenment religion as one that purifies our desires and frees us from idols, René Girard's postsacrificial God who refuses scapegoating in the name of *caritas*, or William James's definition of religion as "the feelings, acts and experiences of individual men in their solitude, so far as they apprehend themselves to stand in relation to whatever they may consider the divine."[8] And, in a more interreligious context, we might want to include here Gandhi's critical revision of Vedanta (beyond caste discrimination) or Vivekananda's related claim that every religion possesses three critically interrelating parts—mythology, ritual, and philosophy.[9] (Philosophy not being the least of these.)

I do not propose to synthesize or classify such diverse definitions, especially at this late stage of my argument. I simply mention these samples to indicate how a critical recovery of religion after religion has many resources to draw from. And I underline the word *recovery;* for this is not a matter of inventing something new but of rediscovering what was always already there *before* religious alienation and abuse. In this sense, the "religionless faith" of Ricoeur and Bonhoeffer is to be understood as a faith purged of the illusions of power, expiation, and escape. And, as such, it need not mean an abandonment of rituals, liturgies, or traditions. All of these, I would argue, can be reinterpreted in the anatheist return. Each brought back to life, for a second time. Transubstantiated, as it were, into something "strange and precious."

Arguably one of the most robust contributions to the contemporary debate on the role of religion and secularity is that made by Jürgen Habermas in his debates with the likes of Derrida and Ratzinger (Pope Benedict). Interestingly, for anatheist purposes, both Habermas and Derrida agree on the central importance of "hospitality" in our modern world. For Derrida it is the best alternative to the friend-foe distinction, given widespread currency by figures like Leo Strauss, Francis Fukayama, and Samuel Huntington and perilously enacted by political figures on both sides of the "axis of evil."[10] Faced with the Huntington thesis that "we only know who we are . . . when we know whom we are against," the ethic of hospitality replies that the stranger is precisely the one who reminds us—not as enemy but as host— that the self is never an autonomous identity but a guest graciously hostaged to its host.[11] Thus, at a practical level, the ethics of hospitality opposes the apocalyptic dualism of pure/impure invoked by Bush and Bin Laden after 9/11 and by several other God-crazed leaders since. Anatheist hospitality opposes such gnostic divides between friend and enemy, where God is always my ally and the Stranger my adversary.

For his part, Habermas cites an ethic of hospitality to overcome the state of nature on the basis of mutual respect.[12] While Derrida acknowledges the deeply "messianic" structure of hospitality as an affirmation of the "impossible," Habermas prefers to sublate and liquefy the religious roots of hospitality into a discourse ethics of rational norms and universalizable laws. He holds that religion, defined as a "comprehensive world-view which claims to structure a life in its entirety," must be translatable into the language of secular society where it can be adjudicated and negotiated. But Habermas does concede that political liberalism goes too far if it maintains that *only* secular reason counts in the public sphere. Religious identity, he admits, is something *other* than socio-normative existence.[13] "The liberal state," he clarifies, "must not transform the requisite *institutional* separation of religion and politics into an undue *mental* and *psychological* burden for those of its citizens who follow a faith" (9–10). And here Habermas introduces what he calls the "institutional translation proviso;" this allows religious believers, who accept that only "secular reasons count beyond the institutional threshold," to express their beliefs in a specifically confessional language if they find "secular translations for them" (9–10). Nontranslatable religious convictions (what Habermas terms private reasons) may thus be admitted to the public sphere for functional and discursive purposes. This admission aims to avoid an unbridgeable chasm between private (religious faith) and public (political reason) and is accompanied, I repeat, with the proviso that religious beliefs remain open to possibilities of further translation and assimilation. Once admitted, under the guise of confessional language, it remains the task of a democratic liberal society to encourage the "religious consciousness to become reflective and the secular consciousness to transcend its limitation in a mutual learning process" (18).[14]

Now, while this seems like a fair carve-up of responsibilities, I think it is really more a one-way street. Close reading shows that for Habermas the goal of such "mutual" learning is for religion to become more and more translatable into the rational normative pedagogy process—not for secular reason to "transcend its limitations." The pedagogy process is surely admirable, but it should, I submit, work in *both* directions at once. Secularity should be humble enough, in other words, to acknowledge the possibility of a certain untranslatable remainder, a *surplus* of meaning that surpasses the limits of normative rationality. For Habermas, it becomes clear, the ultimate goal of a democratic society is to integrate a plurality of faiths and cultures into an institutionalized discourse of deliberative decision making and generally accessible language (10). And here he explicitly cites Judeo-Christianity as a suitable candidate for such progressive pedagogy, since many of its religious legacies have already been translated into core principles of democratic enlightenment.

"For the normative self-understanding of modernity," writes Habermas, "Christianity has functioned as more than just a precursor or a catalyst. Universalistic egalitarianism, from which sprang ideals of freedom and a collective life in solidarity, the autonomous conduct of life and emancipation, the individual morality of conscience, human rights and democracy, is the direct legacy of the Judaic ethic of justice and the Christian ethic of love." This legacy, Habermas adds, "has been the object of a continual critical reappropriation and reinterpretation. Up to this very day there is no alternative to it. And, in light of current challenges of a postnational constellation, we must draw sustenance now, as in the past, from this substance. Everything else is idle postmodern talk."[15]

But the difficulty here (quite apart from the neglect of the Islamic legacy) is, I think, this: how do we react to the radically new and surprising?

How do we respect the stranger without trying to translate him or her into our terms? How do we respond to what we have been calling the anatheist wager (and to what Derrida and Benjamin call the messianic)? In short, it would seem that for Habermas the final aim of philosophical and political reason is, as Eduardo Mendieta puts it, to "completely assimilate, translate, rework and sublate all desirable religious content."[16] But how then can the divine remain a transcendent Other who comes to us? A visitor from outside our home (*unheimlich*), opening doors to novel events and inviting us to epiphanies "never dreamt of in the philosophies" of Horatio or Habermas? How, in a word, is secular reason to account for that aspect of alterity which—precisely as foreign and sacred—always remains partially unassimilable and inaccessible to our normative or normalizing grasp? Can Others only become our guests as *Gästarbeiter* tolerated in so far as they surrender their uniqueness? It is not sure that Habermas's public sphere can really welcome strange gods. He does not seem, in my view, to have a host language to respond to what Benjamin calls the "untranslatable kernel" at the heart of every guest language, namely, that inimitable transcendence which puts us into question, shatters our self-security, and opens us to the incoming Other.[17]

I think another difficulty with Habermas's telos of "universal rational translatability" is that of responding to religions other than the European tradition of Judeo-Christian humanism. What of the religions of the East or, closer to home, the religion of Islam both inside and outside the borders of the Western "postnational constellation"? Are only those believers to be accepted whose translation from faith into reason has "already occurred in the pre-parliamentarian domain, i.e., in the political public sphere itself"?[18] On this score, I think that Lovisa Bergdahl is right to say that Habermas has a limited and somewhat Eurocentric notion of religious pluralism, one that prefers familiar religious strangers to unfamiliar ones. The real task of translation, as Benjamin and Bergdahl note, is to acknowledge the *double* call of the stranger: translate me/do not translate me! For the challenge is to respect "the unfathomable, the mysterious and the poetic" surplus of meanings while making as much sense as we can.[19] In short, the biggest temptation for the translator—in politics no less than in poetics—is to conserve the state presiding in one's host language without allowing it be transformed by the foreignness of the guest tongue.[20] To yield to such temptation is to close the door on the alien. It is to decline interlinguistic and interconfessional hospitality.

IV

If religion is to mean anything in the third millennium, it should, I suggest, mean more than a set of common norms. Such norms are necessary but not sufficient. In searching for a shared "essence" or "universal structure" of religion, it would be folly to neglect what is most strange and different in each faith. Interconfessional hospitality means respecting the otherness of each other as much as acknowledging something common to all. For, without the former, there would be no guest to be invited and no host to receive. In other words, it is not enough to distill the overlapping moral elements of the great religions into one syncretist brew. It is also crucial to acknowledge the very distinct paths that each wisdom tradition takes to reach that shared ethical vision. Without this appreciation of deep confessional and cultural *diversity* there can be no real sense of hospitality at work between religions. For, I repeat, without the recognition of alterity there can be no experience of the stranger and so no opening to what is not ourselves.

But, I hasten to add, alterity is not always on the side of the angels. If religious difference bears the potential for welcoming aliens, it also bears the opposite potential to enclose, exclude, and expel. The double plot of hospitality and hostility does not dissolve as one reaches the roots of diversity; it thickens.

Let me try to put this in another way: if all religions are reduced to the same, there is no way of recognizing the equiprimordial potential for both love and hate inherent in each religion. That is why every religion needs to carry on a radical autocritique of its own violent tendencies if it is to rescue what is genuinely tolerant and emancipatory at its core. In short, any faith must be prepared to purge itself of the inherent temptation to violently impose its own version of the Absolute on others. For only then is it capable of acknowledging the multiple receptions of the Word in faiths not its own. As Anthony Steinbock puts it, obedience to a Word that surpasses human language is the source of both "vertical" *and* "idolatrous" interpretations.[21] Hence the deep ambivalence of such religious terms as *surrender, submission,* and *sacrifice.* There is always a hermeneutic wager. And if one opts to follow the path of hospitality, of listening to others, one must be open to the possibility of discovering in the other faith something that is not—or not yet adequately—discovered in one's own. Believers in the Bible, for example, may well discover in Buddhism a sense of unconditional compassion for "all sentient beings" still dormant or undeveloped in the Abrahamic religions.

Just as Buddhists may discover in biblical religion a greater attention to the realization of a kingdom of justice in history or to the emancipatory power of divine desire.[22]

One might also mention here how Hindu sages like Vivekananda, Tagore, and Ramakrishna confessed that their understanding of Vedantic religion was amplified by their exposure to Abrahamic faiths and practices. (We noted this liberating reinterpretation of Hindu sources in the Gandhi section of chapter 7.) And such gestures of interconfessional exchange between East and West were reciprocated, in turn, by pioneering figures like Abhishiktananda, Bede Griffiths, and Sarah Grant who believed their Christian convictions were greatly deepened (and at times critically revised) by exposure to the Hindu tradition of Advaita.[23]

V

The distillation of all religions into a set of common denominators has its purpose. An impressive example of this is the project of the Parliament of World Religions, convened in 1992, to develop a global ethic of peace, based on the Golden Rule that we should treat all others as ourselves. The project echoed similar attempts to establish principles of interfaith dialogue such as the Snowmass Conference of 1986 and the Scorboro Interfaith movement of the 1990s. These mark crucial steps in the reconciliation of competing and often warring religions in our world. Granted. But anatheism suggests, once again, that there is something else, another step to be taken that supplements the move toward universal principles. And this second step involves a radical descent into the specificities of each spiritual tradition—a descent into difference (in addition to the ascent toward oneness), which seeks, at the root of each religion, a silent, speechless openness to a Word that surpasses us. The anatheist wager is, therefore, that, in the deep belonging to a unique faith conviction, there may arise the humility to counter the violence of exclusivity with a generosity of attention. For if it is true that all religions involve a special acoustic of obedience to a Word beyond our finite language, this may lead to a modest ability to listen to Otherness as much as to a claim that our religion alone has an absolute take on the absolute. Anatheistically understood, verticality leads to latitude.

. . .

Once again, I do not, even in these concluding moves, wish to deny that most religions have, at one time or another, invoked creedal partisanship to prove their superiority over others. *In hic signo. We have God on our side. There is no God in all the earth apart from ours.* These are not catchcries of the past. One need only mention the ongoing struggles between Hindus and Muslims in Kashmir, between Buddhist Singhalese and Hindu Tamils in Sri Lanka, between Muslims and Jews in Jerusalem, between Christians and Muslims in Kosovo—not to mention countless examples of intrareligious wars in places like Northern Ireland, Iraq, and North Africa. These are sorry truths, and there is no point pretending that our secular post-Enlightenment world has exorcised such atavisms. There is, it would seem, a tendency in the "inaugural energy" of almost every religion (with possible exceptions like Buddhism and Jainism) toward some form of exclusivism, exceptionalism, or absolutism.[24] It is one side of the Janus face of religion. But there is, I am arguing, another side: the ability of each confession to delve into its own hidden foundation and discover there, in a moment of bold autocritique, a countervailing drive toward hospitality and healing.

That such hospitality emerges from each religion's unique depths, rather than from a surpassing of these depths, may seem paradoxical. It marks a retrieval of what is best against the very worst that belief can offer: difference cuts both ways. And this is what I might call an anatheist recovery of a religion *before* religion—a recovery stemming from a foundation without secure foundation, namely, a foundation founded on something *other* than itself. It is this mystical *fond sans fond*, I suggest, that ultimately invites our wager that the foreigner has more to offer us than we can ever find in ourselves alone. In this sense anatheism comes before as well as after religion.

VI

And so we return, finally, to the hermeneutic maxim that the shortest route from self to self is through the other. Just as in linguistic translation we discover something in the "guest" language that has never been said in our "host" tongue, so too in confessional translation we may find in another faith something undreamed of in our own. Though, as we have just seen, we have to dwell deeply in our own faith to be able to recognize such disclosure as *new*, as basically *other* than our own. The discovery of the wisdom of the stranger presupposes that the self knows itself as different from the stranger.

Thus certain messages in one's own faith—say, in the case of a Christian, the wise detachment preached in the Sermon on the Mount—may find confirmation of this otherwise "impossible" message in the teaching of a very different tradition, e.g., the Buddhist notions of compassion, detachment, and *sunyata* (the emptying of self). In fact, to pursue this example further, I would say that the biblical message of *kenosis* and the kabbalistic notion of *zimzum* may actually *need* exposure to foreign teachings like the Heart Sutra ("Emptiness is form and form is emptiness") in order to better understand themselves.

Anatheism suggests that religions can best recover their own unique secrets through reciprocal exposure to others. (Just think again of the illuminating readings of the Gospels by Thich Nhat Hanh or of Eastern texts by Thomas Merton.) Reciprocity is the key here. In faith as in love: you discover your true self in the self revealed to you by the beloved. Self-discovery presupposes the discovery of one's other (and vice versa). This other may be a million miles away or in our very midst: a paradox Camus poignantly captures when he writes of those moments when "under the familiar face of a woman, we see as a stranger her we had loved months or years ago, and perhaps come even to desire what suddenly leaves us so alone."[25]

This is where anatheism returns to the appreciation of not just others' theism but of atheism *tout court*. For, in the otherness of the atheist who knows she does not know (unlike the antitheist who knows everything), we encounter an estranging and dispossessive challenge which 1. compels autocritique, and 2. reveals our innermost convictions in a movement of response and recovery. So, rather than too rapidly renouncing our respective convictions—in the name of one global religion or morality—might it not be wise to acknowledge what differentiates us? For in thus recognizing the existence of otherness in each other we may mutually attest to a *surplus of meaning* that exceeds all our different beliefs. A surplus that is Other than every other. More strange than every stranger. This something "more" is what enables humans to do the impossible, to break with conditioned patterns of thinking and behavior. (Any Alcoholics Anonymous member will attest to this.) This discovery of something "different," "ulterior," "more," is stronger, I suggest, when it is made from *inside* each conviction than when imposed from *outside* by some abstract God's-eye view. In short, anatheism proposes the challenging route of embracing complexity, diversity, and ambiguity rather than prematurely endorsing a spiritual Esperanto of global norms. For anatheism the universal can only be reached through singular others—that is, others that are other to each other.

If this is so, it means that the answer to religious conflict requires more than a sociology of comparative religions based on some common "essence." One also needs to take the internal journey to the silent, unspoken root of each religion. For we might then be in a better position to practice a hospitality of translation between different root convictions deeper than a set of universal principles, though in no way counter to it. The road to an ultimate reality preceding and exceeding our belief systems passes through each of these beliefs.

To return, then, to the anatheist wager, we might say that when we translate—interconfessionally—we export ourselves into strangers and import strangers into ourselves. And, in daring to translate across borders, we encounter the limits of translatability. This invariably implies risk, as aptly expressed in Antoine Berman's phrase *l'épreuve de l'étranger*. The process of interreligious hospitality I have been tracing, summons us on a pilgrimage to the secret inaugural moments of different religions rather than to some supertheological summit adjudicating rival claims from On High. For it is in the depths, as Paul Ricoeur insists, that we "touch on something unsaid . . . a mystical ground (*un fond mystique*) of what is most fundamental in each religion and which is not easily translatable into language but rather borders on a common profound silence."[26] In other words, the best way to tackle the violent tendency within religious conviction is to go all the way down to the source that religion does not master and that refuses to be rendered into dogmatic formulae or ideological manifestos. Each religion will have its own unique access to this ineffable genesis point: the work of illumination for the Buddhist, the Prayer of Thanksgiving for the Christian, the learned meditation on scriptural texts for the Muslim or Jew, the practice of yoga for the Hindu. In each case the specific way acknowledges a source it does not initiate or control but heeds with modest vigilance. And it is in this hearkening to a source beyond and beneath oneself, a superfluity one does not possess or manipulate, that we may find new resources for nonviolent resistance and peace.

The most effective antidote to fundamentalist perversions, therefore, may well be to attend to the "deep ground" that no religion can ever fully appropriate. Every religion is capable of taking this action against itself, brushing against its own dogmatic grain, purging itself of its pathologies so as to reach the silent source that not only surpasses but disarms it.[27] This implies a conversion of the heart whereby each religion finds at the ineffable quick of its belief the means to reverse the violent impulses that inform religious claims to master absolute truth. It involves an anatheist moment of critical and therapeutic self-retrieval (what Ricoeur calls "un mouvement de retournement contre la composante de violence d'une conviction").[28] Precisely here we discover a complementary partnership between an inner move to ineffable mystery and an outer move to enlightened awareness. And it is at this anatheist chiasmus, I would argue, that theism and atheism can become, once again, allies.[29]

The autocritique of religious power is, I believe, doubly assisted in this way—from both within and without. And this bilateral gesture is crucial for the critical self-surpassing of religion. In encountering strange Gods we are invited to discover hidden aspects of our own God (often congealed in convention); while the recovery of such hidden origins opens us further to strange Gods. But this two-way encounter does not imply sublation into some all-embracing totality. We are reminded here again of the necessary limits of integration. For at the edge of every liaison between self and stranger there remains that "untranslatable kernel," that irreducible enigma that resists complete assimilation into a home whose doors could be definitively closed. This fundamental alterity is what makes reconciling religions at once necessary and inadequate. There is always something *more* to be said and understood, some inexhaustible residue never to be known. And it is this "more"—which many religions call God—that allows the stranger to remain (in part at least) always strange to us. This is why every authentic religious experience is a *re-legere*, a return again and again from surplus to signification to surplus. An ongoing odyssey of reading that makes translation endless.[30]

All great ethical teachings share a set of precepts—do not kill, tell the truth, be just, look after the weak. What religions, anatheistically retrieved, can add to such shared principles, as inscribed in world charters of human justice, is a deep mystical appreciation of something Other than our finite, human being: some Other we can welcome as a stranger if we can overcome our natural response of fear and trauma. For beyond the indispensable provisions of juridical, ethical, and political peace, there are profound spiritual resources that can bring an extra element to the peace table—the surprise of the stranger, the gracious surplus of faith, hope, and caritas.[31]

VII

So let me try to sum up. If peace is ever achieved on our planet, it will not, I suspect, be brokered solely by global politicians and constitutional lawyers. It will also be a peace brought about by what Karl Jaspers called a "loving combat" (*liebender Kampf*) between different faiths and nonfaiths. Anatheism is not about a facile consensus that ignores the reality of conflicting convictions. It is an effort to retrieve a unique hospitality toward the Stranger at the inaugural scene of each belief. In thus exposing ourselves to the Gods of other traditions we take the risk of dying unto our own. And in such instants of kenotic hospitality, where we exchange our God with others—sometimes not-knowing for a moment which one is true—we open ourselves to the gracious possibility of receiving our own God back again; but this time as a gift from the other, as a God of life beyond death. In losing our faith, we may gain it back again: first faith ceding to second faith in the name of the stranger. That is the wager of anatheism. And the risk. For in surrendering our own God to a stranger God no God may come back again. Or the God who comes back may come back in ways that surprise us.

EPILOGUE

The glory of God is each and every one of us fully alive.

—Irenaeus, AD 185

Some last thoughts *dans l'esprit de l'escalier*—afterthoughts descending the stairwell as one remembers things unsaid.

The first of these is the question of humanism. Why, one might ask, does the stranger have to be a divine other? Why can't it just be human? Or natural? Why is anatheism any more than being nice to your neighbor—something atheists surely do as well as theists or anatheists? What's God got to do with it?

This is a common point that comes up in discussions with atheist colleagues and friends. And it is a fair one. My respectful response is that recognizing something "more" in the stranger than the human is a way of acknowledging a dimension of transcendence in the other that—in part, at least—exceeds the finite presence of the person before me. But I am talking here of a transcendence in and through immanence, which, far from diminishing humanity, amplifies it. If the divine stranger does not enhance one's humanity, inviting it to better things, that is, to a more just, loving, and creative manner of being, then it is not worthy of the name *divine*. The bottom line is: does the Other in the other bring more abundant life or not? Does it invite us to have more hope, charity—and wonder—than we might have if we did not respond to something higher and deeper in the other person than what meets the eye? Something that summons us to greater heights and depths than are available at a purely humanist or naturalist level? This is what I refer to as the call of the "stranger" in the other, and it is a dimension of alterity that invites belief in the *impossible made possible:* namely, the imagination to credit the incredible, the courage to welcome the unprecedented and surprising. Hence my particular choice of scenes of primary natality (Sarah and Mary saying yes to the advent of an "impossible" child) and second natality (Jacob, Jesus, and the Prophet saying yes to the call for new life). But events of the impossible made possible are by no means confined to sacred Scriptures. They can occur at all kinds of everyday levels. Think, for example, of addicts and alcoholics who give up their addictions by acknowledging that they cannot do it "on their own." For many in addiction support groups, healing only comes when one admits one's addictions are "uncontrollable," beyond human willpower, and can only be overcome by surrendering to a "higher power" (however understood). This "higher power," beyond one's human capacities, is another name for transcendence. And I think it is for this reason that Thomas Merton described Alcoholics Anonymous as one of the most important spiritual movements of the twentieth century.

In terms of social and ethical practice, I have tried to show something similar at work in the lives of people like Vanier, Day, and Gandhi, visionaries whose fidelity to something sacred—something graciously greater than themselves—gave them the audacity to transform injustice into justice and the passion to serve others in need. It is this radical and recurring sense of something *more*—something ulterior, extra, and unexpected—that various religions call God.

This book is not interested in the scientific hypothesis of God's existence. Following in the wake of my earlier book, *The God Who May Be,* it does not aim to prove the metaphysical status of a supernatural Being residing in some celestial heaven and superintending the world. Anatheism goes beyond such metaphysical (or pseudoscientific) claims and focuses instead on the meaning of the sacred—after one has abandoned illusions of the Alpha-God—for one's ethical and poetical existence. The wager on the stranger—as infinite Other incarnate in finite others—is a wager based not on a logic of calculation or probability (Pascal) but on a phenomenological testimony of goodness.

Antitheists like Dawkins and Hitchens make the claim that God is not good and that the world would be a better place without faith. If they are right, then we should dispense with the God question for once and all. But what I have been arguing in this book is that the anatheist wager leaves open the option of a second faith that promises the opposite: to increase the good.

How? By choosing "the lowly and despised of the world, those who count for nothing" (1 Cor. 1:28), by choosing to give a cup of cold water to the stranger because the stranger is "more" than me, because the other is other than all I can know, grasp, control, and possess, because the alien signals a dimension of transcendence and ultimacy that surpasses the limits of humanism and naturalism and liberates a space of gratuity and grace. Another space and another time: a time that is usually described, in the Abrahamic traditions, in any case, as an *advent*. A moment that comes *to* us rather than *from* us. For even though the anatheist wager takes the form of a retrieval of second faith, it does so from out of the future, by giving a future to the past, by surprising us in each messianic instant. It is in this sense that I speak of anatheist time as a time of micro-eschatology. A time of epiphanies when the stranger breaks through the continuum of history.

Does this mean that anatheism is against atheism? No, it only means that it discerns between two different kinds of atheism and two different kinds of theism. I make a distinction here, in other words, between anatheist atheism and antitheist atheism, on the one hand, and between anatheist theism and dogmatic theism, on the other. In this sense, *anatheism* might be said to serve more often as an adjective (or adverb) than a noun. For it marks that middle space where theism dialogues freely with atheism. This third space is not, I hasten to add, a static position that risks dogmatism in turn. It is a wagering between belief and nonbelief that never comes to a full stop. (Even Christ, as I repeatedly note, wagered between abandonment and consent in his final moment on the Cross). Far from signaling a lukewarm zone of noncommitment, the anatheist wager is at all times dynamic and attentive, moving intrepidly between engagement and critique, recovery and loss, sadness and joy. Instead of *never* making up its mind, it is *always* making up its mind. The anatheist moment attests to humanity fully alive because acutely aware of the complexity of ultimate things. And it is important to recall that such anatheist moments are not confined to the inaugural scenes of great religions but occur, potentially, in any instant of our everyday lives.

If some atheists wonder what they might get from anatheism, I suggest they might at least find possibilities of retrieving a rich grammar, vocabulary, and imaginary of radical hospitality from traditions not readily available in an exclusively secular discourse. Not to mention the benefit of keeping one's mind open.

Anatheism is more than a question of faith. In addition to belief (with, for some, its voluntarist connotations of choice), anatheism is a matter of hope, love, and wonder. Hope that the stranger is more than we expect. Love of the stranger as infinitely other. And wonder at the very strangeness of it all. Indeed, it is perhaps fitting to end with wonder. For this is the shared founding experience of the spiritual, the philosophical, and the poetic — the spiritual epiphany of welcoming, the philosophical *thaumazein* of questioning, the poetic shudder of imagining. This book has sought to draw from all three, while never forgetting a fourth experience of wonder: namely, the ethical act of transfiguring our world by caring for the stranger as we watch the world become sacred.

NOTES

INTRODUCTION

1. See Nicholas Berdyaev, *Dostoyevsky: An Interpretation*, trans. Donald Attwater (London: Sheed and Ward, 1934), 78–79: "The Faith which Dostoyevsky wished to see established was a free faith, buttressed by liberty of conscience; his own had 'burst forth from a huge furnace of doubt' and he wanted all faith to be tried in the same fire. The Christian world has not known a more passionate defender of liberty of conscience. 'The freedom of their faith was dearer to thee than anything,' says the Grand Inquisitor to Christ, and the words were as applicable to Dostoyevsky himself: 'Thou didst desire man's free love. . . . Man must feely decide for himself . . . having only thine image before him as a guide instead of the rigid law of old'—it is Dostoyevsky's own profession of faith. . . . When the Son of God came into the world 'in the form of a servant' and was tortured by the world on the cross he appealed to the free human spirit. He used no coercion to make us believe in him as in God, he had not the might and majesty of the sovereigns of this world. . . . Therein lies the secret of Jesus Christ, the secret of freedom." Dostoyevsky may also be described as deeply anatheistic in his recognition that, while humans may dwell in the divine and the divine may dwell in the human, they are nontheless not identical. As Berdyaev puts it: "For Dostoyevsky there was both God and Man: the God who does not devour man and the man who is not dissolved in God but remains himself throughout all eternity" (ibid., 64–65). In other words, the human self and divine stranger may indwell in one another but are never the same. The gap—what Gregory of Nyssa calls the *diastema*—between the finite and the infinite is never totally dissolvable: for if it were, divine desire and love of the Other would dissolve also.
2. See Richard Kearney, ed., *Interreligious Imagination*, special issue of *Religion and the Arts* 12, nos. 1–3 (Leiden: Brill, 2008), and "Heart Mysteries," *Japan Mission Journal* 61, no 1 (2007).
3. Michel de Certeau, "Mysticism," *Diacritics* 22, no. 2 (Summer 1992): 24.

4. Jacques Derrida, "Violence and Metaphysics" in *Writing and Difference* (London: Routledge, 1978), 152–153.

5. Ibid., 153; and Emmanuel Levinas, *Totality and Infinity*, trans. Alphonso Lingis (Pittsburgh: Duquesne University Press, 1969), 24.

6. My thanks to my friend and colleague, Paul Freaney, for several of these references.

7. Charles Taylor, *A Secular Age* (Cambridge: Harvard University Press, 2007), 755–765.

8. See our comparison between Gerard Manley Hopkins's poetic witness to the "dark night" and the mystical witness of saints like Teresa of Avila and St. John of the Cross in Richard Kearney, "The Shulammite's Song: Divine Eros, Ascending and Descending," in *Toward a Theology of Eros* (New York: Fordham University Press, 2006), 330f. I think that Keats is referring to a somewhat isomorphic experience — at the level of a mystical poetics — when he speaks of "negative capability" in a letter to his brothers George and Thomas Keats, December, 21, 27, 1817, in the *Norton Anthology of English Literature*, 5th ed. (New York: Norton, 1986), 863. And perhaps Gaston Bachelard is responding to something similar when he writes of a certain kind of poetry responding to a "nascent logos" in the realm of the everyday: "Poetry . . . can only correspond to attentive thought that is enamored of something unknown, and receptive to becoming" (alluding to Pierre Jean-Jouve). See Gaston Bachelard, *The Poetics of Space*, trans. Maria Jolas (Boston: Beacon, 1969), xxvii.

9. See my Epiphanies of the Everyday: Towards a Micro-Eschatology" in John Manoussakis, ed., *After God: Richard Kearney and the Religious Turn in Continental Philosophy* (New York: Fordham University Press, 2006), 3–20. See also Philip Ballinger, *The Poem as Sacrament: The Theological Aesthetics of Gerard Manley Hopkins* (Louvain: Peters, 2000). The poet Patrick Kavanagh describes a similar movement of reaffirmation of the sacred after affliction and abandonment in his poem "The Hospital." Recovering from a near-death experience in a hospital ward in Dublin, he looks out his window at sundry things in the yard below and declares, anatheistically, "naming these things is the love act and its pledge / To snatch out of time the passionate transitory." Rilke has Orpheus testify to another variation on this anatheist recovery when, having reemerged from the dark cave of the underworld, he declares, "To be here is such splendor" (*Sonnets to Orpheus*).

10. Martin Heidegger, "On the Way to Language," cited in Richard Kearney, *Modern Movements in European Philosophy* (Manchester: Manchester University Press, 1987), 41.

11. Ibid., 41–42.

12. See Simon Critchley, "We Can't Believe/We Must Believe," paper presented at the Religion and Politics Conference, Trinity Western University, British Columbia, Canada, March 13–14, 2008.

13. Ibid.

14. Ibid.: "In his compassion for the downtrodden and the poor, but equally in his pity for the hard, empty hedonism of the rich, Christ is the incarnation of love as an act of imagination, not reason, an imaginative projection of compassion onto all creatures. What Christ teaches is love and Wilde writes, 'When you really want love you will find it waiting for you.' The decision to open oneself to love enables

an experience of grace over which one has no power and which one cannot decide."

15. Quoted by Arthur Kirsch in *Auden and Christianity* (New Haven: Yale University Press, 2005), 8. Auden also has this to say about the Christian sacrament of confirmation as a responsibility of second faith: "Confirmation should be postponed until the individual has reached the age of spiritual consent . . . Child confirmation is as absurd as child marriage"(ibid.). Auden was repelled by the gnostic dualism that opposed spirit and flesh, arguing instead for the "binocular vision" of mature faith. In his poem "New Year Letter," he writes of "the gift of double focus / That magic lamp" that "can be a sesame to light" and a remedy against the Devil, "the great schismatic who / First split creation into two" and "who controls / The moral asymmetric souls / The either-ors, the mongrel halves" (ibid., 33). Against all forms of metaphysical or anthropological dualism, Auden prayed that "the shining / Light be comprehended by the darkness" (ibid., 38). Manichaean dualism is, for Auden, a result of the Fall and finds its answering remedy in Christian love. As he famously wrote in September 1, 1939, on the eve of war: "We must love one another or die." I am grateful to my colleague, Kascha Semonovitch, for bringing this text to my attention.

16. Paul Ricoeur, *The Rule of Metaphor*, study 8 (Toronto: University of Toronto Press, 1977), 257f.

17. See further discussions of the problems and limits of translatability in chapter 2 and the conclusion. See also the illuminating analysis by Lovisa Bergdahl, "Lost in Translation: On the Untranslatable and Its Ethical Implications for Religious Pluralism," paper delivered at the Society for Continental Philosophy and Theology Conference at Gordon College, Massachusetts, April 12–13, 2008. This contrasts with Samuel Huntington's notion that the stranger-as-enemy is essential for communal self-identity. See Donatien Cicura, "Identity and Historicity: Hermeneutics of Contemporary African Marginality,"69–75, Ph.D. diss., Boston College, 2008. This analysis may be usefully compared with René Girard's notion of stranger as scapegoat. See "Myth and Sacrificial Scapegoats," in Richard Kearney, *Poetics of Modernity* (Atlantic Heights, NJ.: Humanities, 1995), 136f.

I. IN THE MOMENT

1. G. W. Hegel, "The Spirit of Christianity and Its Fate," in *Early Theological Writings*, trans. T. M. Knox (Pennsylvania: University of Pennsylvania Press, 1975), 209–216.

2. Emmanuel Levinas, *Totality and Infinity*, trans. Alphonso Lingis (Pittsburgh: Duquesne University Press, 2004, 1961), 234; see also my analysis of the face of the other in "Towards a Phenomenology of the Persona," in Richard Kearney, *The God Who May Be* (Bloomington: Indiana University Press, 2001), 9–20.

3. See Jonathan Sachs, *The Dignity of Difference: How to Avoid the Clash of Civilisations* (London: Continuum, 2003). I am grateful to my brother, Tim Kearney, for bringing this text to my attention.

4. Hillel, Talmud, Shabbat 31a. I am grateful to my Boston College assistant, Sarit Larry, for research on these etymologies and bringing several of these passages to my attention.

5. *Eterachthe* is the verb used for Zechariah's reaction to Gabriel in Luke 1:12. This

is the same verb as the one used in Mary's similar reaction in Luke 1:29 (with the addition of the preposition *dia* to indicate "thoroughly," thus *diatarachthe*). The word for "fear" in the same verse is the standard Greek *phobos* (which gives our *phobia*). The passage from Judges 13:6, concerning the annunciation of Samson's birth, is a more complicated story. In the critical edition of the Septuagint—the translation of the original Hebrew into Greek in the second century BC, which the early Christian Church accepted as the official translation—the text is rendered in two alternative versions (apparently because there are some major variants and both versions are supported by major manuscripts). So the A version (referred to by Origen and some other ancient authors) speaks of "the vision of an angel of God" as *epiphanes sphodra*, while the B version (supported by the Codex Vaticanus) has "and his appearance was an appearance of an angel of God," *phoberon sphodra* meaning very terrible or fearful. This ambiguous rendering of the vision as either wondrous epiphany or phobic trauma—or *both*—is very telling for our hermeneutic of the biblical stranger. This ambiguity is powerfully and ironically captured in the poem, "Mary" by Kascha Semonovitch (*Crab Creek Review* [Spring 2009]):

MARY

Let's call her Mary. Let's start when

He rings the door. Everything rings. She hears a flutter
Of wings. His coat hits the floor. The face of God raped Mary
From the door. She had no choice. So she said. No, she said
He was God, and so he was kind. He said, Imagine

How it will be when you are with me. A borrowed story;

He'd overheard it. And heard it working. He brought her lilies,
Stuffed them under her nose. The flesh of her nose sucked a flap
Of skin of the flower in. Stuck. "Aren't they good ?" The angel asked.
The most inimitable gasp.

He was beautiful. Mary was full of fear but oh he was
Beautiful. Smoke curling through his likewise curled hair and his fin-
gers
Round the glass of gin—she'd never—at noon. She thought of
Her betrothed. Who was not here. Who didn't smell so good. He had

Mules. Who doesn't? Angels. People who brings flowers. Who'd touch

A girl like that mid-day. Mary chose grace over fear. Not to call it—but
Joy. Not to call it him but God. Strange. Not to call him
Known but not. Today, she would have read the safety information on
the package,
And taken a full dose. But so it goes.

"Jacob was left alone and a man wrestled
with him." This she'd read. And that was God. So perhaps,
it was always so? She's half thinking now, only half, the white wine lily
door open drapes
refolding gasp through me down the day is cool

And later she shuts the porch against the rain.

6. Michel de Certeau, "The Founding Rupture," cited in Nathalie Zemon Davis, "The Quest of Michel de Certeau," *New York Review of Books* 55, no 8 (2008): 58. Interestingly de Certeau sees the great Christian saints and mystics as visionaries of the epiphany of the Other, in both love and service. He sees Teresa of Avila, for example, as a "wanderer, creating convents across Spain for lovers of God; immersed in daily affairs, she can pass in an instant to ecstatic connection with the beloved Other" (ibid., 60). On the mystical rapport between the human and divine stranger, see Michel de Certeau, *The Mystic Fable*, trans. Michael B. Smith (Chicago: University of Chicago Press, 1992), and *Heterologies: Discourse on the Other*, trans. Brian Massumi (St. Paul: University of Minnesota Press, 1986). See also Michel de Certeau, "Mysticism," *Diacritics* 22, no. 2 (Summer 1992): "For the mystic to "prepare a place" for the Otheris to prepare a place for others. . . . The mystic is only one among many others . . . joining with others and the Other" (ibid., 20).

7. I am grateful to my friend and colleague John Manoussakis for these references to the Greek Orthodox liturgy and also to Luke's Gospel.

8. See commentaries on this passage in Mattew 25 by Gustavo Gutiérrez, *A Theology of Liberation* (New York: Orbis, 1988), 112–116; and by Karl Rahner, "The Unity Between the God of Love and Concrete Love of Neighbour" in *Foundations of Christian Faith* (New York: Crossroad, 2007). See also the commentary of Rahner's account by Thomas O'Meara OP, *God in the World* (Minnesota: Liturgical, 2007). Rahner says of this unity: "The other, which mediates the person to itself, ever more clearly emerges as the personal other whom the person in knowledge and love encounters. The human environment is such only as a human and personal world in which man lives in order to come to himself, so that in love he abides with the other and thereby experiences what is meant by 'God' who is the sphere and the ultimate guarantee of interhuman love" (cited in O'Meara, *God in the World*, 62). This passage from the Gospel of Matthew together with the Sermon on the Mount "leads the hearers from an external religion to an interior orientation, one human and divine. . . . In religion, no scene is more important than the drama of the end of the world, the final judgment on individual life. Curiously, in Jesus' dramatic narrative at the end of the Gospel according to Matthew, people are judged not by religious ideas and rituals but by their human treatment of others . . . the effort (being) to go beneath religion to the reign of God" (ibid., 82–83). See also Julia Kristeva's commentary on Luke's and Mark's notions of "sacrifice" and "serving" the other in *Black Sun*, trans. Leon Roudiez (New York: Columbia University Press, 1992), chapter 5, "Holbein"s Dead Christ." Kristeva makes the following key distinction between Christ as eucharistic service and as expiatory scapegoat: "'Serving,' which in Luke's context refers to 'serving at the table' shifts to 'giving his life,' a life that is a 'ransom' (*lytron*) in Mark's gospel. Such a semantic shift clearly sheds light on the status of the Christly 'sacrifice.' He who gives life is the one who sacrifices himself and disappears so that others might live. His death is neither murder nor evacuation but a life-giving discontinuity, closer to nutrition than to the simple destruction of value or the abandonment of a fallen object. A change in the conception of sacrifice obviously takes place within those texts, one that claims to establish a link between men and God

through the mediation of a donor. While it is true that giving implies deprivation on the part of the one who gives, who gives of himself, there is greater stress on the bond, on assimilation ('serving at the table') and on the reconciliatory benefits of that process" (ibid., 130–131). And Kristeva adds, significantly: "Indeed, the only rite that Christ handed down to his disciples and faithful on the basis of the last supper is the oral one of the Eucharist. Through it, sacrifice (and concomitantly death and melancholia) is *aufgehoben*—destroyed and superseded" (ibid., 131). Kristeva remarks here on the fact that the Latin term *expiare* implies more of a reconciliation—to be welcoming toward another—than a notion of punishment for sins or violent blood sacrifice. It is, she notes, possible to trace the meaning of the word *reconcile* or *atone* to the Greek *allasso*, meaning "to make different," "to change with respect to someone"—the idea of the offering of a gift rather than a ritualistic bloodletting. And yet Kristeva is not sanguine or oblivious to history here. She recognizes that an influential ascetic Christian tradition sacralized the "victimized aspect of that offering by eroticizing both pain and suffering, physical as well as mental, as much as possible" (ibid). And she asks, pointedly, if this oblatory reading is more than a simple medieval perversion of the true Gospel message.

9. Karen Armstrong, *Islam: A Short History* (New York: Modern Library, 2002), 5.
10. Ibid.
11. Ibid., 4.
12. See Qur'an 3:7 and 3:9, cited in Anthony Steinbock, *Phenomenology and Mysticism* (Bloomingto m,..n: Indiana University Press, 2007), 235.
13. Maqbool Ahmed Siraj, "India: A Laboratory of Religious Experiment," in Richard Kearney, ed., *Interreligious Imagination*, special issue of *Religion and the Arts* 12, nos. 1–3 (Leiden: Brill, 2008): 319–328; see also note 9 of my "Introduction" to this volume, 29. See also the pioneering hermeneutic work of Western scholars like James Morris, *Orientations: Islamic Thought in a World Civilisation* (London: Archeype, 2003); and Fred Dallmayr, *Dialogue Among Civilizations* (New York: Palgrave Macmillan, 2002). See the more popular and very influential work by Armstrong, *Islam*, especially her arguments for an enlightened Islamic hermeneutics that refused dogmatic reductionism and emphasized instead the crucial role of symbols in the language of the Qur'an and its central message of tolerance, peace, and respect for the weak and the stranger (dating back to its reclamation of the story of the estranged Ishmael); see, in particular, 30–31, 101–103, and 70–77. On the important historic role of an Islamic hermeneutics of the Qur'an, see Steinbock, *Phenomenology and Mysticism*, 335–337.
14. Siraj, "India," 335f.
15. For the full document issued by the Muslim scholars in October 2007 see http://www: acommonword.com. Several of the key points of this manifesto were in fact anticipated by the interreligious council in Florence in the late fifteenth century and Nicholas of Cusa's text *De Pace Fidei* where Christian-Muslim dialogue finds powerful expression. Nicholas of Cusa played a key role at the Council of Florence by proposing about the union of the Churches on the basis of the highest common denominator, to which several religions were also invited. At the time of the council's conclusions in 1493, Cusa was thirty-eight years old and therefore, compared to the other Church fathers present, a relatively young man. However, if one takes into consideration Cusa's complete works, by which he became, so to

speak, the "gatekeeper to the new era" and a founder of modern natural science and advocate of a revolutionary mystical poetics and interconfessional exchange, then it is not surprising that he should have contributed so much in practice and content, to make the union of the churches possible—even if history failed to realize the promise. His book *De Pace Fidei* is considered to be one of the most pioneering works on interreligious conversation between the Abrahamic faiths. I am grateful to my friend Joseph O'Leary for bringing this and related points on interconfessional hospitality to my attention.

16. See Fred Dallmayr, "Reason, Faith and Politics," in *Dialogue Among Civilizations*, 129. For Averroes important scriptural doctrines like "Creation from nothing" or the "resurrection of the body" called for a broad tolerance of "different readings and construals" (ibid.). Against the orthodox literalists he offered three different possible interpretations advising that "it is every man's duty to believe whatever his study leads him to conclude," and he added that "a scholar who commits an error in this matter is excused, while one who is correct receives thanks and a reward" (ibid.).

17. Ibid., 129f. See also David L. Lewis, *God's Crucible: Islam and the Making of Modern Europe, 570–1215* (New York: Norton, 2008).

18. Dallmayr, "Reason, Faith and Politics," 133. See also Kwame Anthony Appiah, "How Muslims Made Europe," *New York Review of Books* 55, no. 17 (November 6, 2008): 59–62. Appiah writes that in Islamic al-Andalus Christians and Jews were able to "share its manifold intellectual and material treasures. Had the three religions not worked together, borrowing from the pagan traditions of Greece and Rome, what we call the West would have been utterly different. In an age where some claim a struggle between the heirs of Christendom and of the Caliphate is the defining conflict, it is good to be reminded of this history of fruitful cohabitation" (Appiah, 62).

19. See Morris, *Orientations*. This process of mutual exchange is vividly illustrated, for example, in the famous painting by Sultan Muhammad of a Hafiz love-poem on divine imagination (khiyal). See James Morris, "Imaging Islam: Intellect and Imagination in Islamic Poetry, Philosophy and Painting," in Interreligious Imagination, ed. R. Kearney, 294 f.

20. Hafiz, *The Gift: Poems by Hafiz*, trans. David Ladinsky (New York: Penguin, 1999), 47.

21. Ibid., 178.

22. Hafiz, *The Collected Lyrics of Hafiz*, trans. Peter Avery (London: Archetype, 2007), 333.

23. For these and other references to Hafiz on the question of interreligious imagination, see Kascha Semonovitch, "Atheism, Theism and Anatheism in Hafiz of Shiraz," *Other Journal* (April 2008).

24. Hafiz, *The Gift*, 92.

25. Hafiz, *The Green Sea of Heaven: Fifty Ghazals from the Diwan of Hafiz*, trans. Elizabeth Gray (Oregon: White Cloud, 1995), especially the introduction by Daryush Shayegan.

26. Kabir, *Songs of Kabir*, trans. Rabindranath Tagore (Boston: Weiser, 2002), 109.

27. Kabir, *Ecstatic Poems*, trans. Robert Bly (Boston: Beacon, 2004).

28. Emile Benveniste, *Le Vocabulaire des Institutions Indo-Européenes* (Paris: Minuit, 1969), *Indo-European Language and Society*, trans. Jean Lallot (London: Faber

and Faber, 1973), 71. A similar ambiguity may be found in related terms such as *guest*, which derives from the Anglo-Saxon and Germanic terms *Gast*, connoting a ghastly intruder or a healing spirit—in other words holy or unholy ghosts (ibid., 72–83).

29. Ibid., 78. Benveniste begins his account of the process by drawing attention to the element *-pet-* in the word, this "originally meant personal identity. In the family group . . . it is the master who is eminently 'himself'" (ibid., 71). Thus, in the first place, inscribed within the term *hospitality* is a fundamental concern with identity. In this light, it is particularly interesting that this etymology develops in what initially appears to be completely divergent directions. In other words, the word betrays its other, or/and the other is "always already" inscribed within this site of identity. See also here Jacques Derrida's commentary on Benveniste in Jacques Derrida, Anne Dufourmantelle, and Rachel Bowlby, *Of Hospitality*, trans. Rachel Bowlby (Stanford: Stanford University Press, 2000). The traces of contradiction between self-identity and the stranger live on in what Derrida has termed the pact of hospitality, within which one's contradictory status as host and guest is determined. Taking his lead from Benveniste, Derrida outlines how this pact of hospitality, "inscribes the *xenos* in the *xenia*, which is to say the pact, in the contract or collective alliance of that name. Basically there is no *xenos*, there is no foreigner before or outside the *xenia*" (Derrida, Dufourmantelle, and Bowlby, *Of Hospitality*, 29). I am grateful to Aidan O'Malley for this reference. See also our analysis in Richard Kearney, "Aliens and Others" in *Strangers, Gods and Monsters* (New York: Routledge, 2003), 63–82.

30. Benveniste, *Indo-European Language and Society*, 78. This more positive sense of the hospitable host as one who receives and welcomes the "guest" as other, stranger, foreigner in a reciprocal gesture is gradually overcome in the development of anonymous states and regimes: "One of the Indo-European expressions of this institution (of hospitality as reciprocal obligation) is precisely the Latin term *hostis*, with its Gothic correspondent *gasts* and the Slavic *gospodi*. In historical times the custom had lost its force in the Roman world: it presupposes a type of relationship which was no longer compatible with the established regime. When an ancient society becomes a nation, the relations between man and man, clan and clan, are abolished. All that persists is the distinction between what is inside and outside the *civitas*. By a development of which we do not know the exact conditions, the word hostis assumed a 'hostile' flavour and henceforward it is only applied to the enemy" (ibid., 78).

31. Ibid., 75. "[H]*ostis* . . . preserved its ancient value of 'stranger' in the law of the Twelve Tables, e.g.: : *adversus hostem aeterna auctoritas est(o)*" (ibid., 76). In addition to this meaning we find related terms like *hostorium* (a measuring instrument for keeping different entities level) and *hostilina* (equalization or equitable compensation in work)—both connoting a just exchange and reciprocity between self and other. We also find the more ritualistic sense of *hostia* meaning a compensatory offering to the Gods in return for their favors. In contrast to *peregrinus*, the stranger who lived outside the boundaries of the pact or the territory, the *hostis* becomes the stranger who is recognized as having equal rights to those within the state (e.g., Roman citizens). Thus the emergence of a particular notion of hospitality as implying the reciprocity of a compact or agreement, a notion of compensatory exchange reminiscent of Marcel Mauss's famous notion of potlatch—a

series of gifts and countergifts practiced by the natives of Northwest America: a practice of instituting compelling economic and social bonds between tribes and families and their descendants. Benveniste notes accordingly: "]H]ospitality . . . is founded on the idea that a man is bound to another (*hostis* always involves the notion of reciprocity) by the obligation to compensate a gift or service from which he has benefited" (ibid., 77). And he goes on to note that the same institution exists under different names in Greek where the *xenos* is someone bound reciprocally in a pact (*xenia*) under the protection of Zeus Xenios. "The guest (the one received) is the *xenos* and he who receives is the *xendokhos*" (ibid., 78). Hence the Homeric example of Diomedes and Glaucus cited in our text, which exemplifies a symmetrical exchange that is, for Benveniste, contractually binding. And, moving further afield, this notion of mutual giving and return is exemplified in the Iranian term for "guest" (*aryaman*) as "intimate friend," or in the fact that Aryaman is the Indo-Iranian god of hospitality, associated in the Rig Veda with marriage: "Aryaman intervenes when a woman taken from outside the clan is introduced for the first time as a wife into her new family" (ibid., 83). Benveniste concludes his detailed analysis of the various etymological roots of hospitality in different cultures and languages thus: "These terms, far removed from one another, came back to the same problem; that of institutions of welcoming and reciprocity, thanks to which the men of a given people find hospitality in another, and whereby societies enter into alliances and exchanges" (ibid.). Benveniste's sociocultural-linguistic account of the complex and ambivalent genealogy of the terms for hospitality offers a useful "Indo-European" counterpart to our own more "Abrahamic" account in this volume. His sociological and anthropological method complements our own more philosophical and ethicoreligious one (where the asymmetry of a transcendent Other giving itself to the human subject accompanies the symmetry of receiving and loving the Other as oneself or oneself as another).

32. Rudolf Otto, *The Idea of the Holy*, trans. Rachel Bowlby (Oxford: Oxford University Press, 1958). See also a somewhat more sociohistorical approach in Michel de Certeau's *The Mystic Fable* and "Mysticism." "From the beginning," notes de Certeau, "mysticism . . . had for is place an elsewhere and for its sign an anti-society which nevertheless would represent the initial ground (*fonds*) of man" (*The Mystic Fable*, 12). In other words, the mystical is the "strange" and "marginal"—"what becomes mystical is that which diverges from normal or ordinary paths; that which is no longer inscribed within the social community of faith or religious references, but rather on the margins of an increasingly secularized society" (ibid., 13). Mystical otherness is deeply paradoxical: "In one of its aspects, it is on the side of the abnormal, a rhetoric of the strange; in the other, it is on the side of an "essential" that its whole discourse announces without being able to express . . . but it is so in order to speak of what can be neither said nor known . . . what is mystical remains secret and invisible . . . mystical in Greek means hidden" (ibid., 13, 16).

33. See Levinas, *Totality and Infinity*, and his *Otherwise Than Being* (The Hague: Nihoff, 1981).

2. IN THE WAGER

1. For insightful commentaries on this crucial aspect of Ibn 'Arabi's *The Book of Theophanies*, see W. Chittick, *Imaginal Worlds: Ibn al-Arabi and the Problem of*

Religious Diversity (Albany: State University of New York, 1994), 74f; and Henri Corbin, *Alone with the Alone: Creative Imagination in the Sufism of Ibn Arabi* (Princeton: Princeton University Press, 1969), 113, 158–162, and 174–175. I am grateful to Elisabeth Suergiu for bringing these texts to my attention.

2. See Edith Stein, *On the Problem of Empathy*, trans. Waltraut Stein (Washington: ICS, 1989). Stein's aim, in dialogue with the early phenomenology of Husserl and Scheler, is to describe empathy as a real "embodied" connection with the other while retaining the unique difference between self and other. The ethical question arising from this is how to extend empathy (as "in-feeling," *Ein-fühlung*) into the positive disposition of sympathy (as "with-feeling," *Mit-leid* or *Mit-fühlung*) without collapsing the distinction between self and stranger. See also Max Scheler, *The Nature of Sympathy* (London: Routledge, 1970); and Catherine Cornille, "Empathy and Interreligious Imagination" in Richard Kearney, ed., *Interreligious Imagination*, special issue of *Religion and the Arts* 12, nos. 1–3 (Leiden: Brill, 2008): 102–117; see as well Cornille's chapter "Empathy," in Catherine Cornille, *The Im-possibility of Religious Dialogue* (New York: Herder and Herder, 2008). For an interesting discussion of the relationship between empathy and a Levinasian ethics of the hostage as passivity and substitution, see James Mensch, "Prayer as Kenosis," in Norman Wirzba and Bruce Benson, eds., *The Phenomenology of Prayer* (New York: Fordham University Press, 2005). While sympathic to the Levinasian critique of the Western ontology of egoistic totality and sameness, I have some difficulty with his notion of "ipseity as hostage" to the other, a radical passivity and persecution that cannot "evade the neighbor's call" and does not, I believe, sufficiently allow for human freedom and choice in one's response to this call. See my critical objections to Levinas's and Derrida's ethics of unconditional alterity in my chapter, "Aliens and Others," in Richard Kearney, *Strangers, Gods and Monsters* (New York: Routledge, 2003), 63f.

3. Hafiz, *I Heard God Laughing: Renderings of Hafiz*, ed. D. Ladinsky et al. (Walnut Creek, CA: Sufism Reoriented, 1996).

4. Cited in Michel de Certeau, "Mysticism" *Diacritics* 22, no. 2 (Summer 1992): 21. The author also cites other mystics whose love of comic paradox was legendary. Meister Eckhart, for example, observed the following mystical paradox: "God is neither being nor reason; nor does He know this or that. That is why God is empty of all things and why He is all things." And the Sufi mystics, Al-Halladj, calling into question the clerical dogmas of the *umma*: "The intent of this letter is that you explain nothing by God, that you extract not a single argumentation from him, that you do not confess his existence and that you are not inclined to deny it" (ibid., 19).

5. See Jacques Derrida in our critical exchange on this subject at University College Dublin, "Hospitality, Justice and Responsibility: A Dialogue with Jacques Derrida" in Richard Kearney and Mark Dooley, eds., *Questioning Ethics* (New York: Routledge, 1999), 65–83. See also my critique of the lack of hermeneutic discernment in the Derridean and Levinasian accounts of the messianic Other in "Aliens and Others" and in my other interviews with Derrida, notably "Terror, Religion and the New Politics" and "Deconstruction and the Other" in Richard Kearney, ed., *Debates in Continental Philosophy* (New York: Fordham University Press, 2006), 3–15 and 139–156; see also my critical exchange with Jacques Derrida and Jack Caputo, entitled "Desire of God," in *After God: Richard Kearney*

and the Religious Turn in Continental Philosophy (New York: Fordham University Press, 2007), 301–309. Michel de Certeau recognizes that a "mystical life is begun when it recovers its roots and experiences its *strangeness* in ordinary life—when it continues to discover in other ways what has occurred that first time." De Certeau describes this discovery in the form of a hermeneutic "itinerary" of ongoing discernment. The divine that opens out into a precise epiphanic time and place in one's life cannot be confined to that moment. "One cannot arrest him (God) there" (de Certeau, "Mysticism," 19). And it is this gap or surplus that forbids fixation and prompts wise discrimination: "This internal exigency and the objective situation of the experience already allow one to distinguish a spiritual sense of the experience from its pathological forms. A process is 'spiritual' when it is not confined to a single moment, no matter how intense or exceptional that moment may be, when it does not dedicate everything to its revival as if it were a paradise to recover or preserve, when it does not lose its way in imaginary fixations. It is realist, engaged, as the Sufis say, in the *ihlas*—on the track of an authenticity that begins with the relationship with oneself and others. It is therefore discriminating" (ibid.). For de Certeau, the gift of God is always given in a culturally defined language that goes all the way down from the conceptual to the carnal—namely, from official doctrinal and theological references to more basic "codes of recognition, the organization of the imaginary, the sensory hierarchisations in which smell or sight predominate" (ibid., 21). As he puts it, "mystics speak only a received language," however creatively and poetically they rewrite it. And this reception involves a "redirecting of the personal life to the social life" which speaks of the "divine depths" in terms of historical, linguistic and geographical hermeneutic contexts (ibid.). That is why if mystical experience begins with what seems like a "foreign language" of the unfathomable, surprising and unexpected, this "irruption of strange symptoms only signals moments of thresholds that are in fact quite specific" (meaning hermeneutically grounded) (ibid., 17). The epiphanic moments are "like throwing open a window into one's dwelling. . . . the spoken word that pierces the heart, the vision that turns one's life upside down—these are decisive experiences, indissociable from a place, a meeting, a reading, but not reducible to the means that convey them" (ibid.). So that while the mystic can always say "it happened there and then," she also knows that the mystical experience extends beyond any "certain knowledge" of this particular time and space. "The surprise produces strangeness," as de Certeau says, "but it also liberates. It draws to the surface a secret of life and death . . . the unsuspected, that has the violence of the unforeseen, gathers together all the days of existence, as the whistle of the shepherd gathers his flock, and reunites them in the continuity of a disquieting relationship with the other" (ibid., 17–18). And, "the very term 'God' (or 'Absolute'), rather than providing a guidepost for the experience, receives is meaning from this dimension" (of unforeseeable "gift") (ibid., 18). Mystical experience is thus a mediation of the inside and the outside, the transcendent and the immanent, the absolute and incarnate: "Indissociable from the assent that is its criterion, such a 'birth' draws from man a truth that is his without coming from him or belonging to him. Thus, he is 'outside himself' at the very moment that a Self is asserted. A necessity is aroused in him, but under the sign of a melody, a spoken word, or a vision coming from elsewhere" (ibid.).

6. See Anthony Steinbock's insightful analysis of key criteria for genuine revelations

and epiphanies of verticality in his *Phenomenology and Mysticism* (Bloomington: Indiana University Press, 2007), 100–104, 115–125, 132–135. Steinbock is fully aware of the problem regarding the ostensibly isomorphic character of genuinely spiritual and counterfeit experiences of the vertical. He notes, for example, the similarities between the psychotic claims for mystical union with God in Freud's famous case of Schreber and the mystical claims for such union (often of a parallel erotic nature) by celebrated mystics. Which raises the crucial dilemma of telling the difference between Schreber's psychotic fantasies about being invaded by God (ibid., 140–142) and the mystical testaments by the likes of John of the Cross or Teresa of Avila (ibid., 45–66) to feeling similarly overcome and traversed by a divine visitor (see in particular Teresa's famous experience of "transverberation" in *The Interior Castle*). See also our critical discussion with Jean-Luc Marion on how we can discriminate hermeneutically between different appearances of the divine Other: Marion, "Hermeneutics and Revelation," in Kearney, *Debates in Continental Philosophy*, 15–33. On this critical question of hermeneutically discerning the "saturated phenomenon" of divine revelation in Marion, see also Shane MacKinlay, "Eyes Wide Shut," *Modern Theology* 20, no. 3 (2004): 117–118; and Tamsin Farmer Jones, "Apparent Darkness: Jean-Luc Marion's Retrieval of the Greek Apophatic Tradition," chapter 4, "Interpreting Saturated Phenomenality: Marion's Hermeneutical Turn?" Ph.D. diss., Harvard University, 2008. The main difficulty with Marion's account, it seems, is that it is indiscriminate when it comes to an ontological or eschatological encounter with the divine other qua "saturated phenomenon." At best, for Marion, the human recipient of such revelation—what he terms in French *l'adonné*—can merely respond to the event of saturation as one responds to a devastating trauma: not with any discerning interpretation but, at best, by blocking or being bedazzled by this ineluctable force of incoming saturation. The *adonné* is the one who receives the gift whether he likes it or not. (Indeed when Marion speaks of the Annunciation it is analogous to a divine violation or invasion where Mary accepts the gift willy-nilly: Marion speaks, for example of "when" Mary receives the Word, never "if" she agrees to receive it). At best, we have an "endless hermeneutics" *after* the event, but never during the event of saturation itself. Discernment, for Marion, is always derivative, not instantaneous. As he puts it, "I undergo the obscure obligation of letting myself conform to (and by) the excess of intuition over every intention that my gaze could oppose to it"; "Evidence and Bedazzlement," in *Prolegomena to Charity*, trans. Stephen Lewis (New York: Fordham University Press, 2002), 53–70. Responding to the other for Marion—as in somewhat different ways for Levinas and Derrida—is a fundamental traumatism of uncritical subjugation and subjection (analogous to Levinas's *traumatisme originel* in meeting *l'autrui*). It is telling, moreover, that one of the meanings of *l'adonné* in French is "addict," someone who has no control over the substance that is traumatizing and saturating its being. What Marion fails to fully appreciate, in my view, is that one can have *both* a passive *and* an active response to the divine Stranger: a "pathos" of receptivity to the incoming Other and a "poiesis" of hermeneutic agency (choice, imagination, reading, commitment, and humorous/humble consent). Once again, I return to the famous "yes" of Mary and Sarah when they believed the impossible was possible. But such a "yes" to the Stranger also implies the freedom to say "no." Consent is a choice, not servile conformity. Marion's problem with hermeneutically discerning between different kinds of saturated phenomenon (divine revelation or Holocaust trauma, for example, banal evil experiences or exemplary holy ones) is well commented on by Tamsin Farmer Jones ("Apparent Darkness," 244–246, 230–234, 186–191). She suggests supplementing Marion's hermeneutic deficiencies with an apophatic hermeneutics based on the scriptural commentaries and writings of Gregory of Nyssa (ibid., 193–194, 227). In sum, while Marion is correct to talk of a deriva tive hermeneutics of commentary and extrapolation after the event of saturation, he fails to appreciate how hermeneutic interpretation—as a prepredicative carnal response—occurs already in the moment of saturation itself. When one speaks of the three famous modes of response to trauma, for example—as flight, fight, or freeze or, in attachment theory, as hysterical overreaction or constrictive under-reaction—one is already recognizing that humans are choosing different modes of response at the most basic corporeal and affective level, long before reflective consciousness of any kind. And, as noted in chapter 1, the phenomenology of mood, emotion, and feeling, carried out by the likes of Husserl, Scheler, and Sartre, give an additional depth and rigor to such analysis of a primary hermeneutic preunderstanding that antecedes our derivative hermeneutic understanding.

7. Max Scheler, "Love and Knowledge," in Harold Bershady, ed., *On Feeling, Knowing and Valuing* (Chicago: University of Chicago Press, 1992), 147–165.

8. Paul Ricoeur, *Oneself as Another*, trans. Kathleen Blamey (Chicago: University of Chicago Press, 1992), 166.

9. Ibid. Jacques Derrida is even more radical in his deconstructive reading of the role of self as "host" and "hostage" in relations of hospitality toward the stranger. See Jacques Derrida, Anne Dufourmantelle, and Rachel Bowlby, *Of Hospitality*, trans. Rachel Bowlby (Stanford: Stanford University Press, 2000). See also my commentary in "Aliens and Others," and my more detailed discussion of the subject in the previous chapter, this volume, especially notes 27–30.

10. Paul Ricoeur, *On Translation*, trans. Eileen Brennan (New York: Routledge, 2006), 23–24. See also in this connection L-M Chauvet, *Sign and Sacrament: A Sacramental Reinterpretation of Christian Experience* (Minnesota: Liturgical, 1995): for example, Chauvet describes how the self is only rediscovered through deconstructive exposure to the other: "It is 'I' which is possible only in its relationship with what is most different, the YOU (the reverse of 'I'); and it is precisely from this tear of otherness, impossible to mend, that the likeness and the reciprocity permitting communication are born" (ibid., 503). See also Ricoeur's important debate with Hans Küng, on the subject of interreligious exchange in my conclusion, and Maurice Merleau-Ponty on the dialogical character of language as chiasmic reversibility of self and other as discussed in chapter 4, this volume.

11. See Richard Kearney, *Postnationalist Ireland* (New York: Routledge, 1996). In the Northern Ireland peace settlement, it is noteworthy that John Hume, leader of the Catholic community, and David Trimble, leader of the Protestant community, served as hosts for their respective enemies and extremists, bringing the terrorists and paramilitaries in from the cold and away from their guns, though this meant that the hosts ultimately sacrificed themselves for the guests, who then went on to become hosts in their turn (e.g., Martin McGuinness and Ian Paisley) of a further stage of the peace process. One finds similar examples of this phenomenon, I would suggest, in historic figures like Mandela or Gandhi, who likewise engaged in a visionary politics of self-sacrifice and kenosis, what we might call a politics of

vulnerability. See chapter 7, this volume, on Day, Vanier, and Gandhi. In relation to Jewish-Christian dialogue in Warsaw, see Edward Kaplan, "Healing Wounds," in Kearney, *Interreligious Imagination*, 441f.

12. Joseph O'Leary, "Knowing the Heart Sutra by Heart," ibid., 356f. O'Leary suggests, for example, that the Buddhist teaching of emptiness invites Christians to recover their own apophatic and mystical traditions of divine nothingness, just as the *neti/neti* of detachment in the Heart Sutra, opening us to universal compassion, may recall Christians to the radical implications of the Sermon on the Mount or Saint Francis's love of all living beings. On the question of interreligious translation and exchange, O'Leary writes: "It used to be said that a good Catholic needs to be a Protestant, while a good Protestant needs to be a Catholic; today we might add, a sane Christian needs to be a Buddhist" (in order to remain a good Christian!). See Joseph O'Leary, "Towards a Buddhist Interpretation of Christian Truth," in Catherine Cornille, ed., *Many Mansions: Multiple Religious Belonging and Christian Identity* (New York: Orbis, 2002). O'Leary suggests that the Heart Sutra, recited in mantras by the community (*sangha*) as a "skillful means" of compassionate wisdom and practice, reminds Christians of the need to combine teachings with service, thereby opening a practical meeting place between Eastern and Western spiritualities as means of concrete living engagement.

13. See Richard Kearney, *The God Who May Be* (Bloomington: Indiana University Press, 2001), and "Epiphanies of the Everyday," in John Manoussakis, ed., *After God: Richard Kearney and the Religious Turn in Continental Philosophy* (New York: Fordham University Press, 2005). See also Jurgen Moltmann, *The Power of the Powerless* (London: SCM, 1983).

14. See Fred Dallmayr, "Empire and Faith: Sacred Non-Sovereignty," in *Small Wonder: Global Power and Its Discontents* (New York: Rowman and Littlefield, 2005).

15. Max Scheler, "The Meaning of Suffering," in Bershady, *On Feeling, Knowing and Valuing*, 87.

16. See Paul Ricoeur, *Memory, History and Forgetting*, trans. Kathleen Blamey and David Pellauer (Chicago: University of Chicago Press, 2004); and also my discussion of giving a future to the "unfulfilled possibilities" of the past in Richard Kearney, "Capable Man," in Brian Treanor and Henry Isaac Venema, eds., *Passion for the Possible: Thinking with Paul Ricoeur: The New Hermeneutics* (New York: Fordham University Press, 2010).

17. See C. Stephen Evans, ed., *Exploring Kenotic Christology: The Self-Emptying of God* (Oxford: Oxford University Press, 2006); and Sarah Coakley's illuminating chapter, "Kenosis and Subversion: On the Repression of 'Vulnerability' in Christian Feminist Writing," in her volume *Powers and Submissions: Spirituality, Philosophy and Gender* (Oxford: Blackwell, 2002), 3–39.

18. For a very insightful discussion of comparative mystical experience in Jewish, Christian, and Islamic traditions see Steinbock, *Phenomenology and Mysticism*.

19. Teresa of Calcutta, *Mother Teresa: Come to My Light* (New York: Rider, 2008).

3. IN THE NAME

1. Etty Hillesum, *An Interrupted Life* (New York: Owl, 1996), 176. See also Hans Jonas, "The Concept of God After Auschwitz: A Jewish Voice," in Lawrence Vogel, ed., *Mortality and Morality: A Search for God After Auschwitz* (Evanston,

IL: Northwestern University Press, 1966), 138–142.

2. Cited in Nathalie Zemon Davis, "Michel de Certeau's Quest," *New York Review of Books* 2 (2008): 33.

3. Hannah Arendt, "Religion and Politics," in *Essays in Understanding*, ed. Jerome Kohn (New York: Harcourt Brace Jovanovich, 1994), 369.

4. Hannah Arendt, *The Life of the Mind*, ed. Mary McCarthy, 2 vols. (New York: Harcourt Brace Jovanovich, 1978), 10.

5. See Arthur Kirsch, *Auden and Christianity* (New Haven: Yale University Press, 2005); and Kascha Semonovitch, "Arendt, Auden and Anatheism," in *Literary Imagination* (New York: Oxford University Press, 2009). I am grateful to Kascha Semonovitch for bringing my attention to Arendt's discussion of the God question and her friendship with Auden.

6. Arendt, "What Remains? The Language Remains," *Essays in Understanding*, 12.

7. Ibid.

8. Rabbi Irving Greenberg, "Easing the Divine Suffering," in Bob Abernethy and William Bole, eds., *The Life of Meaning: Reflections on Faith, Doubt, and Repairing the World* (New York: Seven Stories, 2002), 69.

9. Ibid., 68.

10. Ibid., 69.

11. Ibid., 72.

12. Emmanuel Levinas, "Useless Suffering," in *Between Us* (London: Athlone, 1997).

13. Emmanuel Levinas, *Totality and Infinity*, trans. Alfonso Lingis (Pittsburgh: Duquesne University Press, 1969), 58.

14. John Llewelyn, *Emmanuel Levinas: The Genealogy of Ethics* (London: Routledge, 1995), 67.

15. Jacques Derrida, "*Sauf le nom (Post-Scriptum),*" in *On the Name*, ed. Thomas Dutoit, trans. John P. Leavey Jr. (Stanford: Stanford University Press, 1995, 1993), 82f.

16. Jacques Derrida, *Spectres of Marx*, trans. Peggy Kamuf (London: Routledge, 1994), 168. My thanks to Neal Deroo for bringing these passages to my attention.

17. Ibid., 169.

18. Ibid., 59.

19. On the question of messianism and eschatology, see also Jacques Derrida, "Deconstruction and the Other," in Richard Kearney, ed., *Debates in Continental Philosophy* (New York: Fordham University Press, 2005), 139f. And see our related analysis of epiphanic and eschatological time in Gaston Bachelard's philosophy of the Instant as a gap within discontinuous time (*pace* Bergson's temporal continuum or *durée*), Richard Kearney, "Bachelard and the Epiphanic Instant," *Philosophy Today*, special Society for Phenomenology and Existential Philosophy issue, ed. Peg Birmingham and James Risser, vol. 33 (Fall 2008): 38–45.

20. Dietrich Bonhoeffer, *Letters and Papers from Prison*, ed. Eberhard Bethge, enlarged ed. (New York: Simon and Schuster, 1971), 279–280. I am grateful to my colleagues Brian Gregor and Jens Zimmerman for bringing Bonhoeffer's writings on "religionless faith" to my attention. See their volume, *Bonhoeffer and Continental Thought: Cruciform Philosophy* (Bloomington: Indiana University Press, 2009).

21. Karl Barth, *The Epistle to the Romans*, trans. E. C. Hoskins (Oxford: Oxford University Press, 1933, 1923), 130–131, 233.

22. Bonhoeffer, *Letters and Papers from Prison*, 280–282.

23. Ibid., 346.
24. See Paul Ricoeur, "The Non-Religious Interpretation of Christianity in Bonhoeffer," in Gregor and Zimmerman, *Bonhoeffer and Continental Thought.*
25. Bonhoeffer, *Letters and Papers from Prison*, 360–361.
26. See John Caputo, *The Weakness of God* (Bloomington: Indiana University Press, 2005); and Catherine Keller, *Facing the Deep* (New York: Routledge, 2002). See also John Panteleimon Manoussakis, *God After Metaphysics: A Theological Aesthetics* (Bloomington: Indiana University Press, 2007), and, as editor, *After God: Richard Kearney and the Religious Turn in Continental Philosophy* (New York: Fordham University Press, 2006).
27. Ricoeur, "The Non-Religious Interpretation."
28. Bonhoeffer, *Letters and Papers from Prison*, 311–312.
29. Ibid., 369–370.
30. Ibid., 361.
31. Cited in Ricoeur, "The Non-Religious Interpretation."
32. Cited ibid.
33. See Paul Ricoeur, *Fallible Man* (Chicago: Henry Regnery, 1967), 215, and *Critique and Conviction* (New York: Columbia University Press, 1998), 145.
34. Ricoeur, "Religion, Atheism, Faith," in *The Conflict of Interpretations* (Evanston: Northwestern University Press, 1974), 441.
35. Ibid., 441–442.
36. See Freud's famous conclusion to *Civilization and Its Discontents*, trans. James Strachey (New York: Norton, 1962), 92.
37. Max Scheler, "Love and Knowledge," in Scheler, *On Feeling, Knowing and Valuing*, ed. Harold Bershady (Chicago: University of Chicago Press, 1993), 160.
38. Richard Dawkins, *The God Delusion* (New York: Mariner, 2008), 23–24.
39. Ricoeur, "Religion, Atheism, Faith," 447. For an excellent critical development of Ricoeur's use of atheism (Freud, Marx, and Nietzsche) as a hermeneutics of suspicion that precedes a second hermeneutics of affirmation (recovering a "second innocence" or "naiveté"), see Merold Westphal, *Suspicion and Faith: The Religious Uses of Modern Atheism* (New York: Fordham University Press, 1994).
40. Friedrich Nietzsche, *The Gay Science*, in *The Portable Nietzsche*, ed. Walter Kaufman (New York: Penguin, 1954), 93–94 (para 341).
41. Ricoeur, "Religion, Atheism, Faith," 448.
42. Ibid.
43. Ibid., 452.
44. Ibid., 454. See also my analysis of the ana-erotic paradigm of mystical experience as a return to a second desire beyond desire in "The Shulammite Song: Eros Descending and Ascending," in Virginia Burrus and Catherine Keller, eds., *A Theology of the Passions* (New York: Fordham University Press, 2006), 306–340.
45. Ricoeur, "Religion, Atheism, Faith," 455
46. Ibid., 460.
47. Ibid., 467. See also Ricoeur, "The Critique of Religion," in Charles Regan and David Stuart, eds., *The Philosophy of Paul Ricoeur* (Boston: Beacon, 1978), 213f. As noted, Ricoeur talks of returning to a second naiveté of authentic faith after the dogmatic prejudices of one's first naiveté have been purged. He speaks accordingly of debunking false religious fetishisms so that the symbols of the eschatological

sacred may speak again. Anthony Steinbock sketches a similar move in his distinction between a genuine "vertical" experience of the sacred and "idolatrous" misconstruals of this in *Phenomenology and Mysticism* (Bloomington: Indiana University Press, 2007), 211–240.

48. Paul Ricoeur, *Vivant jusqu'à la mort* (Paris: Seuil, 2007), 45.

49. See Jacques Derrida, "Violence and Metaphysics," in *Writing and Difference,* ed. and trans. Alan Bass (Chicago: University of Chicago Press, 1978), 131. The full quote is: "No philosophy responsible for its language can renounce ipseity in general, and the philosophy or eschatology of separation may do so less than any other. Between original tragedy and messianic triumph there is philosophy, in which violence is returned against violence within knowledge, in which original finitude appears, and in which the other is respected within, and by, the same."

50. Paul Ricoeur, "From Interpretation to Translation," in *Thinking Biblically* (Chicago: University of Chicago Press, 1998), 331f. See also "La croyance religieuse: Le difficile chemin du religieux," hosted by l'Université de tous les saviors, dir. Yves Michaud, and compiled in *La Philosophie et l'Ethique*, vol. 11 (Paris: Odile Jacob, 2002), especially the section entitled "L'homme capable, destinataire du religieux," 207f.

51. Paul Ricoeur, "A Colloquio con Ricoeur," in Fabricio Turoldo, *Verita del Methodo* (Padova: Il Poligrafo, 2000), 254.

52. Ricoeur, "The Poetics of Language and Myth," in Kearney, *Debates in Continental Philosophy*, 99f.

53. Ricoeur, "A Colloquio con Ricoeur," 255.

54. Ibid.

55. Ricoeur, "The Nuptial Metaphor," in *Thinking Biblically*, 265f. See Ricoeur's final reference to my notion of divine *posse* in one of the last "Fragments" of *Vivant Jusqu'à la mort,* 129–130. This occurs in the context of Ricoeur's discussion of Marc Philonenko's reading of the "Our Father." Remarking that we are concerned in this prayer less with a statement about God's being (the fact that God is) than an invocation to action and doing, Ricoeur sees here a movement beyond a traditional metaphysics of being to an eschatology of *possibilisation:* "Une invocation s'addresse à un Dieu *qui peut ce qu'il fait* [our emphasis]. Dans les demandes en tu, il est demandé à Dieu de faire qu'il règne. . . . Peut-être un Dieu du posse (Richard Kearney). La vision eschatologique est celle d'une complétude de l'Agir" (129–130). Returning to his oft-repeated desire for a hermeneutical rereading of Aristotle's dialectic of possibility and actuality, Ricoeur notes that Christ's appeal to the Father takes the form not just of wish but of expectancy, an act of trust in the accomplishment of action (*agir*). Here Ricoeur sees a "coupling" of capacities, human and divine, seeking to be realized in a "coupling" of actions. "Forgive us as we forgive others," etc. "Le comme opère verbalement ce que la symmétrie inégale des deux agir opère effectivement" (130). Ricoeur concludes with an eschatological reinterpretation of Aristotle's ontology of potency and act, involving a new hermeneutic "coupling," with its own radical charge of semantic interanimation and innovation: "Telle serait la possibilisation d'une énonciation en terme d'agir. Non grec. Mais possibilité d'une réecriture du verbe être à la façon d'Aristote. Etre comme dunamis-energeia. L'agir rend possible cette réecriture de l'être grec. Comme déjà Exode 3, 14–15. Voir Penser le Bible sur 'Je suis qui je serai'" (131–132). In this final reflection on the eschatological "capacity" for pardon, Ricoeur

conjoins his ontological and theological insights into the transformative power of the "possible."

56. Stanislas Breton, *The Word and the Cross*, trans. Jacqueline Porter (New York: Fordham University Press, 2002).

57. Ricoeur, *Vivant jusqu'à la mort*, 76. Other significant contributions to the "God after metaphysics" debate—which emerged in the wake of the "religious turn" in phenomenology (Jean-Luc Marion, Jean-Louis Chrétien, Jean-Yves Lacoste, Michel Henry) and in deconstruction (Derrida)—include the recent work of thinkers like John Caputo, John Manoussakis, and Mark Taylor. These thinkers have explored the idea of a messianicity without metaphysics, calling this, paradoxically but tellingly, a "religion without religion." Caputo's own notion of the "weakness of God" stems from a reading of Christian kenosis in light of a deconstructionist complicity between mysticism and atheism that, as noted, was already identified by Derrida in *Sauf le Nom*. Manoussakis and Taylor develop somewhat different conclusions to their respective books, both titled *After God*, the former veering in a more theistic direction, the later in a more atheistic one.

. 4. IN THE FLESH

1. On the notion of a pilgrim or messianic church that seeks to open particularity to universality, see the following recent commentaries on the revolutionary role played by Paul: Alain Badiou, *Saint Paul: The Foundation of Universalism*, trans. Ray Brassier (Stanford: Stanford University Press, 2003); Georgio Agamben, *The Time That Remains*, trans. Patricia Dailey (Stanford: Stanford University Press, 2005); Slavoj Žižek, *The Fragile Absolute; or, Why Is the Christian Legacy Worth Fighting For?* (London: Verso, 2000); and Julia Kristeva, *Strangers to Ourselves* (New York: Columbia University Press, 1994). It is interesting that these four contemporary retrievals of Paul's messianic message are all by atheists or agnostics. See also contributions by Žižek, Badiou, Daniel Boyarin, Mark Jordan, Karen Armstrong et al. in John Caputo and Linda Alcoff, eds., *Saint Paul Among the Philosophers* (Bloomington: Indiana University Press, 2008).

2. See here the recent attempts to formulate a postmetaphysical understanding of God by thinkers like Jack Caputo, Merold Westphal, Mark Taylor, Jean-Luc Marion, and John Manoussakis. In the wake of the deconstruction of ontotheology by Heidegger, Levinas, and Derrida, these thinkers offer powerful critiques of the metaphysical concept of God as an all powerful substance that causes and thinks itself (*ens causa sui*), a self-sufficient entity with no need to refer to anything or anyone beyond itself. Such an abstract Being does not care for widows, orphans, and strangers. It does not care tout court. This concept of divinity was often invoked as a weapon of ideological authority during the period known as "Christendom." But it involved, I am arguing, a profound misconstrual of Christianity as a doctrine of triumphal exclusivism to the detriment of many dissenting strains of thought both within Christianity itself and beyond it (Christianity having become the mainstream biblical religion in Europe after the marginalization of Judaism and Islam). Christendom, as Kierkegaard observed, compromised Christ's message, turning it into a dogma of force and fear. Notorious for witch hunts, inquisitions, heretic burning, and crusading wars against infidels, it purged "strangers" within and without. It was the antithesis of anathesim.

3. One could cite here mystical reformist figures like Teresa of Avila, John of the Cross, Margaret Porete, and Meister Eckhart whose works were condemned by the Inquisition or Church authorities (even Thomas Aquinas had his works placed on the Index at one point). More recently, one might cite pioneering mystical thinkers, like Teilhard de Chardin and Henri le Saux (Abhishiktananda), whose works were withheld from publication by the Church. It is one of the great ironies of Western Christianity that so many of its followers—of different denominations—seem to have ignored its founder's central message of Word made flesh in the mystical body of the world.

4. Teresa of Avila, *The Collected Works* 3, trans. Kieran Kavanagh and Otilio Rodriguez (ICS, 1980), 5.8. I am grateful to Anthony Steinbock, whose *Phenomenology and Mysticism* examines this question in detail; see Steinbock, *Phenomenology and Mysticism* (Bloomington: Indiana University Press, 2007), 64–65.

5. Teresa of Avila, *The Collected Works*, 1:22, 7–8.

6. Paul Ricoeur, *L'Homme faillible* (Paris: Aubier-Montaigne, 1960), 156.

7. See in particular Edmund Husserl, *Ideas II*, trans. A. Schuwer (Dordrecht: Kluwer, 1989), and *The Crisis of European Sciences and Transcendental Phenomenology*, trans. David Carr (Evanston, IL: Northwestern University Press, 1970). See the excellent commentary by Didier Franck, *Chair et corps: Sur la phénoménologie de Husserl* (Paris: Minuit, 1981) as well as by other French phenomenologists like Jean-Luc Marion in works like *Being Given*, trans. Jeffrey Kosky (Stanford: Stanford University Press, 2002), *In Excess*, trans. Robyn Horder and Vincent Berraud (New York: Fordham University Press, 2003), *The Erotic Phenomenon*, trans. Stephen Lewis (Chicago: University of Chicago Press, 2006), and Jean-Louis Chrétien, *Hand to Hand*, trans. Stephen Lewis (New York: Fordham University Press, 2003). William Desmond also has interesting philosophical points to make about the sacredness of the flesh in his recent essays on "consecration"; see "Consecrated Love," *INTAMS Review* 2 (Spring 2005): 4–17, and "Consecrated Thought," *Louvain Studies*, no. 30 (2005): 92–106. The theme of the "flesh" was largely ignored by Western metaphysics since Plato. This may seem strange given the fact that almost fifteen hundred years of the history of metaphysics comprised what Étienne Gilson called the "Christian synthesis" of Greek and biblical thought. But scholastic metaphysics (with some notable exceptions, like Scotus before scholasticism or Thomas before Thomism!) managed to take the flesh and blood out of Christian incarnation, leaving us with abstract conceptual and categorical equivalents. There were the mystics of course, whose lives and confessions testified, as I am trying to suggest in this volume, to the mystery of transcendent-immanence; but these were invariably sidelined or threatened with the Inquisition or the Index (i.e. Eckhart and the Beguines, John of the Cross, Teresa of Avila, Margaret Porete). The citadel of scholasticism was not breached by their heartfelt heresies. Or, if it was, it remained in proud and sovereign denial. It resisted all such infiltrations of the flesh-invested spirit from without and from within. Even poor Aquinas, as noted, had the mystical harm taken out of him, his initial nerve and brio reduced to a caricature of itself. Aquinas's original doctrine of analogy and his concept of divine simpleness in the *Summa Theologica* (1–1,3) ruled out any of the purchase on a divine essence that would be implied in reducing God to a principle of sufficient reason (Leibniz) or a metaphysical necessity (second-hand scholasticism). In this sense Aquinas, and Bonaventura too, could be said to stand firm against

theodicy. By contrast, the closed edifice of Ontotheology—which admitted subtle thinkers like Aquinas to a systematic caricature—admitted of no gaps, no risks, no wagers. Immune to the daring of quotidian incarnation—the daily coming into flesh of the divine (*ensarkosis,* as Scotus called it)—mainstream metaphysics stood firm, indubitable, *intactus.* So, in terms of Western philosophy at least, it would, I will argue, take Husserl and the modern phenomenological revolution to bring Western philosophy back to the experience of "sacramental flesh," that is, the possibility of acknowledging Spirit in our prereflective lived experience. One might also note here the way in which a thinker like Paul Ricoeur has attempted hermeneutic retrievals of classic thinkers like Spinoza on singularities and *conatus* or Leibniz on *dynamis* in light of a phenomenological awakening to the living body. See also here the work of feminist thinkers Catherine Keller, *The Face of the Deep: A Theology of Becoming* (New York: Routledge, 2003); and Luce Irigaray, *Speculum of the Other Woman,* trans. Gillian C. Gill (Cornell: Cornell University Press, 1985). Nor should we omit reference to Gabriel Marcel's intriguing philosophical reflections on incarnation and embodiment, which exerted a considerable influence on the "religious" phenomenological writings of Ricoeur and Levinas: see especially *Being and Having,* trans. Katherine Farrer (Westminister: Dacre, 1949). See, finally, Steven Schloesser on painting (especially Rouault) and what he calls mystic modernism, in his *Jazz Age Catholicism: Mystic Modernism in Postwar Paris, 1919–1923* (Toronto: University of Toronto Press, 2005).

8. See James Morley, "Embodied Consciousness in Tantric Yoga and the Phenomenology of Merleau-Ponty," in Richard Kearney, ed., *The Interreligious Imagination,* special issue of *Religion and the Arts* 12, no. 1–3 (Leiden: Brill, 2008): 144–163. See also Husserl's statements on God, transcendence, and the absolute cited in my "Hermeneutics of the Possible God," in Ian Leask and Eoin Cassidy, eds., *Givenness and God* (New York: Fordham University Press, 2005), 220f.

9. Maurice Merleau-Ponty, *Phenomenology of Perception* (London: Routledge, 2002), 246. I am grateful to John Panteleimon Manoussakis for this reference; see Manoussakis's extended discussion of this theme in *God After Metaphysics: A Theological Aesthetics* (Bloomington: Indiana University Press, 2007). Merleau-Ponty also has an intriguing notion of "primary faith" that operates at the most basic level of our ordinary perception and requires an interruption of critical non-faith or suspension if we are to return to it as an "engima" or "wonder" after the event. See, for example, the opening section of Maurice Merleau-Ponty, *The Visible and the Invisible,* trans. Alfonso Lingis (Evanston, IL: Northwestern University Press, 1968): "We see the things themselves, the world is what we see: formulae of this kind express a faith common to the natural man and the philosopher— the moment he opens his eyes; they refer to a deep-seated set of mute 'opinions' implicated in our lives. But what is strange about this faith is that if we seek to articulate it into theses or statements, we enter into a labyrinth of difficulties and contradictions." So our world of primary perception is already, at a pre-reflective level of lived experience, a primary faith, which the philosophical moment of questioning interrupts. But this interruption—as formalized in Husserl's reduction and epoché, for example—does not offer answers so much as invite us to think of ourselves as an "enigma" (ibid., 3–4). But this enigma should not be thought of in terms of some abstract intellectual curiosity, nor as an Oedipus riddle to be solved. It is an enigma rather in the sense of a challenge to our preconceived views, an

endless wrestling with the options of meaning and meaninglessness in an effort to see what seeing means, to better understand what belief believes. As such, the philosophical suspension of primary faith introduces a sense of "wonder before what is," which in turn allows for the possibility of a second faith in the wake of philosophical interrogation and poetic wonderment.

10. Merleau-Ponty, *Phenomenology of Perception*, 248.
11. Merleau-Ponty, *The Visible and the Invisible*, as cited in my *Modern Movements in European Philosophy* (Manchester: Manchester University Press, 1986), 88–89.
12. Ibid., 89. Merleau-Ponty is influenced here by Gaston Bachelard's "phenomenology of the elemental," already developed in the years 1938–1948 and brought to fruition in Bachelard's later works like *Poetics of Reverie* (Boston: Beacon, 1971). Bachelard also explored the notion of reversible seeing and reversible speaking in the context of a passive-active acoustic, e.g., "When a dreamer speaks, who is speaking he or the world?" (ibid., 187); or again, on active-passive vision: "everything that shines sees" (ibid., 186). Bachelard also wrote that the poetic reveries of imagination can resacralize the world: "reverie sacralizes its object," elevating it to the level of the poetic as it consecrates the moment of experience" (ibid., 36). Merleau-Ponty explicitly acknowledges his debt to Bachelard in *The Visible and the Invisible*, at page 267, and elsewhere. See also Eileen Rizo-Patron, *"Regressus ad Uterum*: Bachelard's Alchemical Hermeneutics," *Philosophy Today*, special Society for Phenomenology and Existential Philosophy issue, ed. Peg Birmingham and James Risser, vol. 33 (Fall 2008): 21–30.
13. Maurice Merleau-Ponty, "Eye and Mind," in Richard Kearney and David Rasmussen, eds., *The Continental Aesthetics Reader* (Oxford: Blackwell, 2001), 288f.
14. Maurice Merleau-Ponty, *Signs* (Evanston, IL: Northwestern University Press, 1964), as cited in Kearney, *Modern Movements*, 85. But even prior to the language of art, the language of everyday life—what Merleau-Ponty calls primary expression—is a transubstantiation of my relations with others. Language is the "reverberation of my relations with myself and with others"; Merleau-Ponty, *The Prose of the World*, ed. Claude Lefort, trans. J. O'Neill, Evanston, IL: Northwestern University Press), 20. In the art of speaking and listening, intersubjectivity is tensional. "Whether speaking or listening," notes Merleau-Ponty, "I project myself onto the other person, I introduce him into my own self. Our conversation resembles a struggle between two athletes in a tug-of-war. The speaking 'I' abides in its body. Rather than imprisoning it, language is like a magic machine for transporting the 'I' into the other person's perspective" (ibid., 19). Hence the miracle of dialogue: "in the experience of dialogue, there is constituted between the other subject and myself a common ground; my thought and his are interwoven into a single fabric, my words and those of my interlocutor are called forth by the state of the discussion, and they are inserted into a shared operation of which neither of us is the creator. We have a dual being, where the other is no longer for me a mere bit of behavior in my transcendental field, nor I in his; we are collaborators for each other in consummate reciprocity. Our perspectives merge into each other, and we co-exist through a common world. In the present dialogue I am freed from myself, for the other person's thoughts are certainly his; they are not of my making, though I do grasp them the moment they come into being, or even anticipate them. And indeed the objection which my interlocutor raises to what I say draws from me thoughts which I had no idea I possessed, so that at the same time that I had lent

him thoughts, he reciprocates by making me think too" (*Phenomenology of Perception*, 313). But if language as speaking transports the I into the other, as listening it imports the other into the I. This interplay of activity and passivity vis-à-vis the other allows for the possibility of hospitality while preventing the temptation of fusion or projection. The fact that I passively receive the other as stranger—always indirectly and *de biais*—means that I am constantly recalled to my limits. The I cannot encapsulate or appropriate the other through language—unless it ceases to listen, which means ceasing to function as communication. The other who exceeds my limits reminds me of my limits—that is, my hermeneutic situatedness as a listener and speaker in a particular time and place facing a particular other before me who is "not me." This emphasis on hermeneutic difference in the I-Other conversation is, of course, accentuated if the other speaks a foreign language and we are obliged to consciously translate between one lexicon and another. This is why, for Merleau-Ponty, language is the guarantor that subjectivity is always inter-subjectivity (*Phenomenology of Perception*, 421).

15. Merleau-Ponty, *Signs*, cited in Kearney, *Modern Movements*, 83–84.
16. Maurice Merleau-Ponty, "Inaugural Lecture to the "Société Française," in James Eddie, ed., *The Primacy of Perception* (Evanston, IL: Northwestern University Press, 1964), 27f.
17. Maurice Merleau-Ponty, *Nature: Course Notes from the Collège de France*, ed. Dominique Seglard, trans. Robert Vallier (Evanson IL: Northwestern University Press, 1995), 133.
18. Ibid., 137.
19. Ibid., 137–138.
20. Ibid., 138. My thanks to my Boston College colleague Kascha Semonovitch for bringing several of these passages to my attention.
21. Jean-Paul Sartre, "Merleau-Ponty Vivant," in *The Debate Between Sartre and Merleau-Ponty*, ed. Jon Stewart (Evanson, IL: Northwestern University Press, 1998), 611.
22. Ibid., 616.
23. Ibid., 617.
24. Ibid., 617–618. In his autobiography, *The Words*, Sartre admits that he himself replaced religion with a mysticism of literature: "I have been writing for exactly half a century, and for forty years I have lived in a glass prison. . . . I realize that literature is a substitute for religion. . . . I felt the mysticism of words . . . little by little, atheism has devoured everything. I have disinvested and secularized writing: One could say that my metamorphosis started with the transformation of my relationship with language. I have passed from terrorism to rhetoric: in my most mystical years, words were sacrificed to things; as an unbeliever, I returned to words, needing to know what speech meant." As cited in Annie Cohen-Solal, *Jean-Paul Sartre* (New York: New Press, 2005), 357–358). Later, Sartre would replace literature with politics, which then became "everything," the second substitute religion. As described by Sartre, Merleau-Ponty's refusal of atheism and continued fascination with a certain mysticism of in-visible flesh suggests that their attitudes to the sacred were far from identical. Merleau-Ponty did not, it seems, unambiguously replace religion with literature and politics in the same way as Sartre.
25. See Jean-Luc Marion, *On Excess* (New York: Fordham University Press, 2005); and Chrétien's *Hand to Hand*. See also the pioneering writings on sacramental

aesthetics, as a traversal of the secular by the sacred, of flesh by transcendence, by Karmen MacKendrick, *Fragmentation and Memory* (New York: Fordham University Press, 2008); and Regina Schwartz, *Sacramental Poetics at the Dawn of Secularism* (Stanford: Stanford University Press, 2008).

26. See Joseph O'Leary, "Knowing the Heart Sutra by Heart," in Kearney, *The Interreligious Imagination*, 356f.

27. See Julia Kristeva, *Strangers to Ourselves*, and also my dialogue with Kristeva on this subject entitled "Strangers to Ourselves: The Hope of the Singular" in Richard Kearney, ed., *Debates in Continental Philosophy* (New York: Fordham University Press, 2006), 159–166.

28. Julia Kristeva, *Time and Sense: Proust and the Experience of Literature* (New York: Columbia University Press, 1996), 251. Transubstantiation is defined as 1. "The changing of one substance into another"; 2. "The conversion in the Eucharist of the whole substance of the bread and of the wine into the blood of Christ, only the appearances (and other 'accidents') of bread and wine remaining: according to the doctrine of the Roman Catholic Church 1533"; William R. Trumble, *The Shorter Oxford English Dictionary*, 6th ed. (New York: Oxford University Press, 2007), 2349. What fascinates both Joyce and Proust about this process, according to Kristeva, is that such an act, mixing the secular and the sacred, combines both an "imaginary" and "real" character. I would not wish to confine the sense of transubstantion in this essay to the Christian or Catholic only, as I believe it carries a deeply interreligious charge. See, for example, how much of what is said in this chapter about transubstantiation chimes with the mystical Islamic notion of "transubstantial movement" (*haraka jawhariya*), a sacred rhythm of the cosmos, as invoked by Sufi sages from Ibn 'Arabi to Ostad Elahi: "No creature is completely immobile; they are all constantly in a . . . 'trans-substantial movement.' This universal trans-substantial motion exists in all beings and animates the entire universe: This movement is caused by the absolute movement of the Divine Essence to which each being is directly connected. This is the phenomenon that they call the 'immediate connection' between God and each of his creatures, which explains how God is present everywhere in all creation. . . . This trans-substantial movement exists in minerals, plants, animals and in general in every creature"; cited in James Morris, *Orientations: Islamic Thought in a World Civilisation* (London: Archeype, 2003), 81. For the Sufi sages, this mystical cosmic motion of interanimating substances was intuited by the human heart (*qalb*) capable of seeing the deep inner convertibility between finite and infinite forces. Gerald Manley Hopkins would be pleased, I think, as would Joyce, Proust, and Woolf.

29. Kristeva, *Time and Sense*, 246. Michel de Certeau offers an interesting account of the close connection between mystical and carnal experience that I think is as relevant to our reading of philosophers like Merleau-Ponty and Kristeva as to that of writers like Proust, Woolf, and Joyce (chapter 5, this volume): "mystics were drawn away, by the life they lived and by the situation that was given to them, toward a language of the body. In a new interplay between what they recognized internally and the part of their experience that is externally (socially) recognizable, mystics were led to create from this corporeal vocabulary the initial markers indicating the place in which they found themselves and the illumination they received. Just as Jacob's wound in the hip was the sole visible mark of his nocturnal encounter

with the angel, so ecstasy, levitation, stigmata, fasting, insensibility to pain, visions, tactile sensations, odors, and the like furnished the music of the senses with the scale of a specific language"; Michel de Certeau, "Mysticism," *Diacritics* 22, no. 2 (1992): 15. The mystics deployed their own corporeal phenomena as a way of saying the "unsayable." They thus proceeded to a "description that ran the gamut of 'sensations,' allowing us to measure the distance between the common usage of these words and the truth that the mystics, led by their experience, gave to them. . . . The 'emotions' of affectivity and the alterations of the body thus became the clearest indicators of the movement produced before or after the stability of intellectual formulations. . . . Mysticism found its modern social language in the body" (ibid.). There is also a telling analogy, I think, between the mystical experience of carnal hospitality to the Other and what Proust called "involuntary memory" and sensible transubstantiation: "the mystic 'somatises,' interprets the music of meaning with his or her corporeal repertoire. One not only plays one's body; one is played by it, as if the piano or trumpet were the composer and the player only the instrument. . . . Philoxène de Mabboug once dared to say, 'The sensible is the cause of the soul and precedes it in the intellect'" (ibid., 22).

30. Kristeva, *Time and Sense*, 246.
31. Ibid.
32. See ibid., 247: "A state of flesh," writes Kristeva, "appears to underlie the therapeutic act, but it can become a true therapeutic act only if language is led to the reversible and chiasmic sensation that supports it" (what Proust calls the "impression" or "transubstantion"; ibid.). For Kristeva this reversibility of flesh can take the form of 1. a literary act of writing and reading as a "two-sided sensoriality" or 2. a psychoanalytic act of transference and countertransference. Interestingly, neither Proust nor Joyce were insensitive to the powers of psychotherapy, any more than they were to the powers of religion—without practicing either. One thinks of Joyce's exchanges with Jung—when he was "jung and freudened" as he puts it in *Finnegans Wake*—or of Lacan's intriguing pun on Joyce as "sinthome" (*symptôme/ saint-homme* or "holy man"). And one recalls the following observation by Proust in *Contre Sainte-Beuve*: "Reading is at the threshold of spiritual life and can lead us to it though it does not constitute it. . . . For someone who is lazy, books play the same role that psychotherapists do for those afflicted with neurasthenia" (cited ibid., 385). In her reading of Proust, Kristeva cites and comments a number of key passages from Merleau-Ponty's *The Visible and the Invisible*, 246f.
33. Kristeva, *Time and Sense*, 251.
34. Marcel Proust, *Against Sainte-Beuve*, cited in Kristeva, *Time and Sense*, 252. I think Kristeva is close here to the hermeneutic model of extralinguistic ontological refiguration that Paul Ricoeur speaks of in *Time and Narrative*, vol 1 (Chicago: University of Chicago Press, 1984). See Ricoeur's claim, for example, that "what a reader receives is not just the sense of the work, but, through its sense, its reference, that is, the experience it brings to language and, in the last analysis, the world and the temporality it unfolds in the face of this experience" (ibid., 78–79).
35. Max Scheler, "The Sense of Unity with the Cosmos," in *The Nature of Sympathy* (London: Routledge and Kegan Paul, 1954), 87f. For a more contemporary account of the relation between the sacramental, the symbolic, and the liturgical see Mark Patrick Hederman, *Symbolism* (Dublin: Veritas, 2007).

36. Scheler, "The Sense of Unity with the Cosmos," 87.
37. Ibid.
38. Ibid., 88. Scheler's work was informed by Husserl's phenomenological investigations but lacked the rigor of the phenomenological method, opting instead for a more romantic, eclectic, and holistic view of the subject in his writings on feeling and sympathy; see Max Scheler, *On Feeling, Knowing, and Valuing* (Chicago: University of Chicago Press, 1992). Scheler differs from both Merleau-Ponty or Kristeva, however, in that his reading of Francis's notion of the sacramental is a form of Christian apologetics closer to the contemporary Catholic phenomenologist Jean-Luc Marion; see, for example, Jean-Luc Marion, "The Phenomenality of the Sacrament—Being and Givenness," in Bruce Ellis Benson and Norman Wirzba, eds., *Words of Life: New Theological Turns in French Phenomenology* (New York: Fordham University Press, 2009).

5. IN THE TEXT

I am very grateful to all my colleagues in the Meaning and Transcendence Seminar at the Jesuit Institute at Boston College for several of the insights in this chapter, in particular those with whom I had a extensive creative correspondence on Joyce, Proust, and Woolf, namely: Mary-Joe Hughes, Dennis Taylor, Anne Davenport, Tom Epstein, Marty Cohen, Andy Von Hendy, Anne Kearney, Vanessa Rumble, and Kevin Newmark. Much of what follows in this chapter is a development of an anatheist aesthetics that I have attempted to explore elsewhere; see, for example, "Epiphanies of the Everyday: Toward a Micro-Eschatology," in John Panteleimon Manoussakis, ed., *After God: Richard Kearney and the Religious Turn in Phenomenology* (New York: Fordham University Press, 2006), and my related essays, "Traversing the Imaginary: Epiphanies in Joyce and Proust," in Peter Gratton and John Panteleimon Manoussakis, eds., *Traversing the Imaginary: Richard Kearney and the Postmodern Challenge* (Evanston, IL: Northwestern University Press, 2007), "Enabling God," in Manoussakis, *After God*, and "Hermeneutics of the Possible God," in Ian Leask and Eoin Cassidy, eds., *Givenness and God: Questions of Jean-Luc Marion* (New York: Fordham University Press, 2005), 220–242.

1. See Julia Kristeva, "Joyce the Gracehoper," in *New Maladies of the Soul*, trans. Ross Guberman (New York: Columbia University, 1995), 172–188. See in particular her opening statement: "Joyce's Catholicism, which consisted of his profound experience with Trinitarian religion as well as his mockery of it, impelled him to contemplate its central ritual—the *Eucharist*—which is the ritual par excellence of identification with God's body and a springboard for all other identifications, including that of artistic profusion. This ritual is also prescribed by the Catholic Faith. It is likely that the cultural context of Catholicism—which Joyce had completely assimilated—was challenged by a biographical event that endangered his identity and enabled him to focus his writing on the identificatory substratum of psychic functioning, which he masterfully laid out against the backdrop of the grandest religion" (ibid., 173) And she continues: "The obsession that Joyce the 'Gracehoper' had with the Eucharist theme is exemplified by his many references to transubstantiation or to Arius' heresy, to the consubstantiality between father and son in Shakespeare's *Hamlet* and between Shakespeare, his father, his son

Hamnet, as well as to Shakespeare's complete works in the sense of a veritable source of inspiration. Let us recall, moreover, the condensation of 'trinity' and 'transubstantiation; in Joyce's umbrella word 'contransmagnificandjewbangtatiatiality'" (ibid., 174). Pointing out that Joyce had read both Freud and Jung by 1915, Kristeva offers many intriguing psychoanalytic readings of Joyce's eucharistic aesthetic including the following: "In this way can Dedalus-Bloom achieve the plenitude of his text-body, and thus release his text to us as though it was his body, his transubstantiation. The narrator seems to say, 'This is my body,' and we know that he sometimes identifies with HCE in *Finnegans Wake*. As for the reader, he assimilates the true presence of a complex male sexuality through textual signs and without any repression. This is a prerequisite for enigmatic sublimation: the text, which restrains but does not repress libido, thereby exercises its cathartic function upon the reader. Everything is to be seen and all the places are available; nothing is lacking and nothing is hidden that could not indeed be present" (ibid., 176–177). Other informative treatments of Joyce's sacramental aesthetic include William Noon, *Joyce and Aquinas* (New Haven: Yale University Press, 1957); Robert Boyle, *James Joyce's Pauline Vision: A Catholic Exposition* (Carbondale, IL: Southern Illinois University Press, 1978); and J. Houbedine, "Joyce, littérature et religion," *Excès de langage* (Paris: Denoöl, 1984). Although Stephen Dedalus rejects the Eucharist of Jesus for the art of Icarus early in *A Portrait of the Artist as a Young Man*, later in the novel he revisits an aesthetic of the sacred in his reading of Thomistic radiance (*claritas*): "The supreme quality is felt by the artist when the esthetic image is first conceived in his imagination. . . . The instant wherein that supreme quality of beauty, the clear radiance of the esthetic image, is apprehended luminously by the mind which has been arrested by its wholeness and fascinated by its harmony is the luminous silent stasis of esthetic pleasure, a spiritual state like that cardiac condition which the Italian physiologist Luigi Galvani . . . called the enchantment of the heart"; see James Joyce, *A Portrait of the Artist as a Young Man* (New York: Penguin, 1992), 23. It is typical of Joyce's incarnational aesthetic to link Aquinas's transcendental category of beauty here with the more physiological category of heart and flesh. Tellingly, we are told in the concluding lines of *A Portrait* of the wish that Stephen "may learn in [his] own life and away from home and friends what the heart is and what it feels. So be it. Welcome, O life!" (ibid., 275).

2. Conversation with Joyce recorded in Stanislas Joyce, *My Brother's Keeper* (Dublin: Da Capo Press, 2003), 103f. I am grateful to Fran O'Rourke for bringing this passage to my attention.

3. See my "Joyce: Epiphanies and Triangles," in Richard Kearney, *Navigations: Collected Irish Essays, 1976–2006* (Dublin: Lilliput/Syracuse: University of Syracuse Press, 2006), 131f, and "Traversing the Imaginary." On epiphany in Joyce, see also George Steiner, *Real Presences* (London: Faber and Faber, 1989), 112f. On parodied, failed, or deconstructed Eucharists in Joyce's stories—"Sisters," "Clay," and the "Dead"—see the work of theologian Joseph O'Leary, e.g., "Enclosed Spaces in 'The Dead,'" in *English Literature and Language* 34 (Tokyo: Sophia University, 1997): 33–52.

4. James Joyce, *Ulysses* (London: Penguin, 1968), 204. On the subject of the eschatological kiss, see also my comparison between Molly and the bride of the Song of Songs in "The Shulammite's Song: Divine Eros, Ascending and Descending,"

in Virginia Burrus and Catherine Keller, eds., *Toward a Theology of Eros: Transfiguring Passion at the Limits of Discipline* (New York: Fordham University Press, 2006). One might also compare and contrast this kiss with another moment of recollected love in Joyce's story, "The Dead," where Gretta recalls her first love, Michael Fury: a scene that is also associated with a sacramental feast, celebrating the Incarnation of the Word at Christmas

5. See our discussion of Joyce's proximity to Duns Scotus's notions of *haecceitas* (thisness) and *ensarkosis* (the ongoing enfleshment of the divine in the world) in "Joyce: Epiphanies and Triangles," in Kearney, *Navigations*, 131f. See also Gaston Bachelard's notion of poetic reverie as a way of raising limited empirical experiences to the level of consecrated time in *Poetics of Reverie* (Boston: Beacon, 1971), 36, 154, 163, 165. Bachelard also develops a notion of second or poetic naïveté (beyond the natural attitude), in a manner analogous to Ricoeur, when he writes: "It is this naïveté, systematically revealed, which ought to result in a pure reception of poems. In our studies of active imagination, we shall follow phenomenology then as a school of naïveté" (ibid., 4).

6. Rudolphe Gasché, *Inventions of Difference: On Jacques Derrida* (Cambridge: Harvard University Press, 1994), 230. Gasché is here elaborating on Derrida's reading of Joyce in "Ulysses Gramophone," in Jacques Derrida, *Acts of Literature*, ed. Derek Attridge (New York: Routledge, New York, 1992).

7. Paul Ricoeur, "Life in Quest of Narrative," in David Wood, ed., *On Paul Ricoeur* (London: Routledge, 1991), 26.

8. Paul Ricoeur, *Time and Narrative* (Chicago: University of Chicago Press, 1988), 3:170.

9. On this later point see Julia Kristeva, *Time and Sense: Proust and the Experience of Literature* (New York: Columbia University Press, 1996), 3–22. For a eucharistic hermeneutics of reading see also Valentine Cunningham, *Reading After Theory* (Oxford: Blackwell, 2002), 148f. Cunningham states: "Here is a body of text and the text as body , the body of the other, the text as other, to be consumed, ingested, in a memorial act, an act of testimony, of worldly witness. . . . In holy communion the believer is blessed and graced, signed as Christ's own, marked as sanctified. In reading on this [eucharistic model], the reader is, in some way or another, also graced, blessed, marked as the text's own" (ibid.).

10. Søren Kierkegaard, *Repetition* (Princeton: University Press, 1941).

11. James Joyce, letter to his brother Stanislaus, 1905, cited by Declan Kiberd in his introduction to the 1992 Penguin edition of *Ulysses* (London: Penguin, 1992), x. The letter begins: "Do you not think the search for heroics damn vulgar?" For a theological reading of Joyce as a mixing of the sacred with the profane, see Thomas J. J. Altizer, *Living the Death of God: A Theological Memoir* (Albany: State University of New York Press, 2006), especially chapter 3, "Epic Theology," which cites Joyce, Dante, and Blake as poetic examples of the comic immanence of the holy as a *coincidentia oppositorum* of verticality and depth, of light and dark, of theism and atheism.

12. Derrida offers a useful gloss on the ostensibly Hegelian language of Molly/Penelope in an intriguing footnote to his commentary on the relationship between Greek and Jew in Emmanuel Levinas in his "Violence and Metaphysics: An Essay on the Thought of Emmanuel Levinas," in *Writing and Difference* (Chicago: University of Chicago Press, 1978), 320–321. Commenting on a phrase in

Ulysses—"Jewgreek is greekjew. Extremes meet"—Derrida attributes this not only to "woman's reason," as in Joyce's text, but he also identifies Joyce here as "perhaps the most Hegelian of modern novelists" (ibid., 153). The implication seems to be that the discourse of "feminine logic," associated with Molly/Penelope, is one that, for Levinas at least, suggests an "ontological category" of return and closure: namely, Ulysses returning to Penelope in Ithaca, Stephen and Bloom returning to Molly in Eccles Street where they may find themselves "atoned" as father-son, jew-greek, greek-jew, etc. It is not quite clear where Derrida himself stands toward Joyce in this early 1964 text, though it is evident that he thinks Levinas would repudiate the Joycean formula as overly Hegelian and Greek (that is, not sufficiently respectful of the strictly Jewish/messianic/eschatological need for a radically asymmetrical relation of self and other). In his later essay, "Ulysses Gramophone," first delivered as a lecture to the International Joyce Symposium in Frankfurt, 1984, Derrida makes it clear that the "yes" of Molly/Penelope marks an opening of the text beyond totality and closure to an infinite and infinitely recurring "other"; see Jacques Derrida, *Ulysses Gramophone: Deux Mots sur Joyce* (Paris, Galilée, 1987). Even if it is a response to oneself, in interior dialogue, "yes" always involves a relay through an other. Or as Derrida cleverly puts it, *oui-dire*, saying yes, always involves some form of *oui-dire* or hearsay: "A yes never comes along, and we never say this word alone" (ibid., 300). With this relay of self through the other, this willing of yes to say yes again, "this differing and deferring, this necessary failure of total self-identity, comes spacing [space *and* time], gramophoning [writing *and* speech], memory" (ibid., 254). And this "other" clearly implies a reaching beyond the text of *Ulysses* itself to the listener, the reader, an open call for our response.

In this sense I would say that *Ulysses* is, ultimately, an anti-Hegelian book. Molly's finale does not represent some great teleological reconciliation of contradictions in some synthesis of Absolute Spirit, but an ongoing affirmation of paradoxes, struggles, contraries, contingencies, spoken in a spirit of humor and desire. "What else were we given all those desires for . . . ?" asks the polymorphously perverse Molly, a far cry from the Hegelian triumph of Identity. We may conclude, therefore, that the story of struggle and trouble does not end when Stephen follows Bloom out of the library; it only begins. And by the same token, Molly, when she finally arrives, does not dismiss Trinities as such, she simply reintroduces us— along with Stephen and Bloom—to another kind of trinity, one without a capital T and more inclusive of time, movement, natality, and desire (all those things banned from the Sabellian Trinity of self-enclosed Identity parodied by Stephen in the National Library scene). And, one might add, more inclusive of the reader. For, like any epiphany, Molly's too calls out to an open future of readers.

13. See my "Traversals and Epiphanies in Joyce and Proust," in *Traversing the Imaginary: Richard Kearney and the Postmodern Challenge*, ed. John Manoussakis and Peter Gratton (Evanston, IL: Northwestern University Press, 2007), 183–208. Our understanding of eucharistic epiphany in literature is deeply indebted to Proust's understanding of sacred "repetition" over time and space, as articulated in the following passage on the way in which all of Combray appeared in a tea-cup: "What is more, it is when the direct short-circuit between two similar sensations, obtained in happy moments, is supplanted by the long mediation on the work of art, that repetition takes on its full signification, which appeared to me to be summed up in the admirable expression of distance traversed. In happy moments,

two similar instants were miraculously brought together, through the mediation of art, this fleeting miracle is stabilized in an enduring work. Time lost is equated with time regained"; Marcel Proust, *The Captive and the Fugitive* (New York: Vintage, 1996), 664. Such eucharistic epiphanies in literature are a connection across distance in time and space, just as the Christian sacrament is a remembrance of the Last Supper of the past (which itself repeats the Passover), which it repeats forward "*until he (the Messiah) comes*" in the future.

14. See Ricoeur, *Time and Narrative*, chapter 7, "The World of the Text and the World of the Reader," 3:157f.

15. See my discussion of the eschatological temporality of the Palestinian formula in both Judaic and Christian messianism in "Enabling God," in Manoussakis, *After God*, and "Paul's Notion of Dunamis," in John Caputo and Linda Martin Alcoff, eds., *Saint Paul Among the Philosophers* (Bloomington: Indiana University Press, 2009). Our own sketch of micro-eschatological possibility, temporality, and carnality is poetically articulated in the following lines of Denise Levertov's "The Annunciation": "The engendering Spirit / did not enter her without consent / God waited," offering her the "astounding ministry . . . to bear in her womb / Infinite weight and lightness; to carry / in hidden, finite inwardness, / nine months of Eternity; to contain / in slender vase of being, the sum of power— / in narrow flesh, / the sum of light. / Then bring to birth, / push out into air, a Man-child/ needing, like any other, / milk and love." Denise Levertov and Paul A. Lacey, *The Selected Poems of Denise Levertov* (New York: New Directions, 2002), 162–163. Teresa of Calcutta expresses a similar sentiment when she writes of the same reversibility of eucharistic giving: "Into each of our lives Jesus comes as the bread of life—to be eaten, to be consumed by us. Then he comes as the hungry one, the other, hoping to be fed with the bread of our life, our hearts loving, and our hands serving." See also these lines by Yves Bonnefoy in his poem, "Une voix" ("A Voice," 1965) "Oui, je puis vivre ici. L'ange qui est la terre / Va dans chaque buisson et paraître et brûler" (Yes, here I can live. The angel that is earth / Will appear in every bush, and will burn). I am grateful to Anne Davenport and Hoyt Rogers for this reference. See also the interesting phenomenological analyses of epiphany in Anthony Steinbock, *Phenomenology and Mysticism* (Bloomington: Indiana University Press, 2007), 17–25. Finally, see John Manoussakis on the phenomenological distinction between sacred time (*kairos*) and secular time (*chronos*) in John Panteleimon Manoussakis, *God After Metaphysics: A Theological Aesthetics* (Bloomington: Indiana University Press, 2007), 58–63.

16. Contrast this inaugural—and ultimately lost—kiss of maternal "fusion" with the disastrous kiss of "diffusion" that Marcel experiences with Albertine later in the novel. The closest Marcel may be said to come to achieve a eucharistic kiss, beyond these two extremes, might be the brushing of his lips on the table napkin chez les Guermantes, which recalls the meal at the Grand Hotel in Balbec or, perhaps more emblematically, the image of the "star-shaped" crossroads where the two diverging paths of his youth—le chemin de Méséglise and le chemin de Swann—converge almost mystically, chiasmically, "transversally," in the figure of Gilberte's daughter, Mlle de Saint-Loup, at the final party. But this final kiss is a kiss deferred for others, in the future, just as the final meal chez les Guermantes is a feast postponed: his lips touch the napkin but he does not eat. It is significant, I think, that Proust's novel does not end with the epiphanies in the library. Marcel

does not stay in the Guermantes' library anymore than Stephen stays in the National Library after his insight into Hamlet. And though Marcel takes this occasion to announce an extremely elaborate theory of literature and life (as does Stephen), the text does not culminate with theory. Marcel leaves the library (as does Stephen again) and reenters the everyday universe. And it is here, in the midst of the chaos and commotion of a fragmenting Parisian community, that Marcel has what we might consider his ultimate epiphany: his meeting with Mlle de Saint-Loup (Gilberte's daughter).

Mlle de Saint-Loup is to Marcel what Molly (via Leopold) is to Stephen. Both appear at the end of the story and lead the author-artist beyond the vain play of mimetic triangles and abstract trinities back to the ordinary universe of generation and gratuity. Was she not, Marcel says of Mlle de Saint-Loup—"and are not the majority of human beings?—like one of those star-shaped crossroads in a forest where roads converge that have come, in the forest as in our lives, from the most diverse quarters"? And he adds: "Numerous for me were the roads which led to Mlle de Saint-Loup and which radiated around her" (see Proust, *The Captive and the Fugitive*, 502). Marcel then recalls the two great "ways"—the Guermantes Way represented by her father, Robert de Saint-Loup, and the Méseglise Way represented by her mother, Gilberte, the narrator's first youthful love. "One of them took me, by way of this girl's mother and the Champs-Elysées, to Swann, to my evenings at Combray, to Méseglise itself; the other, by way of her father, to those afternoons at Balbec where even now I saw him again near the sun-bright sea. And then between these two high roads a network of transversals was set up" (ibid.). From this emerges Marcel's new vision of life as a large web where the various incidents of time past and time recovered crisscross in a "network of memories" that give us an "almost infinite variety of communicating paths." So that life resurrected in and through literature becomes a palimpsest of chiasmic overlaps and transversals that cannot be brought to a final close. Mlle de Saint-Loup sets up a series of reverberations and recollections that resonate out into the future. She is the only character in the novel not "recalled" from the past as such. She comes to Marcel out of the future, as it were, taking him by surprise. And it is precisely by virtue of her "messianic" advent into Marcel's world that she engenders a new *optique* on the past, the present, and the time-still-to-come.

This new *optique* is what Marcel now calls a three-dimensional psychology, one that leads from life to literature and back again. Marcel's recapture of the different planes and elements of his life, following his encounter with Mlle de Saint-Loup in the party, makes him realize that "in a book which tries to tell the story of a life it would be necessary to use not the two-dimensional psychology which we normally use but a quite different sort of three-dimensional psychology"; a perspective that affords, he says, "a new beauty to those resurrections of the past which [his] memory effected while [he] was following his thoughts alone in the library" (ibid., 505–506). Marcel, like Stephen after his library epiphany, is now ready to "part" with his past so as to regain it. He is prepared to pass from the "see this, remember" (epiphany 1) to the "will see" (epiphany 2). And again, like Stephen, Marcel will be lead to his book and to a life-beyond-the-book by someone with whom he does not actually speak (Molly for Stephen, Mlle de Saint-Loup for Marcel). In Gilberte's daughter, coming to him across the room in the Guermantes salon, Marcel sees the possibility of rebirth and renewal, another's life beginning again and going beyond his own. This young woman, he realizes, is the incarnation of time lost and regained: "Time, colorless and inapprehensible time, so that I was almost able to see it and touch it, had materialized itself in this girl . . . still rich in hopes, full of laughter, formed from those very years which I myself had lost, she was like my own youth" (ibid., 507).

Then comes the moment of decisive *anagnorisis* (see Aristotle, *Poetics* 4.4.1448). While tempted to rejoin his old ambition to compose a great master-piece, which would "realize a life within the confines of a book!"—mimetically drawing "comparisons from the loftiest and the most varied arts" (Proust, *The Captive and the Fugitive*, 507)—Marcel says no. He resists the temptation. "What a task awaited him!" he proclaims, taking his final distance from the persona of the Great Writer, now suddenly displaced into the third person—"How happy would he be, I thought, the man who had the power to write such a book!" (ibid.). But Marcel now knows he is not this man. He is not one of those Promethean roman-tic artists whose will-to-power would construct his work "like a general conducting an offensive" or an architect building a huge vaulted "cathedral," ensuring one's immortality even in the tomb, "against oblivion" (ibid., 508). This Ideal Author of the Ideal Book is not for Marcel. He has learned, like Stephen in the wake of the library episode, to "cease to strive." And, again like Stephen, he has come to disavow "his own theory." He no longer believes in the Gospel of the Absolute Text. Instead, he resolves on a far more modest proposal: to begin a work that will serve not as a text in-itself and for-itself—the Grand Illusion of the self-sufficient Book—but rather as a pretext for the renewed and resurrected life of his readers. Marcel's critical conversion is marked by the seemingly innocuous phrase, "But to return to my own case." The word "But" is all important here. The full passage reads as follows: "But to return to my own case, I thought more modestly of my book and it would be inaccurate even to say that I thought of those who would read it as 'my' readers. For it seemed to me that they would not be 'my' readers but the readers of their own selves, my book being merely a sort of magnifying glass like those which the optician at Combray used to offer his customers—it would be my book, but with its help I would furnish them with the means of read-ing what lay inside themselves. So that I should not ask them to praise me or to censure me, but simply to tell me whether 'it really is like that,' I should ask them whether the words that they read within themselves are the same as those which I have written" (ibid.). The author dies unto himself so as to be reborn in and through his readers. Marcel's literary *metanoia* is complete. The die is cast. This ultimate epiphany expresses itself in a series of descriptions of writing as discovery and disclosure—midwifery, pregnancy, childbirth, mining, incubation, detection, listening, diving, excavation, repetition, revelation. Indeed it confirms Samuel Beckett's own conclusion that, for Proust, "the only fertile research is excavatory"; Samuel Beckett, *Proust* (New York: Grove, 1970), 25. The old romantic delu-sion of art as some fiat of omnipotence gives way to a more humble profession, namely, to an aesthetics of passion rather than imposition, of receptivity rather than volition, of humility rather than hubris. Epiphany as anaphany. In a world, ana-aesthetics. And what do we readers learn from Penelope? What do we stand to gain, if anything, from our traversals of the Joycean and Proustian imaginaries? Less closure and consolation, I would wager, than keen vigilance and excitement before the open interplay between literature and life. Traversing the epiphanies of Marcel and Proust, something about our own sensibilities as readers is more finely attuned, just as something about our imaginations is more enhanced and amplified, graciously opened to new possibilities of being. After such odysseys the world we return to is, surely, never quite the same.

17. Kristeva, *Time and Sense*, 3f.

18. Ibid., 101. Kristeva comments interestingly on Proust's fascination with the Catholic Eucharist and links it with his aesthetic interest in John Ruskin: "For Proust, who was in search of the real presence of signs, the Mass described as taking place in 'the cathedrals that are the greatest and most original expression of French genius' proved to be a living example of the experience sought by his emerging aesthetic. The religion of the 'living God' was thoroughly attractive, and it was the primary source of Proust's interest in Ruskin. . . . Proust was sincerely disturbed by anticlerical laws and by the general anticlericalism of governing bodies. At the same time, he recognized that the *écoles libres* held a sectarian view of Freemasons and Jews and noted that clericalism itself 'had completely freed itself from the dogmas of the Catholic religion. . . . The Christian spirit . . . [has] nothing to do with the partisan spirit which we seek to destroy.' . . . With this in mind we see that John Ruskin (1819–1900) was the writer through whom Proust felt he could reinvigorate the religious aesthetic (or the aestheticized religion, for therein lay the entire question) in a modern and progressive fashion" (ibid., 100–101). Kristeva goes on to argue that Ruskin's seduction was "aesthetic as well as religious. When Proust outlined his nascent conception of life as 'real life' and artistic experience as a real presence, as 'time embodied' and a 'transubstantiation,' he relied on this confirmed socialist, this admired or challenged modern man" (ibid., 101).

19. Kristeva cites this telling passage from Proust's *Contre Sainte-Beuve*: "Crossing a courtyard I came to a standstill among the glittering uneven paving-stones. . . . In the depth of my being I felt the flutter of a past that I did not recognize; it was just as I set foot on a certain paving-stone that this feeling of perplexity came over me. I felt an invading happiness, I knew that I was going to be enriched by that purely personal thing, a past impression, a fragment of life in unsullied preservation. Suddenly, I was flooded by a stream of light). It was the sensation underfoot that I had felt on the smooth, slightly uneven pavement of the baptistery of Saint Mark's" (*Time and Sense*, 107). It is interesting that the other two novels under consideration here also end with touch-stones of a telling kind: the rock of the lighthouse which Mr. Ramsay touches in *To the Lighthouse* and the rock of Gibraltar where Molly's final anamnetic fantasy concludes.

20. Marcel Proust, *In Search of Lost Time*, vol. 6: *Time Regained*, ed. D. J. Enright, trans. Andreas Mayor and Terence Kilmartin (New York: Modern Library, 1999), 290.

21. Ibid., 291.

22. Ibid., 290. Gilles Deleuze makes the point in *Proust and Signs* (London: Athlone, 2000) that Proust's experience of "essences" requires the "style" of art and literature to be brought to expression. Proust speaks here of "a qualitative difference in the way that the world looks to us, a difference that, if there were no such thing as art, would remain the eternal secret of each man." See Marcel Proust, *In Search of Lost Time*, vol. 3: *The Guermantes Way*, ed. D. J. Enright, trans. C. K. Scott Moncrieff and Terence Kilmartin (New York: Modern Library, 2000), 895. In *Time Regained*, Proust famously describes the move from the inner se-

cret essence within each life to the style of literary art as an act of "translation." Deleuze refers to a "final quality at the heart of the subject" due to the fact that the essence "implicates, envelops, wraps itself up in the subject" (Deleuze, *Proust and Signs*, 43) and so doing constitutes the unique subjectivity of the individual. In short, essences may be said to individualize by being caught or inscribed in subjects in what Proust referred to as a "divine capture"; Marcel Proust, *In Search of Lost Time*, vol. 1: *Swann's Way*, ed. D. J. Enright, trans. C. K. Scott Moncrieff and Terence Kilmartin (New York: Modern Library, 1992), 350. The epiphanic translation of essence is also described by Proust as a "perpetual recreation of the primordial elements of nature" (*The Guermantes Way*, 906), implying that the essence retrieves the birth of time itself at the beginning of time. Invoking the Neoplatonic idea of *complicatio*—referring to an original enveloping of the many in the One prior to the unfolding of time (*explicatio*), Deleuze suggests that it is to this original timeless time, complicated within essence and revealed to the artist, that Proust points when he writes of "time regained." And, one might add, it also has echoes of Leibniz's view that each created monad represents the whole created world. Is this not close to what Proust is getting at when he writes of "Combray and its surrounding world taking shape and solidity out of a cup of tea" (ibid., 51). But, in Deleuze's reading of Proust, essence can only recapture this original birth of the world through the "style" of art—expressing that "continuous and refracted birth," that "birth regained" in a substance (words, colors, sound) rendered adequate (Deleuze, *Proust and Signs*, 46).

I think this can be linked with Walter Benjamin's suggestion that Proust's involuntary memory is "closer to forgetting than what is usually called memory," for it is only when we can forget conventional time that we are open to the capture or recall of originary timeless time. Following Proust's hint that "the only true pleasures are the one's we have lost" (Proust, *Time Regained*, 222), Benjamin defines the root of Proust's "elegiac happiness" in terms of "the eternal repetition, the eternal restoration of the original, the first happiness" which occurs in literature; Walter Benjamin, "The Image of Proust," in *Illuminations: Essays and Reflections*, ed. Hannah Arendt, trans. Harry Zohn (London: Pimlico, 1999), 200. Benjamin, like Deleuze, argues that the Proustian translation of essences—which I call epiphany—is only available through the mediation of literature. Indeed Benjamin goes so far as to claim that the "image of Proust is the highest physiognomic expression which the irresistibly growing discrepancy between life and literature was able to assume" (ibid., 197). Proust's use of literary metaphor extended the usual understanding of this trope to mean not just one thing standing for another—a notion deconstructed by Paul de Man's famous reading of Proust—but one thing standing for the world. Or, as Benjamin put it, "an experienced event is finite," but an involuntarily "remembered event is infinite because it is only a key to everything that happened before and after it" (ibid., 198). Commenting on the final meeting between Marcel and Mlle de Saint-Loup—described by Proust in terms of the "star-shaped crossroads" image—Thomas Gunn writes: "Thus the metaphoric, and expressive universe is created, which . . . combines unity and diversity and every element is able to express any other. It is only in remembering and writing that metonymy is transmuted into metaphor. However, this is no longer a metaphor that aims to exclude contingency and metonymy but a metaphor constituted entirely by chance but raised to the level of metaphor with the potential to express the whole world"; Thomas Gunn, "On Proust's Spiritual Exercises," seminar paper, University College Dublin, March 2005.

By contrast, my own reading of epiphany and transubstantiation as a two-way crossover between literature and life follows the more hermeneutic reading of Paul Ricoeur; see Ricoeur, *Time and Narrative*, vol. 2; and Kristeva, *Time and Sense*. As Ricoeur puts it, Marcel's "decision to write has the capacity to transpose the extra-temporal character of the original vision into the temporality of the resurrection of time lost" (Ricoeur, *Time and Narrative*, 2:145), and, so doing, it opens up a return journey to the life of the reader, refigured by the text toward new possibilities of being in the lived world. The reading of the text invites the reader to repeat the "spiritual exercises" performed by the narrator in and through the text, so that "the process of composition, of configuration, is not completed in the text but in the reader and under this condition makes possible the reconfiguration of life by narrative" (Ricoeur, "Life in Quest of Narrative," 26). In short, the hermeneutic reading espoused by Ricoeur, Kristeva, and this author construes epiphany as a double translation between life and literature. Proustian translation would thus take the form of a bilateral "transversal" from life to literature and from literature to life. This seems faithful to Proust's own chiasmic image of the "star-shaped crossroad" where "roads converge . . . from the most diverse crossroads" (Proust, *Time Regained*, 502).

23. Kristeva also identifies nominal associations here with Marie Magdalene in the Scriptures.

24. Marcel Proust, *In Search of Lost Time*, vol. 2: *Within a Budding Grove*, ed. D. J. Enright, trans. C. K. Scott Moncrieff and Terence Martin (New York: Modern Library, 1998), 23.

25. Proust, *Time Regained*, 432.

26. Proust, *Swann's Way*, 95.

27. Benjamin, "The Image of Proust," 210.

28. Walter Benjamin, *The Arcades Project*, trans. Kevin McLoughlin (Cambridge: Harvard University Press, 1999), 69. One might also mention here John Caputo's notion of holy "quotidianism" in *The Weakness of God: A Theology of the Event* (Bloomington: Indiana University Press, 2006), 155f.

29. Proust, *Time Regained*, 509.

30. The point is not that epiphanies never happened before the library scene; it is that Marcel was not yet ready to see and hear them for what they really were. He had not yet, to cite Deleuze, been fully trained in his "apprenticeship to signs." Gilles Deleuze, *Proust and Signs*, trans. Richard Howard (New York: Braziller, 1972), p. 10. And it is not until such apprenticeship is accomplished, through his recapitulative awareness of "being-towards-death" in the library, that Marcel can finally acknowledge the preciousness of even the most banal and discarded events through the lens of time recaptured (*le temps retrouvé*). Art is less a matter of romantic creation than of epiphanic recreation. For, as Marcel asks, "was not the re-creation by the memory of impressions which had then to be deepened, illumined, transformed into equivalents of understanding, was not this process one of the conditions, almost the very essence of the work of art as I had just now in the library conceived it?" (Proust, *Time Regained*, 525). Such epiphanic understanding marks the moment of anagnorisis. Otherwise put, time has to be lost before it can be recovered. Unless the seed dies, accidents cannot be retrieved as essences,

contingencies as correspondences, obsessions as epiphanies. Only through the veil of mortality can the sacred radiate across the profane world that the arrogant repudiate as ineligible for art. It is only after he renounces his promethean Will-to-Write that Marcel's previously in-experienced experience is re-experienced in all its neglected richness. (And the greater the neglect the greater the richness.) For it is precisely the rejected and remaindered events of Marcel's existence that return now, in and through literature, as "resurrections." The three personas of Marcel — as character, as narrator, and as author — seem to crisscross here for the first time, like three Proustian Magi recognizing that the deepest acts of communion are to be found in the most fortuitous acts of ordinary perception.

31. Ibid., 530–531. So what do these Proustian conclusions tell us about epiphany? They indicate, I suggest, that epiphany is a process "achieved" in a series of double moves. First, that of mortality and natality. Second, that of metaphor (the translation of one thing into another) and metonymy (the disclosure of new meaning through the accidental contiguity of contingent things). Third, that of constructing and deconstructing. Moreover, it is in this last double gesture that the text surpasses itself and finally reaches out toward its future readers. For, if we begin with the notion that literature "constructs" an epiphany based on the recreation of impressions recalled in involuntary memory, the literary text, in turn, "deconstructs" itself in order to allow for the recreation of the reader. That is how Penelope's tapestry and Françoise's sewing works — stitching and unstitching, weaving and unweaving, endlessly. In a form of hermeneutic arc, the text configures an epiphany already prefigured by a life that is ultimately refigured by the reader (see Ricoeur, *Time and Narrative*, vol. 2, especially the section entitled "The Traversed Remembrance of Things Past" in chapter 4). And this reader is one who not only co-creates the text with the author but re-creates it again as she returns from "text to action." So that, if epiphany invites a first move from life to literature, it re-invites us to come back again from literature to life. In both Proust and Joyce it is indeed Penelope who has the last word.

Walter Benjamin identifies the Penelope motif of textuality in Proust thus: "For the important thing for the remembering author is not what he experienced but the weaving of his memory, the Penelope work of recollection"; Benjamin, "The Image of Proust," *Illuminations* (New York: Schocken, 1969), 202. Benjamin interprets this Penelope trope in terms of a textual process of weaving-unweaving, forgetting-remembering, composing-disrupting that manages to reveal the extraordinary in the ordinary. Once again, Penelope's fidelity to the epiphanies of the everyday is affirmed: "Can we say that all lives, works and deeds that matter were never anything but the undisturbed unfolding of the most banal, most fleeting, most sentimental, weakest hour in the life of the one to whom they pertain" (ibid., 203). Or again: "Proust's most accurate, most convincing insights fasten on their objects as insects fasten on leaves, blossoms, branches, betraying nothing of their existence until a leap, a beating of wings, a vault, show the startled observer that some incalculable individual life has imperceptibly crept into an alien world. The true reader of Proust is constantly jarred by small shocks" (ibid., 208). This emphasis on the microscopic and minuscule is repeated at the level of language itself where Proust, like Joyce, offers us a subatomic investigation of society in terms of exploring the reverberations and associations of the most everyday words and phrases, what Benjamin calls "a physiology of chatter" (ibid., 206). This reminds me, in turn, of Camus's observation that "all great deeds and all great thoughts have a ridiculous beginning. Great thoughts are often born on a street corner or in a restaurant's revolving door"; Albert Camus, *The Myth of Sisyphus*, in *Basic Writings of Existentialism*, ed. G. Marino (New York: Modern Library, 2004), 448. This passage is followed by Camus's curious eucharistic allusion to the finding in the "body, affection, creation" the "wine of the absurd and the bread of indifference on which [the rebel] feeds his greatness" (ibid., 478). I am also reminded here of this marvelous passage in Aristotle's *On the Parts of Animals* (645a:15–23): "Every realm of nature is marvelous: and as Heraclitus, when the strangers who came to visit him found him warming himself at the furnace in the kitchen and hesitated to go in, is reported to have bidden them not to be afraid to enter, as even in that kitchen divinities were present, so we should venture on the study of every kind of living thing without distaste; for each and all will reveal to us something natural and something beautiful."

32. J. Hillis Miller, "The Rhythm of Creativity: *To the Lighthouse*," in J. Hillis Miller, *Tropes, Parables, Performatives: Essays in Twentieth-Century Literature* (Durham, NC: Duke University Press, 1991), 159.

33. Virginia Woolf, *A Room of One's Own* (London: Hogarth), 102. See Miller, *Tropes, Parables, Performatives*, 169.

34. Erich Auerbach, "The Brown Stocking," in *Mimesis* (New Jersey: Princeton University Press, 1968), 536. See also pages 540, 552.

35. Virginia Woolf, *To the Lighthouse* (London: Harcourt Brace, 1990), 82.

36. The references to Lily leaping into a "gap" and finding the third, final stroke that draws the "line, there in the centre," is interesting when we consider the image of the "wedge," so intimately and recurrently associated with Mrs. Ramsay. This trope carries connotations of a deep inner emptiness or nothingness—as in references to the "wedge of darkness" or the "wedge-shaped core of darkness"—that holds out the possibility of some mystical fullness or completion. When we recall that Lily has been trying to compose a portrait of Mrs. Ramsay and James in the form of a "purple triangle," one might be tempted to construe Lily's finishing brushstroke as the line that completes the two-sided wedge: the missing third side, so to speak. After which she can say, "it was done. . . . I have had my vision" (ibid., 209). Interestingly, this vision coincides with the exact moment that the missing father, Mr. Ramsay, lands on the rock of the lighthouse and finds acknowledgment in the hearts of his children, James and Cam. He is finally accepted back into the picture of mother and child. This is the moment that Lily, on shore in front of her painting, suddenly find's her "razor's edge" balance between "art and Mr. Ramsay." The final "cut" is made. The third stroke applied to the wedge. The triangle completed, work done, novel concluded. This charged figurative imagery of wedge and triangle may be read, I suggest, in aesthetic, psychoanalytic, or Trinitarian terms. Or all three combined. (It is interesting how the same Vedantic trope of the "razor's edge" was also used by Somerset Maugham as title for one of his novels. I am grateful to my colleague, Frank Clooney, for this information.)

37. Woolf, *To the Lighthouse*, 63–64. This approximates to the Buddhist and Hindu view that the sacred is in all sentient beings. See the teaching, for example, of Dilgo Khyentse Rinpoche in this regard: "Pure perception is to recognize the buddha-nature in all sentient beings and to see primordial purity and perfection in all phenomena." See John Makransky, *Awakening Through Love* (Boston: Wis-

dom, 2007), 92. The sacramental reference for all natural things is also evidenced in certain biblical texts, such as the Song of Songs (which Mrs. Ramsay's vision echoes in the final lines just cited), but also in the nature visions of certain Christian mystics like St. Francis, and Hildegarde of Bingen (see in particular her notion of *veriditas*, or the divine "greening" of all things), not to mention Gerard Manley Hopkins or Teilhard de Chardin. Woolf's English Protestant culture may not, however, have made her familiar with such writings. Either way, Woolf's mysticism, however "Asiatic" its allusions at times, remains nondenominational and nonconfessional. One might even say nontheistic or posttheistic—or anatheistic.

38. Virginia Woolf, *Moments of Being*, cited in Martin Corner, "Mysticism and Atheism in *To the Lighthouse*," in *Virginia Woolf's "To the Lighthouse*," ed. Harold Bloom (London: Chelsea House, 1988), 43. In a diary entry of May 9, 1926, Woolf notes how she had quarreled with her husband, Leonard, who "disliked the irrational Xtian in me." *The Diary of Virginia Woolf*, vol. 3: *1925–1930* (New York: Harvest, 1981), 81.

39. The metaphor of the "razor's edge" is a famous verse from Katha Upanishads, 3:16. Here is the full passage, concerning the discovery of the true mystical sense (Atman-Brahman): "Arise! Awake! Pay attention, / When you've attained your wishes! A razor's sharp edge is hard to cross— / That, poets say, is the difficulty of the path." And the passage goes on: "When a man perceives it, / fixed and beyond the immense, / He is freed from the jaws of death" (verse 15); or, again, if a person "proclaims this great secret . . . during a meal for the dead, / it will lead him to eternal life" (verse 17). Eucharistic echoes abound. One might also cite here the mystical notions of immanent-transcendence to be found in Hindu swamis like Ramana and Ramakrishna or Christian-Hindu sages like Abhishiktananda, Bede Griffiths, and Sarah Grant.

40. Woolf, *To the Lighthouse*, 202.

41. Virginia Woolf, *A Writer's Diary: Being Extracts from the Diary of Virginia Woolf* (New York: Houghton Mifflin Harcourt, 2003), 85; see Corner, "Mysticism and Atheism," 48.

42. Ibid.

43. See Miller, *Tropes, Parables, Performatives*, 152–153: "The goal Mrs. Ramsay reaches in the novel is death. The novel turns on the vanishing of her consciousness from the world and from the lives of the other characters." Hence the significance of the "Time Passes" section of the novel, which serves as prelude to Lily Briscoe's finally applying her finishing stroke to the painting in part 3: "the line that stands for the dead Mrs. Ramsay and substitutes for her, that replaces the missing shadow on the step cast by Mrs. Ramsay, the wedge-shaped core of darkness which had been present there when Lily began her painting and Mrs. Ramsay sat knitting the reddish-brown stocking and reading to James" (ibid., 153). Miller extends his reading of Woolf's spiritual-aesthetic vision to her novel *Mrs. Dalloway* in chapter 7 of his work, *Fiction and Repetition* (Cambridge: Harvard University Press, 1982), subtitled "Repetition as the Raising of the Dead." He points out that the narrator of this novel "remembers all and has a power of resurrecting the past in her narration. . . . She rescues [the various characters] from time past and presents them again in language to the reader. Narration itself is repetition" (ibid., 178–179). He compares Woolf's attitude here to that of Proust—whom he reminds us Woolf greatly admired—and he goes on to suggest that the "universal

mind" is, for her, part of the characters' minds and that if one "descends deeply enough into any individual mind one reaches ultimately the general mind of the narrator. . . . Deep down the general mind and the individual mind become one. Both are the same side of the glass, and the glass vanishes" (ibid., 181). This relates back to what Woolf calls her "great discovery" of "tunneling," which she describes thus: "I dig out beautiful caves behind my characters; I think that gives exactly what I want; humanity, humor, depth. The idea is that the caves shall connect" (ibid., 182). But Miller's thesis is that Woolf's narrative not only "repeats" the past but "resurrects" it in another form in the action of the novel (ibid., 191). Like Mrs. Ramsay, Mrs. Dalloway has, as she presides over her dinner party at the conclusion of the novel, the "gift still; to be; to exist; to sum it all up in the moment" (ibid., 193). But Mrs. Dalloway, like Mrs. Ramsay, fails as a single character to bring everything together as she wishes. The sense of communion is only momentary at best and is interrupted by the news of Septimus's suicide and by her recognition of the real "mystery" of the "privacy of the soul" triggered by her observing the old lady next door climbing her stairs to her room (ibid., 196). Hence Clarissa's sobering insight, again akin to Vedantic wisdom, that "death was an attempt to communicate; people feeling the impossibility of reaching the centre which, mystically, evaded them; closeness drew apart; rapture faded, one was alone. There was an embrace in death" (ibid., 197). But Clarissa's recognition of her kinship with Septimus's death (Woolf describes her as Septimus's "double" in the preface to the Modern Library edition) is not the last word. The party ends and the various characters leave. It is the narrator who therefore serves to revive the pasts of the characters themselves in what Miller calls a "double resurrection." As he puts it: "The victory of the narrator is to rescue from death this moment and all the other moments of the novel in that All Soul's Day at a second power which is literature" (ibid., 199). In other words, literature as tunneling, preservation, and repetition—that "creative power," as Woolf once remarked, "to bring the whole universe to order" (ibid., 201). For writing is the only action that exists "simultaneously on both sides of the mirror, within death and within life at once" (ibid.). Whence Miller's intriguing conclusion that "the novel needs for its structural completeness two opposite but similar movements, Septimus's plunge into death and Clarissa's resurrection from the dead. Mrs. Dalloway is both of these at once: the entry into the realm of communication in death and the revelation of that realm in words which may be read by the living" (ibid.). And, while he admits that the relationship between literature and life remains ultimately "undecidable" in Woolf, he ventures this bold hypothesis: "The possibility that repetition in narrative is the representation of a transcendent spiritual realm of reconciliation and preservation, a realm of the perpetual resurrection of the dead, is more straightforwardly proposed by Virginia Woolf than by most of her predecessors in English fiction" (ibid., 262). But I would suggest that to the "double resurrection" of 1. the past repeated in the character's minds and 2. the character's minds repeated in the narrator's universal mind might be added a third resurrection—the repetition of these two resurrections in the mind of the reader.

44. Martin Corner, "Mysticism and Atheism."
45. Woolf, *To the Lighthouse*, 192.
46. Ibid., 161.
47. Georges Didi-Hubermann, *Confronting Images* (Pennsylvania: Penn State Uni-

versity Press, 2005). I am grateful to my colleague Stephen Schloesser for this reference. See also Gaston Bachelard's notion of a similar sacramental aesthetic in his reading of "elemental participation" (based on Greek notion of *methexis*— e.g., 1 Cor. 10:16–17) over against "mimetic representation." His account of the material imagination paved the way for Merleau-Ponty's "flesh of the world." See Eileen Rizo-Patron, "*Regressus ad Uterum,*" *Philosophy Today,* special Society for Phenomenology and Existential Philosophy issue, ed. Peg Birmingham and James Risser, vol. 33 (Fall 2008): 21–30; and her Ph.D. thesis, "Through the Eye of a Needle: Hermeneutics as Poetic Transformation," Binghamton University, 2005. Ann Arbor, MI: ProQuest Information and Learning, 2006. UMI no. 3203890.

48. Woolf, *To the Lighthouse,* 207.

49. Ibid., 180.

50. Corner, "Mysticism and Atheism,"

51. Corner concludes as follows: "what is Virginia Woof saying about atheism and its relationship to mysticism? As far as atheism is concerned, her central insight is that if it is to progress beyond the stage of the 'little atheist' it must be a faithfulness, moral as well as theoretical, to the nonhumanity of the world. She presents it as a training of the whole person toward a comprehended truth, a truth which must be grasped emotionally as well as intellectually. And this is a process which involves risk; only when a person is able to leap from the pinnacle of the tower, away from whatever limited certainties are available—the self-protective ego, the familiar life—does the process achieve its fulfillment. And here a paradox appears which connects Mr. Ramsay with Lily, the atheist with the mystic. Without God, the leap ought to end in disaster, in the chaos of that void which Virginia Woolf evokes so powerfully in part 2 of *To the Lighthouse.* But those of her characters who succeed in facing the world nakedly and without evasion are shown to discover, mystically or otherwise, that they are not leaping into a void. Something emerges to meet them—the rock beneath Mr. Ramsay's feet, the reality 'at the back of appearances,' the ordinary world transfigured into miracle and ecstasy, and for Virginia Woolf herself that abstraction which nevertheless resided in the downs near Rodmell and beside which nothing mattered. This is the key to her atheist mysticism. For her, atheism was the renunciation of inappropriate expectations toward the nonhuman world; but it was also a condition of that purified perception which would reveal the world as ordinary and yet miraculous, as nonhuman in its otherness and yet beyond everything worth our attention" (ibid., 51). For a more ecological account of Woolf's vision of cosmic interconnection, explicitly related to the ontology of flesh and entwining in Merleau-Ponty, see Louise Westling, "Virginia Woolf and the Flesh of the World," *New Literary History* 30, no. 4 (1999): 855–875. Westling cites Woolf's 1908 vision of a "symmetry by means of infinite discords, showing all the traces of the minds passage through the world, [achieving] in the end, some kind of whole made of shivering fragments." She also makes much of Woolf's famous claim in 1925 that "life is a luminous halo, a semi-transparent envelope surrounding us from the beginning of consciousness to the end." She endorses the view that for Woolf, as for Merleau-Ponty, the world is no longer to be conceived in terms of a Platonic/Cartesian dualism but rather a "sacramental engagement within the body of the world," as a "pulsating field of mind and matter in which everything is interconnected" (ibid.).

51. See Jean-François Lyotard's intriguing comments on *ana* and *post* in the post-

script to Jean-François Lyotard, *The Postmodern Condition: A Report on Knowledge*, trans. Geoff Bennington and Brian Massumi (Minneapolis: University of Minnesota Press, 1984).

6. IN THE WORLD

1. Dietrich Bonhoeffer, *Ethik*, ed. E. Bethge, vol 6 of the *Bonhoeffer Werke* (Munich: Chr. Kaiser, 1998), 44f. I am grateful to Jens Zimmerman and Brian Gregor for bringing this and other related passages to my attention.
2. Stanislas Breton, *The Word and the Cross* (New York: Fordham University Press, 2002), 114, 84f.
3. Stanislas Breton, "On the God of the Possible," in John Manoussakis, ed., *After God: Richard Kearney and the Religious Turn in Phenomenology* (New York: Fordham University Press, 2006), 167–184.
4. Gianni Vattimo and Richard Rorty, *The Future of Religion*, ed. Santiago Zabala (New York: Columbia University Press, 2005), 35. See also Gianni Vattimo, *Being Not God* (New York: Columbia University Press, 2008). One might recall here Dietrich Bonhoeffer's affirmation of the sacred in the secular, albeit it in a more explicitly Christological vein: "Secular and sacred are not opposed but find their unity in Christ. . . . That which is Christian is to be found only in the natural, the holy only in the profane." Bonhoeffer, *Ethik*, 44f.
5. Vattimo, *The Future of Religion*, 36. See also, in this regard, Jean-Luc Nancy, *La Déclosion: Déconstruction du Christianisme* (Paris: Galilée, 2005); and Thomas Altizer, *Living with the Death of God*, "Foreword" by Mark Taylor (Albany: State University Press of New York, 2006).
6. Arthur Kirsch, *Auden and Christianity* (New Haven: Yale University Press, 2005), 9.
7. Réne Girard, *The Scapegoat* (Baltimore: John Hopkins University Press, 1986). See also my "Strangers and Scapegoats," in Richard Kearney, *Strangers, Gods, and Monsters* (New York: Routledge, 2003), 23f, and "Myth and Sacrificial Scapegoats," in Richard Kearney, *Poetics of Modernity* (Atlantic Heights, NJ: Humanities, 1995), 118f. It is noteworthy that Samuel Huntington also advances a theory of natural and cultural division between the community and the Other, but, unlike Girard, he does not see a spiritual faith in grace and forgiveness as any kind of response to this condition of human conflict.
8. Gilles Deleuze and Felix Guattari, *A Thousand Plateaus* (Minneapolis: University of Minnesota, 1987), 122.
9. See Max Scheler on St. Francis, "A Sense of Unity in the Cosmos," and "Ordo Amoris," in *The Nature of Sympathy* (London: Routledge and Kegan Paul, 1954).
10. On the Prophet's vision of the Lote Tree as an image of mystical ultimacy located in "the eye of the heart," see Hannah Merriman, "The Paradox of Proximity to the Infinite," in Richard Kearney, ed., *The Interreligious Imagination*, special issue of *Religion and the Arts* 12, no. 1–3 (Leiden: Brill, 2008): 329–342. See also Anthony Steinbock, *Phenomenology and Mysticism* (Bloomington: Indiana University Press, 2007), on the relationship of *fana*, mystical annihilation of self, and *baqa*, the return to a second self in a world of renewed "subsistence" through divine grace (109–111).

11. See the discussion of this theme in my essay, "On Terror" in Kearney, *Strangers, Gods and Monsters*, 111–115.
12. Gerhard Lenski, *The Religion Factor* (New York: Doubleday, 1961).
13. Rodney Stark and William Bainbridge, *The Future of Religion* (Berkeley: University of California Press, 1985), 1.
14. C. Wright Mills, *The Sociological Imagination* (Oxford: Oxford University Press, 1959), 32–33. I am most grateful to my friend, Fred Dallmayr, for many of the references and citations that follow.
15. Charles Taylor, *A Secular Age* (Cambridge: Harvard University Press, 2007).
16. Raimon Panikkar, *Worship and Secular Man* (Maryknoll, NY: Orbis, 1973), 2; see Fred Dallmayr, *Dialogue Among Civilizations: Some Exemplary Voices* (New York: Palgrave Macmillan, 2003), 191.
17. Dallmayr, *Dialogue Among Civilizations*, 195, n. 15.
18. See Abdolkarim Soroush, *Reason, Freedom, and Democracy in Islam*, trans. Mahmoud Sadri and Ahmad Sadri (New York: Oxford University Press, 2000), 55–56; see Dallmayr, *Dialogue Among Civilizations*, 176.
19. Ibid., 177.
20. Ibid. See Steinbock, *Phenomenology and Mysticism*, 133–134, on the Islamic mystic Baqli.
21. Abdolkarim Soroush, *Reason, Freedom, and Democracy in Islam*, as cited in Dallmayr, *Dialogue Among Civilizations*, 180.
22. See James Morris, *Orientations: Islamic Thought in a World Civilisation* (London: Archeype, 2003); and Maqbool Siraj, "India: A Laboratory of Inter-Religious Experiment," in Kearney, *The Interreligious Imagination*, on this hermeneutic retrieval of alternative readings of Islam to the official Western verdict conveyed by the "clash of civilizations" thesis popularized after 9/11 and the Middle East wars by Samuel Huntington and the neoconservative lobby in the U.S.
23. Dallmayr, *Dialogue Among Civilizations*, 146.
24. Ibid., 173.
25. Hannah Arendt, *Crises of the Republic* (New York: Harcourt Brace Jovanovich, 1972), 229.
26. Lahouari Adi, cited in Dallmayr, *Dialogue Among Civilizations*, 173.
27. Ibid., 173, n. 8.
28. See my introduction to *The Interreligious Imagination*; and also, in the same issue, Eileen Rizo-Patron, "Promises of Advent: North and South," 434–457.
29. See Scarboro Missions Statement, "Principles and Guidelines for Interfaith Dialogue," http://www.scarboromissions.ca. This document is inspired by Thomas Keating's *Snowmass Conference Report* (1984) of the international monastic interreligious movement. Keating is a Trappist monk who has made a major contribution to the centering prayer movement and to interfaith spirituality. He is convener of the Snowmass Conference and a member of the international monastic interreligious movement. He authored the following report:

> "A report on an experience of on-going inter-religious dialogue might be helpful at this point. In 1984, I invited a group of spiritual teachers from a variety of the world religions—Buddhist, Tibetan Buddhist, Hindu, Jewish, Islamic, Native American, Russian Orthodox, Protestant, and Roman Catholic—to gather at St. Benedict's Monastery in Snow-

mass, Colorado, to meditate together in silence and to share our personal spiritual journeys, especially those elements in our respective traditions that have proved most helpful to us along the way. We kept no record and published no papers. As our trust and friendship grew, we felt moved to investigate various points that we seemed to agree on. The original points of agreement were worked over during the course of subsequent meetings as we continued to meet, for a week or so each year. Our most recent list consists of the following eight points:

1. The world religions bear witness to the experience of Ultimate Reality to which they give various names: Brahman, Allah, Absolute, God, Great Spirit.

2. Ultimate Reality cannot be limited by any name or concept.

3. Ultimate Reality is the ground of infinite potentiality and actualization.

4. Faith is opening, accepting and responding to Ultimate Reality. Faith in this sense precedes every belief system.

5. The potential for human wholeness (or in other frames of reference)—enlightenment, salvation, transformation, blessedness, "nirvana"—is present in every human person.

6. Ultimate Reality may be experienced not only through religious practices but also through nature, art, human relationships, and service of others.

7. As long as the human condition is experienced as separate from Ultimate Reality, it is subject to ignorance and illusion, weakness and suffering.

8. Disciplined practice is essential to the spiritual life; yet spiritual attainment is not the result of one's own efforts, but the result of the experience of oneness with Ultimate Reality.

At the annual Snowmass conference in May 1986, we came up with additional points of agreement of a practical nature:

A. Some examples of disciplined practice, common to us all:
    1. Practice of compassion
    2. Service to others
    3. Practicing moral precepts and virtues
    4. Training in meditation techniques and regularity of practice
    5. Attention to diet and exercise
    6. Fasting and abstinence
    7. The use of music and chanting and sacred symbols
    8. Practice in awareness (recollection, mindfulness) and living in the present moment
    9. Pilgrimage
    10. Study of scriptural texts and scriptures

And in some traditions:

    11. Relationship with a qualified teacher
    12. Repetition of sacred words (mantra, japa)
    13. Observance of periods of silence and solitude
    14. Movement and dance
    15. Formation of community

B. It is essential to extend our formal practice of awareness into all aspects of our life.

C. Humility, gratitude, and a sense of humor are indispensable in the spiritual life.

D. Prayer is communion with Ultimate Reality, whether it is regarded as personal, impersonal, or beyond them both. We were surprised and delighted to find so many points of similarity and convergence in our respective paths. Like most people of our time, we originally expected that we would find practically nothing in common. In the years that followed, we spontaneously and somewhat hesitatingly began to take a closer look at certain points of disagreement until these became our main focus of attention. We found that discussing our points of disagreement increased the bonding of the group even more than discovering our points of agreement. We became more honest in stating frankly what we believed and why, without at the same time making any effort to convince others of our own position. We simply presented our understanding as a gift to the group."

30. See Abhishiktananda's reading of Advaita presented by Shirley De Boulay, "Aranachula," in Kearney, *Interreligious Imagination*, 197f.

7. IN THE ACT

1. Julia Kristeva, *Strangers to Ourselves* (New York: Columbia University Press, 1994).
2. Dorothy Day, *The Long Lonliness* (New York: Harper, 1952), 148.
3. Gary Wills, "The Saint of Mott Street," *New York Review of Books* 41, no. 8 (1994): 47–48.
4. Dorothy Day, *Living with Christ* 9, no. 4 (2008): 76.
5. William R. Trumble, *The Shorter Oxford English Dictionary*, 6th ed. (New York: Oxford University Press, 2007), 988.
6. Day, *Living with Christ*, 79. See also William Desmond, "Consecrating Peace: Reflections on Daniel Berrigan as Witness," in James Marsh and Anna Brown, eds., "On Standing Somewhere: Daniel Berrigan's Impact on Catholic Social Thought" (forthcoming, 2010).
7. John of Damascus, *On the Divine Images*, trans. D. Anderson (New York: St. Vladimir, 1980), para. 16, p. 23. I am grateful to my friend and colleague Mary Anderson for this passage. See also her interesting commentary on an incarnational and sacramental aesthetics in chapter 3 of her "Thou Art: The Subject of Christ" (doctoral thesis).
8. David Tracy, "Writing," in Mark Taylor, ed., *Critical Terms for Religious Studies* (Chicago: University of Chicago Press, 1998), 388–389.
9. Fred Dallmayr, "Empire and Faith," *Dialogue Among Civilizations: Some Exemplary Voices* (New York: Palgrave Macmillan, 2003), 203.
10. Ibid.
11. Charles Taylor, *A Secular Age* (Cambridge: Belknap, 2007).
12. Ibid.
13. Jean Vanier, "Where the Weak and the Strong Dance Together," in Bob Abernethy and William Bole, eds., *The Life of Meaning: Reflections on Faith, Doubt,*

and Repairing the World (New York: Seven Stories, 2007), 372. See also "Interview with Jean Vanier" in Timothy Kearney, *The Prophetic Cry* (Dublin:Veritas, 2000).

14. Vanier, "Where the Weak and the Strong Dance Together," 374.

15. Ibid ., 375.

16. Ibid., 373.

17. Ibid., 376.

18. Fred Dallmayer, "Freedom East and West," in *Dialogue Among Civilizations: Some Exemplary Voices* (New York: Palgrave Macmillan, 2003), 211.

19. Fred Dallmayer, "What Is Self-Rule? Lessons from Ghandi," in *Dialogue Among Civilizations*, 217.

20. Ibid., 219.

21. Ibid., 222, n. 11.

22. Ibid., 217.

23. Siddartha, "Open Source Hinduism," in Richard Kearney, ed., "Interreligious Imagination," special issue of *Religion and the Arts* 12, nos. 1–3 (Leiden: Brill, 2008), 34–41.

24. See Bede Griffiths's comparative analysis of the relationship between the sacred and the secular in an East-West context in *River of Compassion* (New York: Continuum, 1987).

25. Ramashray Roy, *Self and Society: A Study in Gandhian Thought* (Sage, 1985) as cited by Dallmayr in *Dialogue Among Cilvilizations*, 223, n. 12.

26. Dallmayr, *Dialogue Among Civilizations*, 18, n. 5.

27. Ibid., 218.

28. Ibid., 225, n. 15.

29. Ibid., 220.

CONCLUSION

1. Max Scheler, "Negative Feelings and the Destruction of Values: Ressentiment," in Harold Bershady, ed., *On Feeling, Knowing and Valuing* (Chicago: University of Chicago Press, 1993), 116–146.

2. Ibid., 132.

3. Ibid.

4. John Cornwell, *Darwin's Angel: A Seraphic Response to the God Delusion* (London: Profile, 2008). See Richard Dawkins, *The God Delusion* (New York: Mariner, 2008). Despite the dismissive, mocking tone of much of Dawkins's diatribe, it turns out that the main target of his critical ire is in fact largely what I have been critiquing as the Omni-God of metaphysical might and magic, namely, "the interventionist, miracle-wreaking, thought-reading, sin-punishing, prayer-answering God of the Bible" (ibid., 41). Dawkins calls an act of "high treason" any attempt to confuse this divine Master of Ceremonies with the "pantheist" God of Spinoza and Einstein, who he decides is not a God of faith or love at all, but merely a "poetic synonym" for the laws of nature and therefore "sexed-up atheism" (ibid., 40). I agree that the two Gods should not be mixed up, but I am not sure that the God of pantheism—or what I prefer to call panentheism—is not a God eminently worthy of anatheist wagers. There is room for meaningful dialogue here I think. Dawkins's language sometimes borders on vitriolic abuse—as when he accuses

creationists of trampling "their dirty hobnailed boots" all over science's turf! (ibid., 92). But I fully agree with him, for example, when he robustly rebukes Richard Swinburne for his apologetic account of horrors like the Holocaust and Hiroshima as wonderful "opportunities for courage and sympathy" (ibid., 89). When Dawkins critiques theism for being fundamentalist and literalist—that is, the denial that we are dealing with interpretations of written texts (ibid., 118–120)—he is pushing an open door as far as anatheism is concerned (which starts with a hermeneutic wager regarding any holy word). Likewise when he appears to support Nehru's and Gandhi's ideal of a "secular India," which fosters religious pluralism: "what it means is that it is a state which honors all faiths equally" (ibid., 68). Dawkins says his hero, Jefferson, would approve; but the tenor of Dawkins's overall argument appears very much at variance with this appeal for a tolerance of many faiths and religions. Basically, my difference with Dawkins and Dennett is that they interpret the God question as a God hypothesis about the scientific origin of the universe, where the bottom line is Darwinism versus creationism (ibid., 81). If it is a matter of counting the scientific evidence for evolution, Dawkins and Dennett are pushing another open door. And if one's idea of God is no more than a magical "superintendent" of the universe (ibid., 75–78), then it is fair to compare it to a "flying spaghetti monster" (ibid., 78). But is this an accurate account of what millions of believers actually hold when they devote their lives to the holy love and service of others? My purpose in this book has not been to prove (or disprove) God's metaphysical existence as some sort of superterrestrial Being, but to show—with the help of phenomenological and hermeneutical methods—the "meaning" of the "God event" at a practical, poetic, and mystical level. In short, our question is how does the encounter with the stranger—as radically other, alien, transcendent, "more"—effect our lives for better (or for worse). This is the essence of the anatheist wager. A matter of interpreting and choosing whether what many call by "divine names" (the radically Other) brings life or death, love or hate. It is not at all concerned with metaphysical or physical proofs for God's existence that rely upon laws of probability. (And here we differ also from the calculations of Pascal's wager.) Anatheism is not at odds with science and the natural world; it simply asks how we respond to the radical surprise of the Stranger as an invitation to faith, to make the impossible possible, to bring justice where there is war, love where there is hate, wisdom where there is ignorance. If anatheism has nothing positive or persuasive to say to this, it is not worth a grain of salt, and this book has been in vain.

5. Daniel Dennett, *Breaking the Spell: Religion as a Natural Phenomenon* (New York: Viking, 2006), 4. My difference with Dennett and Dawkins is not with biological Darwinism but with social, political, or spiritual Darwinism. Is natural selection of the fittest more likely, I ask, to yield to a loving and just society than hospitality to the radical stranger who comes to us from beyond us and calls us to goodness? My thanks to Kascha Semonovitch for this reference.

6. Ibid., 5.

7. Dennett says as much in his introduction to *Breaking the Spell*. It is to be noted that the contemporary critique of religion also finds influential voices outside Anglo-Saxon thinking; see for example, Michel Onfray, *Traité d'athéologie: Physique de la métaphysique* (Paris: Grasset et Fasquelle, 2005). I am grateful to Christian Aubin for bringing my attention to Onfray's work. For a contrary reading of the

origins of atheism and theism see Patrick Masterson, *Atheism and Alienation: A Study of the Philosophical Sources of Contemporary Atheism* (Notre Dame, IN: University of Notre Dame Press, 1971).

8. William James, *The Varieties of Religious Experience* (New York: Penguin, 1982), 31, cited in Dennett, *Breaking the Spell*, 11.

9. Swami Vivekananda, *Karma Yoga* (1896) in *The Complete Works* (New York: Vedanta, 2000), 1:72.

10. Jürgen Habermas and Jacques Derrida, *Philosophy in a Time of Terror: Dialogues with Jürgen Habermas and Jacques Derrida*, ed. Giovanna Borradori (Chicago: University of Chicago Press, 2003), 55f. See also Hent de Vries and L. E. Sullivan, *Political Theologies: Public Religions in a Post-Secular World* (New York: Fordham University Press, 2006); this volume soberly demonstrates how excessive the political take on religion has become. I am grateful to Lovisa Bergdahl for several of these references.

11. Samuel Huntington, *The Clash of Civilizations and the Remaking of the World Order* (New York: Simon and Schuster, 2003), 21. I am grateful to Donatien Cicura for this reference—see his "Identity and Historicity in African Philosophy," Ph.D. diss., Boston College, 2008. Cicura states: "According to Huntington, the process of creating enemies is an inherent component of the process of being a self, of acquiring or appropriating an identity. Identity is made of allies (those who belong to my group) and enemies (those with whom I compete either individually or as a member of a group). In this line of thought, Huntington's idea of identity is analogous to the interpretation Francis Fukuyama gave of Plato's *thumos* in *The End of History and the Last Man* (New York: Penguin, 2002). "Human beings identify themselves in thyumotic terms, that is, they need self-esteem, recognition, and approbation. To this extent, conflict with an enemy reinforces the above qualities in a group and procures comfort and a sense of gratification" (Cicura, "Identity and Historicity," 75). As Huntington himself puts it: "The need of individuals for self-esteem leads them to believe that their group is better than other groups. Their sense of self rises and falls . . . with the extent to which other people are excluded from their group." See Samuel Huntington, *Who Are We? The Challenge to America's National Identity* (New York: Simon and Schuster, 2004), 25. For recent critiques of this adversarial model of politics and religion, see Amartya Sen, *Identity and Violence* (New York: Norton, 2007); Homi K. Bhabha, *The Location of Culture* (London: Routledge, 1994); Martha Nussbaum, *For Love of Country* (Boston: Beacon, 2002); and Richard Kearney, chapters 1, 3, and 5 ("Strangers and Scapegoats," "Aliens and Others," and "On Terror") in *Strangers, Gods and Monsters* (New York: Routledge, 2003), 23–140.

12. Habermas and Derrida, *Philosophy in a Time of Terror*, 55.

13. Jürgen Habermas, "Religion in the Public Sphere," *European Journal of Philosophy* 14, no. 4 (2006): 6.

14. Cited and commented on by Lovisa Bergdahl, "Lost in Translation: On the Untranslatable and Its Ethical Implications for Religious Pluralism," *Journal of Philosophy of Education* 43, no. 1 (2009): 31–44. I am grateful to Lovisa Bergdahl for bringing these arguments and texts to my attention.

15. Jürgen Habermas, "A Conversation About God and the World," in Eduardo Mendieta, ed., *Religion and Rationality: Essays on Reason, God and Modernity* (Oxford: Blackwell, 2000), 148–149. On the need for a complementary rational dialogue

between secular and religious citizens, see also Jürgen Habermas and Joseph Ratzinger, *The Dialectics of Secularization* (San Francisco: Ignatius, 2006), 43–47.

16. Eduardo Mendieta, "A Conversation About God and the World," in Mendieta, *Religion and Rationality*, 163.

17. See Walter Benjamin, "The Task of the Translator," in *Illuminations: Essays and Reflections*, ed. Hannah Arendt, trans. Harry Zohn (New York: Harcourt Brace Jovanovich, 1973); and Jacques Derrida, *The Ear of the Other: Otobiography, Transference, Translation* (New York: Schocken, 1985).

18. Habermas, "Religion in the Public Sphere," 10–12; see also Jürgen Habermas, *Between Naturalism and Religion* (Cambridge: Polity, 2006); cited and commented on by Bergdahl in "Lost in Translation," 3.

19. Benjamin, "The Task of the Translator," 70. On the limits of interreligious translatability as both a possibility and impossibility of symmetrical dialogue, see Catherine Cornille, *The Im-Possibility of Religious Dialogue* (New York: Herder and Herder, 2008). See also Edith Stein in *On the Problem of Empathy*, trans. Waltraut Stein (Washington, DC: ICS, 1989); here she talks about our phenomenological encounter with the other as a "primordial experience of the non-primordial," that is, as a direct sense of the indirectness and elusiveness of the "stranger" within every person we encounter, be they familiar or foreign. On this theme, see also Max Scheler, *The Nature of Sympathy*, and Derrida's discussion of Husserl's Fifth Cartesian Meditation in 'Hospitality, Justice and Responsibility,'" in Richard Kearney and Mark Dooley, eds., *Questioning Ethics* (London: Routledge, 1999), 66–83.

20. Benjamin, "The Task of the Translator," 75, 81.

21. Anthony Steinbock, *Phenomenology and Mysticism* (Bloomington: Indiana University Press, 2007), 211f.

22. Paul Ricoeur, "Entretien Hans Küng–Paul Ricoeur: Les religions, la violence et la paix. Pour une éthique planétaire," *Arte* 5 (April 1996), as published in *Sens*, no 5 (1998): 211–230.

23. See my introduction ("Journey to the Heart") in Richard Kearney, ed., *Interreligious Imagination*, a special issue of *Religion and the Arts* 12, nos. 1–3 (Leiden: Brill, 2008): 3–33.

24. Ricoeur, "Entretien Hans Küng–Paul Ricoeur." See also Cornille's illuminating discussion of the question of interreligous dialogue as a "hospitality to difference" in *The Im-Possibility of Religious Dialogue*, 177–179.

25. Albert Camus, *The Myth of Sisyphus*, in Gordon Marino, ed., *Basic Writings in Existentialism* (New York: Modern Library, 2004), 441f.

26. Ricoeur, "Entretien Hans Küng–Paul Ricoeur."

27. Ibid.: "non seulement ce message me dépasse mais aussi il me désarme."

28. Ibid.

29. Ibid.: "Je crois que nous avons besoin de la parole de l'*Aufklärung*. Et la grande chance du christianisme c'est d'avoir été confronté dès le début, grâce à la Grèce et à tout l'héritage du rationalisme, à ce conflit de ce que j'ai appelé le conflit de la conviction et de la critique. C'est dans la mesure où nous menons ce combat de l'intérieur de la conviction, et avec l'appui de ceux du dehors, et du dehors de toute religion, que nous avons besoin de l'athée, pour nous comprende, nous croyants, et pour comprendre les autres croyants qui sont dans d'autres croyances que notre croyance."

30. Benjamin, "The Task of the Translator." Contrast this with Jürgen Habermas's view of translation between religions as a process of mutual public exchange and exposure in "Religion in the Public Sphere." The anatheist approach seeks a middle route between the positions of Habermas and Benjamin.

31. This "extra element" is what I have been describing as something "more." William James has some interesting observations on this "more": "[The Individual] becomes conscious that this higher part is coterminous and continuous with a MORE of the same quality, which is operative in the universe outside of him, and which he can keep in working touch with, and in a fashion get on board of and save himself when all his lower being has gone to pieces in the wreck." William James, *Varieties of Religious Experience* (New York: Penguin Putnam, 1958), lecture 20, "Conclusions," p. 419. Or again: "The 'more,' as we called it, and the meaning of our 'union' with it, form the nucleus of our inquiry. Into what definite description can these words be translated, and for what definite facts do they stand? It would never do for us to place ourselves offhand at the position of a particular theology, the Christian theology, for example, and proceeding immediately to define the 'more' as Jehovah, and the 'union' as his imputation to us of the righteousness of Christ. That would be unfair to other religions, and from our present standpoint at least, would be an over-belief." Ibid., p.421. I would add that the "more" need not only be identified with a transcendent divinity but may also be experienced in the human stranger *beyond* our borders or the stranger *within* our borders of nation-state or community of loved ones. Or even within ourselves. The "more" as stranger goes all the way down—to the very least of beings, human, natural, or sacred. If we choose to call it "God"—as most religions and faiths do—it is a "more" always available in the "less." A "surplus" that excludes nothing or nobody. A transcendence enfleshed in immanence.

INDEX

Abraham, 3, 25, 45, 76; choice and, 44; cruelty and, 20; desert strangers and, 8, 17–20, 51, 109, 152; divine stranger and, 17–20; hospitality and, 19; Mount Moriah and, 19; as prophet of strangeness, 19; temptation and, 19; as wanderer, 19

Abrahamic faiths, xv, 3, 22–23, 137, 143; history of, 5; defining moments of, 7, 184; dialogue and, 50–52, 149–151; and non-Abrahamic, 51–52, 149–51, 161, 163; as Religions of the Book, 17; divine strangers and, 17–39; *via negativa* and, 55–56

absolutism, xiii, xiv, xviii, 5, 16, 145, 149, 177, 80

abyss, 71, 98

Adi, Lahouri, 148–49

Adieu (Derrida), 63

Adore Te Devote, Maundy Thursday hymn, 28

advena/advent, 21, 183–84; space of, 109–10; of the stranger, 160; writing and, 103

aesthetics, 101; anatheism and, 10–14, 130; Greek, 9; mystical, 126–27; sacramental, 41, 98–99, 102, 113, 118, 208–9n25, 229n7; Wilde and, 13

After God (ed. Manoussakis), 52

Agamben, Giorgio, *The Time That Remains* by, 107

a-gnosis, 8, 38

Agnosticism, xvi, 102; inquiry and, 4; abandonment and, 9; in Wilde, 13–14

akasa, 16

Akbar, and interspiritual philosophy, 33

Alcoholics Anonymous, 178, 183

Al'farabi, 33

"Allah-Rama," 37

allogenes, 29

Al Qaeda, 32, 138–39; *see also* 9/11; bin Laden, Osama; terrorism

alterity, 50, 151, 175, 183; advent of, 4; ego and, 48; enigmas of, xvi; sacred, 43; *see also* stranger, the; other, the

Amnesty International, xiii

amor mundi, 60, 133–34, 166

anabasis, 12

ana-gnorisis, 8, 217n16

anakaiphaleosis, 75

ana-thema, 86

ana-theos, 3, 27, 75, 86

anashim, 19

anatheism, 69, 75–76, 137; *ana* of, 7, 13, 25, 75, 130; in art, 10–16, 103–4; Auden and, 15, 135, 189n15; Averroes

and, 34; before/after religion, 177;
Bonhoeffer and, 66–71; Christian,
25; commitment and, 44; Derrida
and, 65; different from atheism, 16,
166–67; distinct from *anamnesis*, 7;
epistemology and, 5; eschatological
faith and, 75, 166; existential desire
and, 75; and Father, 76; as freedom of
belief, 16; versus historical dialectic,
xvi; historical precedents for, 7–8;
over hypothetical synthesis, 6; and
journey toward Other, 55; Kristeva
and, 96; modern authors and, 102–4,
108, 126–27; moments of, 5, 55, 129;
movements of, xviii, 167; mystical,
126–27; option of, 39, 74, 130; postfaith and, 61, 130; as posttheism, 57;
religion/art and, 129–130; as repetition and return, 7–8, 108, 129; sacramental moment of, 153, 155, 161;
secularity/secularization and, 139–42,
149, 166; as space of belief, xiv, 81,
130; of stranger, 53–54, 151; versus
theistic perversions, 52; theo-erotic
dimension of, 63; three arcs of, 152;
time and, 184
Arendt, Hannah, 59–60; on *amor mundi*,
60; on death of God, 59; *Eichmann in
Jerusalem* by, 59; on the political, 66,
148; on problem of evil, 59
Aristotle, 9, 79; Arendt on, 60; on comedy, 107–8; on *katharsis*, 10–11; on
phronesis, 60, 147; *Poetics* by, 170,
217*n*16; Ricoeur on, 203*n*55
Assisi, Saint Francis of, 23, 99, 136–37,
156
atheism, xi–xiii, 39, 54, 56, 86, 102; as
a-theism, 39; belief after, 74; critical
and iconoclastic, 39, 171; Derrida on,
63–64; and dialogue, xvii; dogmatic,
16, 68; faith and, 13–14, 74; Freud/
Nietzsche and, 72; Levinas on, 62;
militant, 3, 16, 89, 153, 166; nihilism
and, 73; politics and, 4; "religious
meaning of," 71, 76; Ricoeur on, 71;
as separation, 62; as part of theism,
16; *tout court*, 178; Western understanding of, 4

Athens/Jerusalem, 9–10
Auden, W. H.: Arendt and, 59–60; on
belief, 15; on "Christian heresies,"
135–36; on confirmation, 189*n*15;
on Eucharist, 135; on Freud, 135; on
Jesus, 135–36
Augustine, Saint, 152, 169; on *Facere
veritatem*, 44; on questioning, 8
Averroes (Ibn Rushd), 33, 146–48, 169,
193*n*16; *The Book of Differences (Fasl
al-maqal)* by, 34
Avila, Teresa of: on divinity, 5, 166; on
mystical experience, 86; on "transverberation," 47

Bachelard, Gaston, 97, 207*n*12
Baqli, Ruzihan, 8
Barth, Karl: Bonhoeffer and, 66; *The
Epistle to the Romans by*, 66
Beauvoir, Simone de, 89
Beckett, Samuel, 111, 117, 217*n*16
Being and Time (Heidegger), 107
belief, *see* faith
Benedict, Pope, 33–34, 172
Benedict, Saint: on guests as Christ, 29;
on hospitality, xii; legacy of, 30; *Rule
of St. Benedict* by, 29
Benjamin, Walter, 117; Arendt and, 59;
on language, 174; and "messianic
justice," 144; on Proust, 116, 219*n*22,
221–22*n*31; and time, 105, 107; and
translation, 233*n*19; on "weak messianism," 54, 59, 65
Benveniste, Emile: Derrida on, 194*n*29;
on etymology of host/guest, 38,
194*nn*29, 30, 194–95*n*31
Bergdahl, Lovisa, 174, 189*n*17
Bergson, Henri, 42, 107
Berman, Antoine, 179
Bhagavad Gita, 163
bin Laden, Osama, 46, 158, 172; *see
also* Al Qaeda; 9/11; terrorism
Biruni, 35
Bonaventure, Saint, 56
Bonhoeffer, Dietrich, 65–71, 76, 170;
on Christianity, 70, 133–134, 171;
execution of, 69–70; Nazis and, 65;
on "nonreligious" faith, 65–67, 85,

93–94; on "polyphony of life," 70
The Book of Differences (Fasl al-maqal) (Averroes), 34–35
The Book of Theophanies (Ibn 'Arabi), 41
Botticelli, Sandro, 23–24, 46
Breton, Stanislas, 80, 133–35
Brigid of Kildare, Saint, 101
Brothers Karamazov (Dostoyevsky), 28
Bruno, Giordano, 33
Buddha, the, 48, 49
Buddhism, 4, 52, 77, 150, 175–79; on emptiness, 16; on "void," 50–51
Bultmann, Rudolph, 67
Bush, President George, 138, 154, 158, 172

Camus, Albert, 89, 178
Caputo, John, 144; on divine weakness, 68, 136; on religion, xiii; *The Weakness of God* by, 136
Cendres (Derrida), 63
certainty, 3; abandonment of, 7; "objective," 68
Certeau, Michel de: on Jesus as "Other," 27; on mystical experience, 9, 191n6, 195n32, 197n5
Chagall, Marc, 18, 41
Chrétien, Jean-Louis, 95
Christianity, 52, 99, 179; Abrahamic legacy in, 23; Bonhoeffer on, 70; and *caritas*, 55; drama of stranger in, 23–30; Habermas on, 172–74; and hospitality, xiii; "irreligious," 66–67; nonviolent, 136; and peace in Ireland, xiii; service of, 29; as summons to *kenosis*, 55; "of this world," 69; vocation of, 85–86
Circumfession (Derrida), 62–63
"A Common Word," 33–34
condition, human, 60
Confucianism, 150
Council of Florence, 33, 192–93n15
Corbin, Henri, 35
I Corinthians (1:28), 184; (11:25–26), 54; (12), 134
Corrigan, Miread, xiii
Critchley, Simon, 13–14

Cusa, Nicholas of: Council of Florence and, 33, 192–93n15; on *docta ignorantia*, 8, 168–69

Dalai Lama, 50, 51
Dallmayr, Fred, 145–46; on Averroes, 34, 193n16; on Day, 157–58
Damascus, John of, 156
David, 21; House of, 9
Dawkins, Richard, xi, 22, 73, 137, 167–68, 170, 183–84, 230–31n4
Day, Dorothy, 5, 183; on Eucharist, 156; on God, 155–59; and Gospel, 154–55; homeless/poor and, 154–59; hospitality and, 154–59; politics of, 154, 157–59; *The Long Loneliness* by, 154
death: Abraham and, 19, 45; angels and, 38–39; Benjamin and, 59; Bonhoeffer and, 65, 133–34; Day on, 154; Dennett on, 169; God brings life or, 5, 19, 54, 61, 63, 67, 69, 142, 181; Hillesum and, 53, 58; Hopkins on, 12; of Jesus, 26–27, 54–55, 70, 76, 134, 137, 191n8; Joyce on, 107–8; Kabir and, 37; mystical experience and, 197n5, 223n39; and nothingness, 129; Proust on, 110–11, 113–16, 118, 220n30; of religion, 66, 71, 73, 139; Ricoeur on, 76–81; stranger and, 45, 231n4; Woolf on, 119, 123–24, 126, 128, 223–24n43; *see also* God
deconstruction, xv, 45, 152, 204nn57, 2
Deleuze, Gilles, 136, 218–19n22
democracy, 5; fundamentalism and, 158–59; Habermas on, 173–74; Islam and, 143–49; the sacred and, 145
Dennett, Daniel, xi, 137, 167–69
Derrida, Jacques, 62–65, 106–7, 136; *Adieu* by, 63; on ascesis, 64; atheism and, 63; *Cendres* by, 63; *Circumfession* by, 62–63; deconstruction and, 64; on divine "name," 63; on hospitality, 63; and Kearney, xiv; on the messianic, 63–64, 144, 172, 174; on Other, 64; on religion, xiii, 63–65; *Sauf le Nom* by, 63; *Shibboleth: For Paul Celan*, by, 63; *Spectres of Marx* by, 107; *tout autre est tout autre*, 45, 64

Descartes, René, 55, 93

desire, 87–88, 108, 171, 214*n*12; beyond, 202*n*44; human and divine, 63, 79–80, 176

Deuteronomy: (10:18), 21; (16:11), 21; (24:17), 21; (26:5), 21; (27:19), 21

dialogue: and postmodern age, xiii; *dialogizomai* and, 25; interreligious/interconfessional, xii, 4, 33, 50–51, 149–51, 176–81; in Islamic tradition, 33–34; Parliament of World Religions and, 176; Scorboro Interfaith movement and, 176; as semantic exchange, 51; Snowmass Conference and, 176; as translation, 51; as welcoming of difference, 51

Didi-Hubermann, Georges, 125–26

Dionysius the Areopagite, 8

discernment, 44–47

dispossession: existence and, 5; poetics and, 13; self-, 48

Dostoyevsky, Fyodor: on beauty, 41; *Brothers Karamazov* by, 28; on faith and doubt, 6, 187*n*1; *The Idiot* by, 41; on Jesus, 28; Kristeva and, 97; on torture, 60

doubt, 95; Arendt on, 59; Descartes', 55; and Dostoyevsky, 187*n*1; and faith, 56

Duino Elegies (Rilke), 38

Eckhart, Meister, 8–9, 43, 63, 69, 99, 196*n*4, 204–5*n*3; on *Abgeschiedenheit*, 127

eesh/iysh, 22

ego, 162, 225*n*51; alter, 16, 104; refiguration of, 47–48; super, 72–73; and totality, 196*n*2

Eichmann in Jerusalem (Arendt), 59

elachistos, 28

Elijah, 51, 106, 127

embodiment: epiphany and, 52; eucharistic, 91–92; flesh and, 87–88, 105; hermeneutics and, 40–41, 46; of infinity, 166; sacramental experience and, 4, 88–94; sacred, 26; Scheler/Francis on, 99–100; *see also* flesh, incarnation

empathy: anatheist movements and, xviii; Edith Stein on, 42, 50; meta-

phor and, 42; as "primordial encounter," 50; sympathy and, 42

Enlightenment, the, xi, 139; atheists, 22; faith and, xvi, 167; positivists, 72

epiphany, 128; Beckett on, 111; cultural conditions of, 7; Derrida and, 64; of divine eros/natality, 25; as embodiment of sacred, 52, 103; eschatology and, 52–53; eternity in, 5; Eucharist and, 108–9, 156–57; figures of, 85–100; God and, 98–99; Jesus's love and, 27; Joyce on, 103–10; light of, 27; modern artists of, 41, 103; in Proust, 110–17; rebirth and, 109; of renewal, 137; stranger and, 129, 149, 184, 185; triadic model of, 109–10

epistemology, 5, 54

The Epistle to the Romans (Barth), 66

Esau, 20

eschatology, 166; epiphany and, 52–53, 105; *eschaton* and, 54, 79; and faith, 75; and future/past, 54; micro-, 52, 184, 215*n*15; *of the possible*, 79–81; realized in alien, 29

eternity, 5, 106, 121–22, 156

ethics, of alterity, 196*n*2; biblical, 9; of compassion, 150; global, 151; of hospitality, 49, 149–51, 172–73; imagination and, 41; Levinasian, 196*n*2; sacramental, 133–37

Eucharist, 85, 153; Breton on, 134–35; host (*hostia*) and, 156; imagination and, 102–3; in Joyce, 103–7; in Woolf, 120–23, 127; *see also* sacramental, the; transubstantiation

evil, 135, 138–39, 148; "axis of," 138, 172; problem of, 58–60, 69, 73, 75; world, 158

existence, 197*n*5; comedy of, 43; of God, 183, 196*n*4, 231*n*4; Habermas on, 172; incarnate, 4; "miracle" of, 94; of otherness, 178; play of, 118; profane, 130; refigured, 117; and service, 158; strangeness of, 160; *thisness* of, 95–96; word of, 75

existentialism, xv

Exodus: (3:14), 79; (3:15), 9, 43, 78; (22:20), 17, 20

faith: act of, 41; after religion, 66; as art of the impossible, 14; Averroes on, 34, 193n16; beyond faith, xix, 3, 9; Bonhoeffer on, 65–71; circumcession and, 56; deconstructive, 65; Derrida on, 63–65; discernment and, 44; doubt and, 56; as endless hermeneutics, 14, 180; Enlightenment and, xvi; genuine, 168; of Islam, 30; leap of, 44; in messianicity, 64; politics and, 141–42; postatheistic, 71; postcritical, 71; post-Holocaust, 61; postmetaphysical, 134; metaphor and, 15–16; mysticism and, 9; reason and, 146; not reducible to fiction, 15–16, 102; secular, 69; as summons, 67; transcendental, 64; "without religion," 4, 64, 85, 171

Feuerbach, Ludwig, xii

flesh, *art of,* 111; of art, 90; divine and, 91–92; as "element," 90, 97; holiness in, 5; invokes word, 139–40; Joyce on, 105; Kristeva on, 97–98; Merleau-Ponty on, 88–91; "miracle" of, 90; phenomenology of, 87–96, 130; in Proust, 111; sacred moments and, 7, 103; word made, 24, 29, 107–8, 110, 118, 124, 128, 135, 156; *see also* embodiment.

foreigner, in ourselves, 96; *see also* other, the; stranger, the

freedom: of belief, 16; and choice, 40, 75; Christianity and, 173, 187n1; and dialogue, 149; evil and, 148; of expression, 143; and faith, 74; human, 56, 196n2; intellectual, 34; political, 162; and responsibility, 62; spiritual, 164

Freud, Sigmund, xi, 68, 71, 74, 167; atheism and, 72; Auden and, 135; on God as Father, 57, 72; *The Interpretation of Dreams* by, 46–47

Freud and Philosophy (Ricoeur), 79

Fukuyama, Francis, 6, 172

Gandhi, Mohandas Karamchand, xiii, 5–6, 51, 183; on caste system, 162–63, 171; "Hind Swaraj" by, 162–63; on the interreligious, 163–65; on sacrifice (*sacer-facere, yajna*), 163; on secular-

ity/sacredness, 162–63; on self, 162; sociopolitical engagement of, 161–65

Genesis, (1), 9; (3:15), 54; (18:14), 18; (27), 109; (32:24), 22

gharib, 32

Ghazali, 35

Gide, Andre, 14–15

Girard, René, 136, 171; *The Scapegoat* by, 136

God: *adito devo bhavah* and, 164; as *advena,* 57; agape/eros and, 135; body and, 90–94; as *causa-sui,* 8, 122; "death of," xi, 58, 59, 69, 72–73, 133, 165; departure from (*a-dieu*), 39, 62; desire and, 63, 79–80; as *dieu capable,* 78–81; disappearance of, xvi; existence of, xii, 72; face of, 20, 22; as Father, 55, 56, 128; of fear, 139; in flesh/blood, 57, 87; freedom and, 162–63; as gift, 69, 197n5; as guest, 29, 35–36, 59, 63, 155–56, 159–60, 164–65; Holocaust and, 58–62; *l'homme capable* and, 80; of hospitality, 139; as host of hosts, 35–36; of interconfessional hospitality, 52; laughter and, 13, letting go of, 3, 98–99, 181; of life, 69; of love over fear, 19; as lover, 36–37; mercy of, 20–21; metaphysical categories of, 52–53, 67, 96, 126, 183; as monarch or stranger, xi, 53; as "more," 180; name of, 21, 45, 57, 63, 167; nature and, 92–93; nonmetaphysical, 66, 73, 96, 130; of *ontotheology,* 73; postdogmatic, 52; postwar rejection of, 59; "powerless power" of, 4, 58, 61; presence of, 70–71; Qur'an and, 32, 143–149; religion and, xi, 80; resurrection and, 69, 74; return to (*hors-dieu*), 39, 142; self-emptying of, 52–53, 77, 80, 91, 126, 133–36; of sovereignty/theodicy, 52, 53, 146, 167; strangeness of, xiv, 4, 7, 56; as stranger, 22, 146, 149, 153, 155, 159–60, 180; as stranger at door, 37, 59; struggles with (*contre-dieu*), 39, 62; suffering, 61, 67; as "surplus," 80, 180; as symbol, 76; as *ta me onta,* 136–37; theodicy and, 53, 58, 59, 61,

73, 80; of Totality, 61; of triumph,
xiii, 53, 58; truth and, 44, 143–44;
violence and, 45–47; as "voyaging
friend," 36; as "Yahweh," 18–20, 54;
world and, 141, 147
The God Who May Be (Kearney), xiii,
xvii, 52, 183
Good Friday Peace Agreement, xiv, 50,
199–200n11
Good Samaritan, story of, 29
Grayling, Anthony, 139
Grand Mufti of Sarajevo, 33, 50
gregoresai, 46
Gregory of Nyssa, 8; *on diastema*, 55–56,
187n1
Greenberg, Rabbi Irving, 60–61
Griffiths, Bede, 51, 176
guest, as angel, 18–20; becomes host,
29; enemy and, 38; as God/Lord,
29, 45; *hostis/hospes*, 38; love of, 29;
in our midst, 37; primal encounters
with, xvii; Stranger as, 15–16; uninvited, 129; *xenisthenta* and, 27–28; *see
also* stranger, the; other, the
guha, 16

Habermas, Jürgen, 172–74, 232n10,
233–34n30
Hafiz of Shiraz, 137; on divine humor,
43; on hospitality, 35–36; poetry of,
35–36
Hagar, 17–18, 20
Hallaj, 35
Hanh, Thich Nhat, 50, 51, 178
Harris, Sam, 139
Heaney, Seamus, xi, xiv
Hegel, George Friedrich Wilhelm, 6,
108, 167; on Abraham, 19; Merleau-
Ponty and, 95
Heidegger, Martin, xviii, 107; *Being
and Time* by, 107; on *Dasein*, 88; on
God of metaphysics, 8, 73; on herme-
neutics, 46; on Hölderlin, 12–13; on
ontotheology, 73
Heimliche, das, 12–13
hermeneutics, 64, 95, 102, 151; begin-
ning/Word and, 38, 169; bodily, 40,
46; circle of, xvii–xviii; cross-reading

in, 50–52; divine encounters and, 22;
faith and, 14, 171; of God, 4; Islamic
poets and, 35–37; name of, 4; poetics
and, 11, 95, 103, 130; and Qur'an,
30–32, 34–35, 192n13; of *reaffirmation*, 153; sacramental, 105–6, 127;
"seeing as," 40–41, 45; of suspicion,
72–73, 152–53; and textual interpretation, xv, 127, 130, 145, 169–70; transcriptural reading in, 50–51; wagers
of, xvii, 22, 24, 169, 175, 231n4; of
weak divinity, 136
Hillesum, Etty, 57, 67, 70, 128; on God,
53, 58–59; as host, 59; at Westerbrook,
58–59
Hinduism, 4, 36, 37, 52, 137; on duty,
150; Gandhi and, 162–65; on *guha*,
50; "open source," xiii, 163–65; texts
of, 33, 176; Trimurti and, 51; yoga
and, 179
Hitchens, Christopher, xi, 22, 137,
167–69, 183–84
history, 161, 184; end of, 167; fallacy
of, xvi, 54; justice in, 176; Kristeva
on, 192n8; of metaphysics, 205n7;
philosophical story and, xviii; versus
story, 170
Hitler, Adolph, 60, 170; *see also* Holocaust, the
Hölderlin, 12–13
holiness, 5
Holocaust, the, xvi , 6, 16, 58–62;
Auschwitz and, 57–60, 61, 65; Dawkins on, 230n4; Derrida on, 63; Nazism and, 65–68, 135–36, 138
Homer, *The Odyssey* by, 49, 107, 127,
195n31
Hopkins, Gerard Manley, 129; on epiphany, 41; on the sacred, 11–12; *The
Wreck of Deutschland by*, 12
hospitality, 47–48, 50, 137, 172; absolute, 64; in ancient literature, 49;
over charity, 155; Christianity and,
xiii; double direction of, 28; etymology of, 38, 194nn29, 30, 194–95n31;
eucharistic, 49, 157; *frères hospitaliers*
and, 161; Homer on, 49; hostility
or, 3, 19–20, 47, 154, 160–61, 170;

interreligious, xiv, 48–52, 149–51, 174–77; interspiritual, xii, 50–52; and Irish artists, xiv; justice and, 20–21, 47; Kearney on, xvi; kenotic, 181; requires imagination/trust, 22; role of knowledge in, 47–48; law of, 135–36; limits to, 48; linguistic, 49; love and, 47; preferential option for, 54; radical, 184; risk of, 47–48; Socratic welcome and, 49; over sovereignty, 54; Sufi mystics on, 35–36, 49; translation and, 48; transubstantiation and, 129; unconditional, 48; Val de Grâce and, 161; *xeneia/xenizo/xenizein* , 27–28

host: divine stranger as, 27–28; as God/ Lord, 45; guest and, 15–16, 29; as *hostia*, 156; *hostis/hospes*, 38, 94; in Jewish commemoration, 19–20; provision and, 21–22; self as, 41–42

Hudgins, Andrew, 24

humanism, 140, 142, 158, 174, 182–84

Hume, John, xiii

humor, 42–44; Bergson on, 42; in Christian Scriptures, 42–43; as humility, 43; *humus* and, 42; possibility/impossibility and, 42

Huntington, Samuel, 172

Husserl, Edmond, xviii; on the body/*Leib*, 87–88; on epoché, 8, 87; Merleau-Ponty and, 95–96; on *natural attitude*, 87–88

Ibn 'Arabi, 35, 41, 99, 137; *The Book of Theophanies* by, 41

The Idiot (Dostoyevsky), 41

Ignatius, Saint, 45, 170

imagination, as *darshan*, 52; epiphany and, 52; ethics and, 41–42; eucharistic, 102; hermeneutics and, 52, 96, 130; hospitality and, 184; Ibn 'Arabi on, 35, 41; in Islamic understanding/practice, 33, 36, 41; Jesus and, 28; and narrative, xvi, 130; poetic, 14–15, 96, 130; power of, xvi; primal moment of, 40–42; sacramental, xvi, 52, 85–100, 101–2, 127–130; sacred, 133; and stranger, xviii, 133; in Wilde, 13–14

immanence: comic, 213*n*11; divinity and, 20–21; Greeks on, 9; transcendence and, 77, 85–87, 94–95, 99–100, 102, 124, 127, 133, 166, 182, 205*n*7

incarnation, 93, 103, 126, 141, 205–6*n*7; Auden on, 135; Joyce and, 212*n*1, 213*n*4; as *kenosis*, 52–53, 156, 160; *see also* transubstantiation; Eucharist

in-nocens, 8

In Search of Lost Time (Proust), 110

In Search of Times Past (Proust), 112–13

instant, 44, 107, 184; of *anagnorisis*, 8; belief and, 7; wagers and, 40

interpretation: body and, 46; space of, xvii; *see also* hermeneutics; meaning

The Interpretation of Dreams (Freud), 46

intersubjectivity, 94, 207–8*n*14

Irenaeus, 137, 182

Isaac, 3, 109; as gift, 19, 45, 76; as "the one who laughs," 19

Isaiah, 136

Ishmael, 20

Islam, 4; Al Qaeda and, 32; Andalusian philosophy and, 33; branches of, 32; democracy and, 143–49; Enlightenment and, 32; faith of, 30; God and, 143, 146–49; and Hindu texts, 33; hospitality and, 31–32, 35–37; against idols, 55; on Indian subcontinent, 33; interreligious belonging and, 37; and *islam*, 30; Lote Tree and, 51; and Mughhal empire, 33; and 9/11, 30; pluralism and, 35; poets of, 35–36, 43, 49; primary scene of, 30; progressive, 35–36; Scripture of, 30; as stranger, 32; Sufi, 35–37, 43, 49, 145; traditions of, 32–35; Wahhabism and, 30, 32; *see also* Muhammad; Qur'an, the

Israel, 17, 20–22, 73, 138; Holy Stranger of, 46; "house of," 67

Jacob, 5, 20, 22–23, 41

Jainism, 150, 177

James, William, 171, 234*n*31

Jaspers, Karl, 141, 181

Jesus Christ, xv, 21, 45, 49, 51, 76, 109; Abraham and, 43; as alien/foreigner, 26–28; Auden on, 135; baptism of,

54; Bonhoeffer on, 69; choice and, 44; Critchley on, 13–14; on Cross, 184; cult of, 112; Day on, 155–58; doubt and, 6, 44; at Emmaus, 27; forgiveness and, 48; Gandhi on, 164; as healer, 29, 157; as hermeneutic event, 28; Hopkins on, 12; humor and, 42–43; "least of these" and, 55; relatives and, 28; Ricoeur on, 77–78; scapegoating and, 78; self-emptying of, 55, 77–78; Sermon on the Mount and, 153, 164, 178, 191n8, 200n12; as stranger, 14–15, 27–29, 46; temptations and, 28–29, 45–46; translation and, 27; as "watchful," 46; as Way, 55; as Way of Stranger, 29; Wilde on, 14; *see also* Incarnation; word

Job, 20, 76, 136

John: (1:15), 54; (6:51), 155; (13), 54; (14), 157; (18:20), 157

John the Baptist, 25, 54

John of the Cross, 8, 69, 99

John Paul II, Pope, 50

Jonah, 51

Joseph, 23

Joseph of Arimathea, 27–28

Joyce, James, 10, 77, 101–10; *A Portrait of the Artist as a Young Man* by, 103–4; epiphanies and, 103–10, 129; on God, 110, 118, 160; influence of, xviii; Kristeva on, 97–98; transubstantiation in, 103–10, 113; *Ulysses* by, 102–10, 117, 127

Judaism, 4; Arendt's experience of, 60; gift of, 62; Greenberg on, 61; against idols, 55; kabbalistic, 178; Levinas on, 62; Talmud and, 169; Torah and, 169

Judges (13:2–25), 25

Julian of Norwich, 8, 69

Kabir Das: on "dual religious belonging," 36; poetry of, 35–37

kairos, 105–7, 109–10, 115, 141, 215n15

Kant, Immanuel, 149; Arendt on, 60; on not-knowing, 8

katabasis, 12

Kearney, Richard: academic training of, xi–xiv, xvi–xvii; 52, 183; *Heidegger et*

la Question de Dieu by, xiii; "hermeneutic situation" of, xv; on hermeneutic wagers, xvii, 40; on Irish literature, xiv; *Poétique du Possible* by, xiii, xvii; and postmodern ideas, xv–xvi; religious upbringing of, xiv; *Strangers, Gods, and Monsters* by, xiii; *The God Who May Be* by, xiii, xvii; *The Interreligious Imagination: A Hermeneutics of the Heart* by, xiii, 6; *Traversing the Heart* by, 6

Keats, John, on "negative capability," 11

kenosis, 77, 80, 91, 94, 124, 178, 181; Christian summons to, 55, 133–37; Day and, 157; Incarnation as, 52–53; of "truth," 126; Vanier and, 159–60

kerygma, biblical, 74

khora/chora, 25–26, 56, 136

Kierkegaard, Søren, 93; "fear and trembling" and, 45; on Jesus, 43; on "objective uncertainty," 8; on repetition, 7, 106–7; on "scandalous strangeness," 28

King Jr., Martin Luther, xiii

Kristeva, Julia, 4, 87, 102–3; aesthetics of, 96–100; anatheism and, 96, 112–17; on Joyce, 97–98; on Merleau-Ponty, 97–99; on Proust, 97–99, 111–17; sacramentality and, 96–100, 153; *Strangers to Ourselves* by, 96; *Time and Sense* by, 97, 113–15; on transubstantiation and, 96–99, 209n28, 210n29, 211–12n1, 218n18

Kung, Hans, 150–51

Lasch, Christopher, 171

Le Saux, Henri, 51

Letter to Olga (Pasternak), 40

Levertov, Denise, 24, 215n15

Levinas, Emmanuel: on atheism, 61, 170; Derrida and, 65, 136; on face, 20, 65; on God as absolute Other, 61, 171; on Judaism, 62, 171; Kearney and, xiv

Lévi-Strauss, Claude, 48

To the Lighthouse (Woolf), 102, 118–27

liturgy, 102, 127, 129, 156, 171; Auden on, 15; Joyce and, 103–5; religious dialogue and, 51

logos, 9, 90, 93–94, 188*n*8
The Long Loneliness (Day), 154
Love and Knowledge (Scheler), 47
Luke (1:15), 25; (10:25–36), 29; (17:18), 29
Luria, Rabbi, 99
Luther, Martin, 67
Lyotard, Jean-François, 65

McBride, Sean, xiii
Magi, 25
Mandela, Nelson, xiii
Marion, Jean-Luc, 95, 198–99*n*6
Mark (8:27), 54; (8:30–33), 55; (9:24), 6; (10:37–44), 158; (14:39), 46
Marx, Karl, xi, 71
Mary, 3, 109, 114; Annunciation and, 8, 23–26, 41, 46, 190–91*n*5; chooses grace over fear, 24; fear/consent of, 25; Hopkins on, 12; humor and, 42; Kascha Semonovitch on, 190–91*n*5; as *khora*, 26; Renaissance painting and, 25
Matthew (1:24), 55; (3:15), 54; (5:43–48), 29; (20:28), 156; (25:35–44), 29; (25:41), 28
meaning: of being, 79; epiphany of, 109; Holocaust and, 59–60; human and divine, 34, 152–53; of religion, 175–77; *surplus of*, 178; textual, 106, 109; and transcendence, xiv; *see also* hermeneutics; interpretation
Mecca, 31
memory: Christianity and, 54; Derrida on, 107, 214*n*12; Eucharist and, 77; Joyce on, 216*n*16; Kristeva on, 97; Proust on, 97, 110–14, 210*n*29, 219*n*22, 220*n*30, 221*n*31; Woolf on, 124–27
Merleau-Ponty, Maurice, 87, 102–3, 111, 117; xviii, 4; on "acosmism," 92–93; aesthetic of transubstantiation and, 90–92, 156; on Christianity/churches, 92–93; on Kierkegaard, 93; *Nature* by, 92–94; on painting, 90–91; on perception, 46, 113; phenomenology of flesh and, 88–94; *Phenomenology of Perception* by, 88–89; on

"primary faith," 206–7*n*9; *Signs* by, 90–93; *The Visible and thè Invisible* by, 89–90
Merriman, Hannah, 35
Merton, Thomas, 51, 178, 183
messiah, 154; *see also* incarnation; Jesus Christ; messianic, the; "messianism"
messianic, the, 54, 59, 107, 144; Derrida on, 63–65, 78, 136, 144, 172, 174, 196–97*n*5; horizons, xv; time, 105, 184; universality, 64; way, 55
"messianism": Derrida on, 64, 107; "weak," 54, 65
metanoia, 44
metaphor: faith and, 15–16, 94; imagining Other and, 42; metonymy and, 117–18; in Proust, 98, 112–13, 117–18; "tensional" model of, 10; translation and, 15
metaphysics: categories of, 52–53, 103; dualisms of, 4, 99; end of, 59; on God, 52–53, 59, 65–67, 73, 86, 92; phenomenology and, 87; Heidegger and, 8
Mills, C. Wright, 140
Mirabai, 36–37
modernity, 101; belief and, 7; "disenchantment" and, 57, 113
monotheism, 22, 65, 92
Morris, James, 35
Moses, xv, 44, 49, 54
Muhammad, the Prophet, xv, 3, 147; like Abraham and Mary, 32; choice and, 44; divine voice and, 8, 30–32, 45, 137; on Mount Hira, 30, 44, 51; sixteenth-century painting of, 31; *see also* Islam
mysticism: apophatic, 11, 63, 96; Buddhist, 127, 137; Certeau, on, 9, 191*n*6, 195*n*32, 197*n*5; Derrida and, 63–64; divine visitation and, 47; holiness and, 5; history of, 8–9; and Islam, 32, 137; Jewish, 137; monastic/mendicant, 85; Saint Francis and, 99–100; Steinbock on, 55–56, 197–98*n*6; Sufi, 35–37, 137; in Woolf, 122–23, 126–27

narrative: hermeneutics and, xvii, 102;

identity and, 60; Kearney on, xvi, 102; Master, 6; testimony and, xvii; voice, 119

natality, 43, 183; Annunication and, 25; pact of, xviii, 89; second, 58, 183

nature: Merleau-Ponty on, 92–93; Scheler/Francis on, 99–100

Nature (Merleau-Ponty), 92–93

Nazi/Nazism, *see* Holocaust

New Age spirituality, 6, 142

Nietzsche, Friedrich, 65, 68, 70–74, 167–68; on God, xi–xii, 67; Merleau-Ponty on, 92; *see also* nihilism

nihilism, 66, 68, 69, 73, 168; atheistic, 133; Merleau-Ponty on, 93; *see also* Nietzsche, Friedrich

9/11, xii, 30, 73, 227n22; and rhetoric, 158, 172; *see also* Al Qaeda; bin Laden, Osama; terrorism

Noah, 51

Novalis, 97

Nyma, Choqui, xv

The Odyssey (Homer), 49, 107, 127, 195n31

Office of the Greek Orthodox Matins of Good Friday, 27–28

ontology, 54, 78, 95; Judeo-Christian, 92

ontotheology, 73, 204n2, 205n7

Origen, 48

Other: absolute, 62; acoustics of, 8, 176; advent of, 46; as alien/foreigner, 20–21, 26–27, 29, 62, 153–54, 161, 175; arrival of, 25, 180–81; brings life, 45; divine, 14, 19–21, 45, 180–181; empathy and, 42; enigma of, 45; face of, 45, 145; as guest, 62, 174; house of, 35–36; imagination and, 41–42; infinite/finite, 183; Jesus as, 27–29; loving the, 21; no appropriation of, 15; perception and, 40–41; poetics and, 11, 14, 106; primal encounter with, xvii; metaphor and, 42; new encounter with, xviii; religious, 138, 149–51; sacredness of, 55; self becomes, 48; shock of, 63; *see also* stranger; foreigner

Parsons, Talcott, 139–40

Passover: Eucharist and, 110, 121; prayer of, 20, 54; promise and, 105

Pasternak, Boris, *Letter to Olga* by, 40

Paul, Apostle, 67, 74, 128; *kairos* and, 106–7

Peniel. 22

peregrinus, 21

I Peter (2:4–5), 112

phenomenology, 99, 167, 183; "epoché" and, 8, 87, 141; of the flesh, 87–88, 95, 130; Keaney on, xv; Merleau-Ponty and, 88–92, 95; method of, 4, 95

Phenomenology of Perception (Merleau-Ponty), 88–89

Philippians (2:5–11), 156

Plato: on anamnesis, 7; Platonism and, 89, 98

pluralism, xiv, 35, 146, 158, 174

poetics: Aristotle on, 10–11; and belief, 15–16, 130; Islamic/mystical, 35–37; romantic, 10–15; of the uncanny, 12–13

Poetics (Aristotle), 170, 217n16

A Portrait of the Artist as a Young Man (Joyce), 103

power, 14, 38, 72, 146–48, 160, 167; of God, 4, 45, 52–53, 66–69, 80, 126, 134, 165; Hillesum on, 58–59; Other and, xviii; of the powerless, 52–56, 68–69, 86

postmodernism, 65; dogmas of, xiii; ideas of, xv

poststructuralism, xv

promise, 105; Derrida on, 64–65; God as, 53; God's to Moses, 54; Mary and, 24; revelation of, 19; Ricoeur on, 78–79; transcendence in, 92; truth and, 44

Proust, 101–2, 106; epiphany in, 110–17, 215–17n16; eroticism in, 112–13; *In Search of Lost Time* by, 110; *In Search of Times Past* by, 112–13; John Ruskin and, 112–113; Kristeva on, 97–99, 111–17; on memory, 110–13; philosophical readings of, 117; repetition and, 214n13, 217n16, 219n22, 223–24n43; sacramental idioms in,

110–18; signs and, 98–99; *Time Regained* by, 102, 110, 114, 117
Psalm 119, 19

Qur'an, the: God and, 32, 143–49; and Hadith, 30; "Heart" (*al-qalb*) and, 35; hermeneutics and, 30–35; fundamentalist interpretations of, 30; metaphorical readings of, 34–35; poets on, 36; revealed, 30, 137–38; Soroush on, 143–44; *see also* Islam

Ramadan, 30
Reformation, the, 140
Reign of Terror, 16
relativism, xviii, 145
religion, xiv, 16, 38, 85, 125, 128, 141, 175, 180, 227–29n29; and absolutism, 145; anatheism and, 6, 144, 166–70, 176–80; Arendt on, 59; art and, 14, 98–102, 130; beyond religion, 136; biblical, 19, 176; Bonhoeffer on, 65–71; critiques of, 57, 72, 130, 139–40, 152–53, 167–70, 231n7; danger of, 53; Derrida on, 64, 232n10; Girard on, 136–37; God without, xi, 80; Habermas on, 172–74, 232n10, 233–34n30; and the holy, 38; hospitality and, 48–52, 167, 175, 177; hostile, xiii; Kristeva on, 98, 210n32, 211–12n1, 218n18; Merleau-Ponty on, 93–95; mysticism and, 9; non-Christian, xii, 33, 234n31; Pannikar on, 140–42; perversions of, 179; and politics, 138, 141, 158–65, 172–74, 232nn10, 11; primary scene of, 7, 184, 191n8; and *re-legere*, 180; Ricoeur on, 71–78; sacramentality and, xvi; Sartre on, 208n24; and triumphalism, xii, 58; violence and, 22, 39 177, 179–80; Wilde on, 13–14; *see also* Abrahamic faiths; Buddhism; Christianity; Confucianism; dialogue; Gandhi; Hinduism; Islam; Jainism; Judaism; "religion without religion"; "religious turn"; sacred, the; secularism/secularity; Sihkism; Zoroastrianism
"Religion, Atheism, Faith" (Ricoeur), 71

"religion without religion," xiii, 64, 204n57
"religious turn," xi, 204n57
Rembrandt, 27
Renaissance, the, 140
repetition, 25, 75; art and, 90–91; brute, 48; *forward*, 54; in Joyce, 103–7; Kierkegaard on, 7, 106–7; messianic, 118; narration as, 223–24n43; in Proust, 214n13, 217n16, 219n22, 223–24n43; reading and, 121; and return, 7, 13; in Woolf, 124, 223–24n43
Ricoeur, Paul, xiii, xiv, xvi, xviii, 65, 85, 128, 151, 170; anatheism and, 75–76, 86; critical hermeneutic of, 74; on *d'où parlez-vous?*, xi, xv; on dying, 77–78; on Eucharist, 77–78; *Freud and Philosophy* by, 79; on God as *dieu capable*, 78–81; on grace, 77–78; and hermeneutic wagers, xvii; 45; on "interconfessional hospitality," 48–49; on linguistic and eucharistic hospitality, 49; on metaphor, 10; on ontology/theology, 78; on philosopher/preacher, 77; on the "possible," 203n55; on postreligious faith, 71–74, 93–94, 171, 202–3n47; on refiguration, 47–48, 106; on religion, 71–73, 168, 179–80; "Religion, Atheism, Faith" by, 71; on *taboo/escape*, 71–74; *Thinking Biblically* by, 79–81; on translation, 49; *Vivant jusqu'à la mort* by, 76–77
Rilke, Rainer Maria, 16, 38, 41, 188n9; *Duino Elegies*, 38
Rosa Mystica, 12
Rosenzweig, Franz, 99
Rouault, 41
Rublev, Andrei, 25–26, 109
Rufi,TK 35
Rule of St. Benedict (St. Benedict), 29
Russell, Bertrand, xii
Ruth, 20–21

sacramental, the, 4, 103; imagination, xvi, 52, 85–100; love and, 163; return, 85–87; vocation, 85–87
sacred, the, 105, 185; and profane, 36; return of, 103, 126; in secular, 11–12,

57, 130, 139–42, 152, 162, 164–66; as strangers, 26–27, 152; "things themselves," 167
Samson, 25
Sarah, 17–19, 23; laughter of, 18–19, 24, 42–43, 109
Sartre, Jean-Paul, xii, 89; on emotions, 46, 88; on Merleau-Ponty, 94–96; "Merleau-Ponty Vivant," 94–95
Sauf le Nom (Derrida), 63
Saul, 20
The Scapegoat (Girard), 136
Scheler, Max, 168; on feelings, 46, 88; 211*n*38; *Love and Knowledge* by, 47; on Saint Francis, 99–100
Second Council of Nicea, 156
A Secular Age (Taylor), 11, 140, 158
secularism/secularity: anatheist task and, 141–42, 167; Gandhi on, 162–65; humanism and, 140; Islam and, 143–49; "laicism" (*laïcité*) and, 140; Mills on, 140; Pannikar on, 140–42; sacramentality and, 140–42, 153–54, 158–59; *saeculum*, 140–41; syncretism and, 142, 175; Taylor on, 140, 158–59
Sefer Ha-Hinukh, 20
self, the, 178; Chauvet on, 199*n*10; and host, 41, 172; refigured, 47–48; and stranger, 15, 19, 50, 56, 62, 145, 152, 177
sensible, the, 88–95, 210*n*29; eucharistic character of, 96, 102
Septuagint, 9, 190*n*5
Shibboleth: For Paul Celan (Derrida), 63
Shiko, Dara, 33
Signs (Merleau-Ponty), 90–93
Sihkism, 150
Sirach 4, "On Wisdom," 17
Siraj, Maqbood, 32–33
Socrates: on not-knowing, 7–8; Stranger and, 152
Solomon, King, 21, 49
Song of Songs, 20–21, 23, 105, 108; (8:5–7), 79
Soroush, Abdolkarim, 32, 143–46, 171
Specters of Marx (Derrida), 106–7
Spinoza, Baruch, 85
Stalinism, 16, 66, 68, 138, 170

Stein, Edith, on empathy, 42, 50, 88
Steinbock, Anthony, 55–56, 175, 197–98*n*6
Stevens, Wallace, 3, 13
stranger, 67, 71, 94–95, 151; as *allogenes*, 29; as angel/*anthropos*, 22, 30; as *Atman*, 162; before Jesus, 29; calls for justice, 21; comedy and, 43; commitment to, 44; Deuteronomy and, 21–22; divine, 14–15, 27–28, 30–32, 41, 43–45, 162; epiphany and, 129, 149; exteriority of, 62; face of, 24, 149; God as, xi, 4, 15–16, 122, 146, 149, 153; Greek/Jewish traditions on, 9–10; as Guest, 15–16, 60; *hospes*, 28; humanism and, 182–83; in Islamic tradition, 35–37; Jesus as, 27–29; in Judaic tradition, 17–21; love of, 185; as "more," 184–85; Muhammad and, 30; name of God and, 21; orphan, widow and, 4, 21, 94–95; persecution and, 58; primal encounter with, xvii, 40–41; re-cognition of, 46; resists translation, 42; responses to, 4, 48; sacred, 3, 23, 26–27, 54, 61, 105, 133, 152, 159–60; scene of, 7; service to, 54, 164; as threat, 20–21; trusting the, 36, 44; as uninvited one, 21–22, 160–61; Way of, 29; as *xenos*, 28; *see also* foreigner; guest; other, the
strangeness, 104; divinity and, xiv; Kierkegaard on, 28; shock of, 9–10
Strangers to Ourselves (Kristeva), 96
Strauss, Leo, 172
Sukkot, Jewish festival of, 19–20
sunyata, 16
Swaraj, 162–65

Taoism, 150
Taylor, Charles: on Hopkins, 11–12; *A Secular Age* by, 11, 140, 158, 170; on secularism, 158–159; on testimony, xvii
Teilhard de Chardin, 99
teleology: anatheism eschews, 6, 167; theism and, 53
Teresa of Calcutta, 56, 156, 160–61
terrorism: Sartre on, 208*n*4; *see also* Al Qaeda; bin Laden, Osama; 9/11

testimony: of goodness, 183; Hopkins and, 12; and narrative, xvii, 125–26; of sages and saints, 6; truth and, 44

theism, xi, 54, 56, 63, 68, 86, 96, 102; and dialogue, xvii; dogmatic, 3, 6, 57, 166; nature and, 92–93; politics and, 4; post-, 57; postreligious, 74; teleology and, 53; Western understanding of, 4

theology: apophatic, 63–64; dualist, 66; end of, 59; epiphany of stranger and, 7; of fulfillment, 6; of liberation, 29, 93, 154; ontology and, 78–79

theophany, 29

Thinking Biblically (Ricoeur), 79–81

Time and Sense (Kristeva), 97, 113–15

Time Regained (Proust), 102, 110, 114, 117

The Time That Remains (Agamben), 107

To the Lighthouse (Woolf), 102

tolerance: Averroes on, 193n16; Dawkins and, 231n4; democracy and, 145; reason/faith and, 169; Qur'an on, 192n13

Torah, 22

tragedy, Greek, 10–11

transcendence, 9, 158; Gandhi on, 162; immanence and, 77, 85–87, 91, 94, 99–100, 102, 124, 127, 166, 182; as surplus of meaning, xiv, 182; Merleau-Ponty on, 90–92; promise and, 91

translation, 112; between Islamic/Hindu texts, 33; between science/faith, 169–71; between self and stranger, 15–16, 42; of ideologies/hearts, 50; interreligious hospitality and, 48–52, 173–74; Ricoeur on, 49

transubstantiation, 127–30, 219n22; Kristeva on, 96–99, 209n28, 210n29, 211–12n1, 218n18; language and, 207n14; transtextual, 128; *see also* Eucharist

trinity: Christian, 51, 109; icon of, 25–26, 109; in Joyce, 211–12n1, 214n12; of strangers, 25

truth, 134, 164; of art, 13; claims, 10–11, 95, 151, 170, 180; divine, 32; God and, 44, 143–44, 170; Jesus as, 55;

metaphysical, xvii; and mysticism, 9, 197n5, 210n29; narrative, 107; poetics and, 170; and power, 74; Proust on, 113; and reason, 34; search for, 7–8, 168; as transformation/*troth*, 44; Woolf on, 123, 126, 225n51

Tyagananda, Swami, xv

Ulysses (Joyce), 102–10, 117, 127

Unheimliche, das, 12–13

Vanier, Jean, xiii, xviii, 5, 183; L'Arche and, 159–61

Vattimo, Gianni, 133–35

violence: Derrida on, 203n49; of exclusivity, 176; of interpretation, 169; non-, 151, 164; religious, 138, 177, 179; strangeness and, 197n5

Vivant jusqu'à la mort (Ricoeur), 76–77

Vivekananda, Swami, xiii, 50–51, 171, 176

The Visible and the Invisible (Merleau-Ponty), 89–90

The Weakness of God (Caputo), 136

Weber, Max, on "disenchantment," 57, 139

Wiesel, Elie, 58, 61

Wilde, Oscar, 13–14

Wittgenstein, Ludwig, 8, 169

Woolf, Virginia, 98–99, 101–2; atheism and, 119, 123, 225n51; on God, 124; and indirect discourse, 119; on "it," 119, 124–27; mysticism and, 122–23; and nothingness/"wedge," 222n36; on narrative voice, 119; and the sacred, 222–23n37; *To the Lighthouse* by, 102, 118–27

word: diversity and, 175–76; of faith/existence, 75, 137; made flesh, 24, 102, 107–10, 118, 124, 128, 135, 137, 156

World Council of Churches, 50

World Parliament of Religions, 50

The Wreck of Deutschland (Hopkins), 12

Zechariah, 25

Zeus, as *Xenios*, 49

Zoroastrianism, 150